D0843312

Belk Center
706 Hillsborough Street
Raleigh NC 27603

THE AGILE COLLEGE

The Agile College

How Institutions Successfully Navigate Demographic Changes

NATHAN D. GRAWE

JOHNS HOPKINS UNIVERSITY PRESS | *Baltimore*

© 2021 Johns Hopkins University Press
All rights reserved. Published 2021
Printed in the United States of America on acid-free paper
9 8 7 6 5 4 3 2 1

Johns Hopkins University Press
2715 North Charles Street
Baltimore, Maryland 21218-4363
www.press.jhu.edu

Library of Congress Cataloging-in-Publication Data

Names: Grawe, Nathan D., author.
Title: The agile college : how institutions successfully navigate demographic
    changes / Nathan D. Grawe.
Description: Baltimore : Johns Hopkins University Press, [2021] |
    Includes bibliographical references and index.
Identifiers: LCCN 2020018803 | ISBN 9781421440231 (hardcover) |
    ISBN 9781421440248 (ebook)
Subjects: LCSH: Education, Higher—Demographic aspects—United States. |
    Educational change—United States. | Education, Higher—Aims and
    objectives—United States.
Classification: LCC LC69 .G73 2021 | DDC 371.829/00973—dc23
LC record available at https://lccn.loc.gov/2020018803

A catalog record for this book is available from the British Library.

To Heather, Hannah, Toby, Caleb, and Noah—
Soli Deo Gloria

CONTENTS

This work would not have been possible without support from so many. I thank Dean Beverly Nagel and the Faculty Grants Committee at Carleton College for a faculty development grant that provided additional time for the project. Similarly, I am grateful to donors whose gifts to the Ada M. Harrison Distinguished Teaching Professorship of the Social Sciences provided time and financial support. Numerous higher education leaders shared the insights and experiences that form the backbone of this project, including: John Barnhill, H. Scott Bierman, Barbara Brittingham, Lisa Bunders, Ace Charette, Terri Curry, William Deeds, Randall Deike, Pam Eddinger, Scott Friskics, John Fuchko III, James Galbally Jr., Ross Gittell, Jonathan Green, Nancy Griffin, Dennis Hanno, Kedra Ishop, W. Joseph King, Michael Kyle, Cindy Lopez, Jon McGee, Amy McGovern, Jeff Morgan, John Neuhauser, Jason Nicholas, John Reynders, Connie Richardson, Abu Rizvi, David Robinson, Rebecca Silbert, Jay Simmons, Joy St. John, Martin Sweidel, Lara Tiedens, Mary Wagner, Richard Wagner, Meridith Wentz, Hope Williams, and Edward Venit. The proactive, constructive work being done by these leaders, their colleagues, and so many colleges and universities inspires confidence in the future. The initial conception of the book began in a conversation with Paul Grawe. Michael Hemesath and Greg Rawski provided invaluable feedback on earlier drafts. Wei-Hsin Fu and Greg Sharpe provided assistance with GIS software. I am grateful for the organizers and participants connected to the many data sources used in this work. Without them, work like this would be literally impossible.

Most of all, I am grateful to Heather, Hannah, Toby, Caleb, and Noah. They have been understanding when long work hours have been inconvenient. And without their emotional support, I'd never have reached the end. As always, Heather filled in the gaps and held us together when I could not be there. I love you all!

Finally, the editorial team at Johns Hopkins University Press has been top-notch. Greg Britton's patient guidance and support has improved the final product significantly. And the production team has led me through the numerous details necessary for turning a manuscript into a book. I cannot thank them all enough.

THE AGILE COLLEGE

Introduction

A S DEMOGRAPHIC FORCES promise to reshape the size and composition of future cohorts of college-going students, many institutions recognize the need to take proactive measures that ensure their sustainability and effectiveness for the future. Of course, institutions are perpetually evolving. What makes the current demographic challenge a bit different is its magnitude. From a peak just prior to the financial crisis in 2008 through 2017, the number of babies born in the United States fell by more than 500,000 (Centers for Disease Control and Prevention 2013, 2019). At the same time, migration and fertility patterns continue to remake the population, producing declining shares of non-Hispanic whites and residents of the Northeast—that is, moving away from populations that have disproportionately attended colleges in the past. As if concerns about the domestic market for higher education were not enough, we have also witnessed a recent decline in new international student enrollments (Institute of International Education 2019). While international enrollments make up about 5% of all US enrollments, the 10% decline in new international undergraduate students seen between the 2015–16 and 2018–19 academic years reminds us that we cannot necessarily count on larger international student numbers to offset domestic declines.

Although these threats to future enrollment are real, it is possible to imagine thoughtful institutions coming through the trials of the next decade as more vibrant and effective versions of themselves. Venit (2018) explains how this might be, drawing on Taleb's (2012) conception of antifragility. "Much like the Hydra of Greek mythology or the skeletons in our body," Venit writes, "antifragile systems not only survive being stressed, they actually become stronger because of it." He wonders whether the higher education system and its institutions might be (or become) antifragile. Is it possible that the reforms taken now to mitigate the pressure of demographic change—reforms that expand the reach of our recruitment by improving access, increase retention and persistence through better and more equitable student experiences, enhance pedagogies to meet the needs of the next generation of students and workers, curtail inefficient expenditure patterns where warranted, and exploit the benefits of cooperative efforts across institutions—might lay the foundation for a stronger future in higher education?

When I discussed this possibility with Barbara Brittingham, who has witnessed more than her share of demographic challenges as president of the New England Commission of Higher Education, she reasonably noted the limitations of the skeletal analogy. After all, skeletons are antifragile only for certain levels of stress; in the stresses of an automobile accident, the body breaks. This observation calls to mind the quip of the physicist who notes that speed doesn't kill: acceleration—or the change in speed—is the real culprit. Brittingham clearly has an argument. At some point, enrollment declines overwhelm even the best institutional practices. But contemplating the stress of a car crash introduces additional observations. Modern safety equipment is designed to lengthen the time over which energy is absorbed in a crash, effectively reducing rates of deceleration. Similarly, institutions have some control over how much deceleration they experience. Waiting to take action until 2030, only after demographic changes are fully upon us, necessarily implies making large adjustments in a short period of time. On the other hand, by setting out on a path for change today, it is possible to design and implement institutional changes over more time and so reduce the inherent stresses. This is particularly true in the context of long-term commitments such as capital investments and tenure.

This book is intended for institutions determined to take proactive measures in the face of the difficulties that lie ahead. Unfortunately, there is no formulaic path forward. The best way through the coming years depends on contextual details surrounding geographic markets, the students we serve, the strengths of our faculty and staff, the programs we offer, governance relationships with faculty and staff, facilities we own, and so much more. Rather than attempt to identify a one-size-fits-all strategy that can't possibly address the variety of circumstances faced by more than 4,000 degree-granting institutions, the chapters that follow provide a plethora of examples drawn from institutions of all types and sizes. Chapter 5 describes how these stories were collected and how they might be used to inform institutional practice. Rather than to dictate a plan, the intent of these examples is to provoke campus conversations about how demographic change can best be addressed within a given institutional context. While readers might find some of the initiatives described here to be useful models, few are likely to be successful without revision that reflects local context and broader strategies. Even more likely, consideration of a range of choices made by other schools may prompt altogether novel programs that grow from and suit the particulars of institutional strengths and limitations.

Possible tactical responses to demographic change are numerous, but they can be categorized usefully into a small number of conceptual categories. Chapters 6 through 11 consider each broad category in turn. If student recruitment pools are declining, one solution is to recruit more effectively (chapter 6). By out-recruiting peers in traditional markets, extending outreach into new markets, or identifying underserved student groups so as to expand access, institutions may continue to enroll the same number of students despite a shrinking pool of prospective students from which to draw. While offices of admissions and marketing clearly play an important role in bringing in the class, in a time of secular decline we must recognize a logical tension with adopting recruitment as the primary (much less sole) response to demographic change. Unless recruitment initiatives attract students who would otherwise not attend college (a distinct minority today), each student gained is lost by some other institution. Assuming that other institutions are just as eager to maintain enrollments, those following this path should expect intense competitive pushback. So, it is critical not to overestimate the role of recruitment in offsetting declines in prospective student numbers. Acknowledging this caveat, the chapter explores innovations in admissions and financial aid designed to increase enrollment rates.

Bringing students to campus is only the beginning of the enrollment process. With fewer young people available to recruit, some institutions are placing renewed attention on retention (chapter 7) to shore up flagging matriculations. While many institutions are creating enrollment management offices with responsibilities that include retention, the most interesting retention initiatives emphasize engagement with the entire campus. After all, for most students the point of greatest institutional contact lies outside an administrative office.

One of the most important points of student contact, of course, is the classroom. With that in mind, some institutions are responding to demographic changes with an emphasis on pedagogical and program reform (chapter 8). Depending on the institutional context, professors and learning support staff are being engaged for a range of purposes. At some, the shifting composition of students raises questions about effective and inclusive teaching practices. At others, technology is being used to provide new student learning opportunities or to reduce costs. Still others look to create and articulate deeper connections between learning on campus and life after college, a response to students' and parents' desire for greater "relevance" in coursework that has the potential to engage students more deeply with their learning and the institution.

While some institutions' best responses may be sufficient to maintain enrollments at prior levels, for others the best path forward will include rethinking size or scope. Done well, budget reprioritization, downsizing, mergers, and consolidation can reduce costs, enhance educational effectiveness, and communicate institutional identity (chapter 9). Just as predicted by Moody's Investors Service (2015), we have seen a meaningful increase in institutional closures in the past few years. According to the National Center for Education Statistics (NCES 2018, table 317.50), 20 nonprofit institutions closed their doors in 2016–17, up from an average of 5 closures per year in the previous six years. (Closures have increased even more dramatically among for-profit institutions, totaling 92 in 2016–17, up from just 15 three years prior. However, closure activity among for-profits is more likely the result of distinct competitive market forces in that subsector than evidence of demographic change.) As demographic pressures intensify, more institutions will surely confront existential questions.

In too many cases, the challenges of enrollment disruption will be layered on top of long-standing structural problems. According to Parthenon-EY (2016, 2), an analysis of financial and enrollment trends suggests that "800 institutions face critical strategic challenges because of their inefficiencies or their small size." Specifically, they find that more than 35% of institutions face at least three of the following threats: enrollments fewer than 1,000, no online programs, annual tuition increases of more than 9%, a discount rate above 35%, tuition dependence above 85%, endowment income less than one-third of expenses, debt payments larger than one-tenth of expenses, and deficit spending. The potential immediacy of some threats is perhaps amplified by current fiscal conditions. In fiscal year 2017, about one-quarter of private nonprofit schools ran deficits (Lederman 2018). The Parthenon-EY authors argue that heavy tuition dependence at institutions with fewer than 5,000 students make these institutions particularly sensitive to periods of nonincreasing enrollment. While institutional closures receive disproportionate attention, retrenchment may be more relevant for a larger number of institutions. Whether discontinuing majors, shrinking through attrition, or simply seeking efficiencies through budget cuts, colleges may find contraction an important part of the puzzle as they navigate coming changes.

Some institutions may prepare for declining demand by committing to a path of enrollment growth (chapter 10), even though it is admittedly a higher-risk strategy. Among highly selective institutions, demographic change actually suggests a rising market that will allow expansion (insofar as they desire it for other mission-driven reasons) despite the aggregate decline in prospective students. The more common and interesting case, however, are less selective schools that seek to overcome declining net fee income per student (which is likely to accompany increased competition in light of demographic weakness) by attempting to increase enrollments. Obviously, this is not a strategy that can be successful at all institutions if the total number of college attenders is falling. But institutions that manage to achieve dominance within their market may yet find a growth path despite general decline.

All of the approaches identified above are distinctly individualistic, focused on a single institution. However, some responses to the shared challenges of demographic change are collective (chapter 11). A range of joint efforts aims to assist higher education as a whole as we seek to attract students, including (1) constructively engaging efforts to reform student debt, (2) encouraging a regulatory environment conducive to increasing international student enrollments, (3) collaborating in admissions, and (4) developing institutions capable of providing bridge funds to schools attempting to make investments in structural changes. As the number of young people declines, it may be natural for competitive feelings to increase between peer institutions. Indeed, many of the strategies discussed here involve heightened competition. But even as institutions pursue individual ends, collaboration reflecting the collective interests shared across institutions may ultimately be critical.

Before sharing examples of institutional response, however, the next chapters explore how newly available data affect Higher Education Demand Index (HEDI) projections presented in Grawe (2018). Chapter 1 briefly recaps how the HEDI combines Census Bureau population figures with estimates of college attendance from longitudinal surveys conducted by the Department of Education. Two significant updates to the data have become available since the original work in Grawe (2018): subsequent waves of the American Community Survey allow forecasts to be extended into the mid-2030s and, more importantly, the release of the High School Longitudinal Study (HSLS) provides updated information on college-going patterns. The HSLS records college choices of students in the high school graduating class of 2013, a significant postfinancial crisis update to the Education Longitudinal Study used in Grawe (2018), which covered the 2004 graduating cohort. Critically, this update captures significant recent increases in college-going among Hispanics. In addition, the chapter summarizes current trends in immigration, migration, fertility, and college attendance that are relevant to HEDI projections.

In the context of evolving trends, chapter 2 explores the resulting, updated HEDI projections, disaggregating two-year from four-year schools and, in the latter group, institutions with regional and national markets (these groups being divided by rankings in *US News & World Report*'s lists of top national colleges and universities). The overall picture from today through the early 2030s looks much as reported in Grawe (2018). However, the additional years of data allow us to see a more distant time horizon. A brief increase in births in 2014 portends a temporary and incomplete recovery in 2031 and 2032, before the onset of continued decline in 2033. As in Grawe (2018), the data point toward a more sanguine path for selective institutions.

Chapter 2 reports updates of the original HEDI analysis in Grawe (2018), and chapter 3 presents new projections. These analyses differentiate demand for public, private, and for-profit institutions; separately consider first-time matriculants, transfer students, and dual enrollees; divide students by their propensity to persist; and consider the sensitivity of the projections to patterns of migration and immigration. While the resulting findings lend additional nuance, the projections do not upend the original analysis in chapter 2. Finally, chapter 4 takes a detailed look at the important dimension of race/ethnicity.

As these first four chapters make clear, the pace of demographic change has been unusually swift in recent years with serious implications for higher education demand. In addition to persistent shifts in the population across race/ethnicity and geography, as the next chapter describes, the fertility rate has fallen persistently and deeply since the onset of the Great Recession. These trends each present challenges to traditional practices in higher education. (Though, on a positive note, the recent surge in college attendance among Hispanics offers hope—at least for institutions that are able to adapt to new market realities.) Despite the real challenges that lie ahead, the examples described in later chapters demonstrate that as disruptive as recent demographic shifts can be, schools that constructively engage the changing environment can emerge stronger as a result. Armed with projections of the future and proactive examples, higher education can prepare to meet the needs of the next generation of students.

PART I | DEMOGRAPHIC PRESSURES

ONE

Evolving Demographic Trends

IN RECENT YEARS, news stories and research have repeatedly high-lighted demographic trends reshaping prospective student pools. Migration has steadily drawn families out of the Northeast toward the South and Southwest—patterns reinforced by flows of immigrants into the country. And for years, fertility among Hispanics has far outpaced that of the population as a whole. In other words, movements into and around the country have combined such that prospective student pools are persistently shifting away from groups traditionally connected to higher education. Grawe (2018) explores how these existing, persistent demographic forces were further complicated by the 10% reduction in fertility that accompanied the Great Recession.

Total fertility rates have been particularly low in the higher education strongholds of New England. To replace the population without adding new people from other areas, on average, about 2.1 children must be born to each woman (one to replace the woman, one to replace a paired man, and a bit more to account for mortality and nonfecundity). The Centers for Disease Control and Prevention (CDC) (2010) reports that in 2007, as the country sat on the precipice of economic slowdown, the total fertility rate for the country as a whole stood just above this replacement rate. However, in each of the New England states—Maine, Massachusetts, New Hampshire, Rhode Island, and Vermont—women, on average, were having fewer than 1.8 children over the life cycle. In fact, Vermont led the country with the lowest total fertility rate in 2007 at just 1.715 babies per woman, and the other New England states claimed spots 2 through 5 on the list of least fertile states in the union. The consequences of this low level of fertility are evident in current enrollment challenges in the region in general and in Vermont in particular, where, between 2016 and 2019, four colleges closed, two merged, and another made plans to merge in 2020 (Education Dive 2019). As uncertainty related to the economy increased during the Great Recession, many young couples chose to avoid pregnancy, initiating a serious fertility decline. By 2011, when the recovery had begun to take hold, the nation's total fertility rate had fallen by more than 10% in just three years, to a level well below replacement (CDC 2013).

As a result, because children get older one year at a time, we can anticipate an abrupt drop in the prospective student pool in 2026, an 18-year-delayed reminder to campuses of the budget cuts in the fallout of the recession itself. The Western Interstate Commission for Higher Education (WICHE) was the first to warn of decreases in the number of high school graduates. The 2012 WICHE *Knocking on the Door* report noted that demographic softness in the Midwest and Northeast presaged persistent decline in K–12 students, and it documented how the national reduction in births beginning in 2008 predicted that much of the nation would join in the Northeast's downward trend in the mid-2020s.

At this point, it is important to pause and recognize two things. First, demographic challenges are present, not future, issues in higher education. For the decade between 2009–10 and 2019–20, WICHE (2016) figures that the number of high school graduates declined by 7% and 8% in the Midwest and Northeast regions, respectively.[1] While the rate of change might be modest, the 2012 WICHE report provides important context: the decade of decline begun in 2009 followed impressive increases in high school graduates during the prior 15 years—

almost 30% in the Northeast and more than 15% in the Midwest. To the extent that practices at many institutions in these parts of the country had been built on the experience of expanding prospective student pools, the declines they have recently lived through would surely create enrollment and financial hardship. A reading of higher education news sources certainly suggests that many schools in these regions continue to struggle to adapt to a new environment in which student numbers are in persistent decline. So, as we look forward to nationwide challenges due to declining fertility, we should recognize that the difficulties are hardly novel to our colleagues in much of the northeast quadrant of the country.

Second, as important as it is to recognize that the effects of fertility decline are already being felt, it is even more critical to note that these challenges can be foreseen. While many have been shaken by recent reports of enrollment shortfalls at Midwest and Northeast schools, as early as 2012 WICHE was warning of "dwindling production" (defined by declines of 15% or more) of high school graduates in the District of Columbia, Maine, Michigan, New Hampshire, Rhode Island, and Vermont (p. xii). Reporters who cover enrollment challenges in higher education could have done much worse than using the 2012 WICHE forecasts to guide their geographic focus in identifying campuses to feature in 2020 stories.

As social science research is wont to be, the WICHE report was cautious and reserved in tone, focusing more on the near- and midterm forecasts. For example, many of the report's analyses described anticipated changes in the number and composition of high school graduates through 2024–25—ending just before the impacts of the evolving birth dearth. And the authors noted that "as with any forecasting effort, the further out in time one looks, the less accurate the projection is likely to be" (3). Such carefulness is entirely appropriate for researchers.

But some readers were quick to see the serious implications for the tail end of the WICHE forecasts (which, in the December 2012 report, extended through 2027–28). For instance, the *Chronicle of Higher Education* ran a front-page story, including a centerfold spread titled

"Colleges, Here Is Your Future," that featured a map in which much of the Northeast dripped with red ink (Lipka 2014). The lede paragraph warned, "Until just a few years ago, colleges could anticipate classes of high-school graduates each bigger than the last. . . . But those days are over." While much could change from the early 2010s through the mid-2020s, we could be quite sure that native children would not be added to the cohorts born in prior years.

In Grawe (2018), I argued that while the WICHE data played an indispensable role in sparking conversations within higher education, many administrators were likely to be reluctant to use forecasts of high school graduates for high-stakes planning without additional information. Two facts allowed readers of the WICHE work to question the relevance for their own campuses. First, no college or university serves a representative slice of the American population—or even the population of high school graduates. Each school serves a niche market. And so it is possible that the market trends for a particular college or even a large set of similar schools might diverge from those of the population as a whole. Second, the probability of college attendance in general (and even more so, the attendance at institutions of a given type) varies dramatically by demographic subgroup. Using data from the Department of Education's Education Longitudinal Study (ELS) of 2002, I showed that it is fairly easy to identify demographic subgroups whose probabilities of attending some types of colleges and universities differ by 10-fold or even 30-fold (Grawe 2018). Taken together, these facts might lead some to question whether analyses of high school graduates speak directly to their institutional context.

In response to these concerns, my work refined head count forecasts by accounting for the probability of college attendance, allowing that probability to differ by basic demographic characteristics: sex, race/ethnicity, geographic location (both Census division and whether in a major metropolitan area), parent education, family income, family composition (i.e., whether living with both parents, mom alone, dad alone, or neither), and nativity. The probability models were estimated using ELS data and then applied to population counts provided by the Census Bureau's American Community Survey (ACS).[2] The result was the Higher Education Demand Index (HEDI), which projects the number of 18-year-olds living in 64 locations—states and metropolitan areas—whose demographic characteristics suggest they will attend college (in various forms) in future years.[3] Because the restricted portion of the ELS includes detailed information on exactly what postsecondary institutions a student has attended, the HEDI creates distinct projections for a range of institution types, from two-year schools to highly selective four-year institutions. Projections were created for the 28 largest metropolitan areas plus residual portions of states.[4]

To make HEDI's basic approach more concrete, consider a simple example. Suppose a population of current 18-year-olds is made up of six people, each with a 50% chance of attending college. Over the next five years, we expect the population of 18-year-olds to fall to only five people, two of whom are certain to attend while the other three attend with a 67% probability. In the current cohort, the expected number of new, traditional-aged college students is 3 (or $0.5 + 0.5 + 0.5 + 0.5 + 0.5 + 0.5$).[5] Looking forward five years, while we expect the population to fall, the expected number of college students holds steady at 3 (or $1 + 1 + 0.67 + 0.67 + 0.67$). As this simple example makes clear, the composition of the prospective pool is as important as its size when we think about future college-going populations.

The resulting HEDI projections in Grawe (2018) provided new insights even as they reinforced the important messages in the WICHE forecasts. Among the nuances, the model found that the rising education level of parents combined with an increase in the Asian American population suggest a general growth trend in the market for selective higher education. The decline in births around the financial crisis foreshadows a reversal of this trend in the mid-2020s, but the overall picture for this part of the market remains positive. Second, all subsectors can expect greater diversity in student pools. While this trend is driven by rising shares of Hispanic students in all subsectors, diversification at highly selective colleges and universities particularly reflects increasing shares of Asian American students. Finally, for all subparts of higher education, the rise of first-generation students may be coming to an end as previous decades' efforts to increase access have produced increasingly educated cohorts of parents. As important as these nuances are, the HEDI ultimately confirms concerns raised by WICHE's work. For the vast majority of higher education, adjustments for the propensity to attend college do not erase the challenges of demographic weakness that are already evident in the Northeast and Great Lakes regions and will spread to the rest of the country in the next decade.

Of course, forecasts necessarily involve assumptions. In the case of the HEDI, the key assumption might be summarized this way: the world will continue to function as it has in the recent past. Jon McGee, author of *Breakpoint* and former vice president for planning and strategy at the College of Saint Benedict and Saint John's University (MN), aptly captures the limitations of forecast modeling.[6] In McGee's reliably pithy way, he notes that models are, at their core, if-then arguments. "If the 'if' fails, then the 'then' fails." Still, forecast work, such as that done by WICHE (2016) and me, provides a valuable baseline from which we can adjust our thinking in light of new information on the "ifs."

Since the completion of work on Grawe (2018), new trends have emerged that suggest that the original HEDI forecasts should be updated. The next sections explore recent evolutions in the trends of immigration, migration, fertility, and college attendance rates. While none suggest a wholesale rethinking of the original projections, recent years have revealed significant changes for both better and worse.

Immigration

The rhetoric of politicians of all stripes might lead one to believe that the magnitude and nature of immigration has been fundamentally altered by the current presidential administration. A look at the data suggests that, despite some important, late-breaking trends, to date it appears that the absence of new legislation has limited the effect of the executive branch. Of course, just as President Barack Obama did later in his term, President Donald J. Trump may increase his use of executive action to address immigration. But for now, what has changed and what remains more or less the same?

The number of persons newly obtaining lawful permanent resident status has fallen by 7% from the last year of President Obama's term to the first year of President Trump's (Department of Homeland Security [DHS] 2018a; 2018b). While decreased immigration flows were seen from all regions, the reduction was somewhat less pronounced in movements from Africa and North and South America, and somewhat more pronounced in immigrants originating in Asia and Europe. With only five quarters of final data under the Trump administration, it is difficult to know whether these changes constitute a modest level adjustment or the beginning of a more pronounced trend. Notably, under both administrations, while Mexico is the largest single sending country, immigrants from Asia outnumber those from Central and South America by around 30%. As a result of this trend, Cohn and Caumont (2016) anticipate that Asian immigrants within the US population will outnumber Hispanic immigrants (regardless of legal status) by the middle of the century.

In addition to those gaining lawful permanent resident status, immigration totals are influenced by those entering without permission. Undocumented immigrant flows are heavily influenced by economic conditions in the United States. After decades of near-continual increase, Pew Research Center estimates suggest that the difficult economic environment created by the financial crisis led to a 7.5% reduction in the number of unauthorized immigrants residing in the United States (Krogstad et al. 2019). Since the onset of the economic recovery, Pew researchers estimate that this population slowly drifted downward from 11.4 million in 2009 to 10.5 million in 2017 for a total decline of nearly 15% since the prerecession peak. Of course, despite more than a decade of talk in Washington about reforming the immigration system and resolving the debate around the status of these individuals, most analysts doubt that congressional leaders will reach an agreement that settles the question any time soon.

Recent analysis of Census Bureau survey data by Frey (2019a) raises questions about reductions in immigration accomplished through changes in the implementation of immigration law that are described in Tavernise (2019). Frey finds that the number of foreign-born residents of the United States grew by only 200,000 between 2017 and 2018. This compares to increases of between 450,000 and 1 million in each of the previous five years. The lower growth is attributable to declines in the recorded number of noncitizens, about half of whom are believed to be undocumented. While it is possible that these survey results point to substantial changes in immigration practices, we must also remember the limitations of surveys. Government surveys in particular can be perceived as threatening to immigrants in general and undocumented immigrants in particular. Release of the *2018 Yearbook of Immigration Statistics* by the Department of Homeland Security will provide additional context from administrative records.

Though the HEDI focuses entirely on domestic demand for higher education, the subject of international student demand is clearly related. While this topic is considered in depth in chapter 11, it is important to note here recent developments. According to the Institute of International Education (IIE) (2019), the number of new international undergraduate student enrollments has fallen for three years straight—from 2016–17 to 2018–19—a notable break from a persistently positive trend. The three-year decline in new enrollments now totals more than 10%. While the total number of international students enrolled at US institutions has only fallen 3% (because newly enrolled students are only one of several cohorts of students enrolled at any point in time), the decline in new enrollments is notable because we have seen increases every year since 1979–80 with the exception of the three years following the 9/11 attacks.[7] The recent deviation from trend suggests we may be entering a new period in which international student enrollments stagnate or reverse, creating even greater dependence on a domestic student market that we expect to weaken in the next decade.

Interstate Migration

In the country as a whole, the interstate migration rate has been more or less steady for the past decade (Frey 2019b). However, the model relies on the rates of movement to and from specific locations, and focuses in particular on migration of children. So, while work like Frey

(2019b) suggests stability in total migration, we must look a little more closely to discern any changes relevant to higher education. According to the 2016 and 2017 ACS, migration patterns among children have shifted slightly over the past five years, though the big picture remains the same: population is shifting out of the Northeast and West Coast toward the southern and southwestern portions of the country. The data show a net out-migration of approximately 0.4% per year from New England. More modest (0.1% to 0.2%) out-migration is also seen in the Middle Atlantic, East North Central, and Pacific divisions. To put these rates into perspective, if out-migration persisted at an annual rate of −0.3%, then 5% of the population would be lost over a period of 18 years. While this loss may not be catastrophic on its own, it certainly does not provide any help in the context of low fertility rates discussed in the next section. These out-migrations are generally consistent with those observed in the 2011 ACS and incorporated in the original HEDI model (Grawe 2018).

Net in-migration has recently boosted child populations in the Mountain West and Southeast, where the annual rates of increase are 0.5% and 0.2%, respectively. In these areas, the net in-migration of children somewhat offsets the effects of lower fertility rates. While these regions were net recipients of children in the 2011 ACS as well, in that year movement into the Mountain West was more muted. This difference is of modest import due to the small population in the Mountain West; despite a lower in-migration rate, in absolute numbers nearly twice as many young people moved into the Southeast as into the Mountain West. While the West South Central (home to Texas) continues to draw children, both the 2016 and 2017 ACS suggest the rate of inflow has moderated somewhat. On the whole, the story of child migration is largely a continuation of established migration patterns between the states.

Fertility

When fertility fell during the Great Recession, economic uncertainty seemed a likely driving force. Since then, the labor market has clearly improved. In 2019, the unemployment rate fell as low as 3.5%—a level not seen since 1969. Unemployment among Blacks and Hispanics established lows never recorded since measurement began for these subgroups in 1973. While labor force participation remains below prerecession levels, since 2016 participation among those 25 to 54 years old has rebounded, regaining about nearly all of the ground that was lost. At the time that the original HEDI projections were created, fertility looked like it had found its bottom. In 2014, the last year for which data was available, the total fertility rate increased relative to 2013, albeit by a meager one-quarter of 1%. More recent data, however, show that despite encouraging economic news, fertility continues to plumb new depths.

Final fertility figures are now available through 2018 (CDC 2019) and show that the total fertility rate has fallen to 1.73 births per woman—a record low and 18.5% off the 2007 peak (CDC 2013, 2019).[8] Not only is fertility lower than prerecession levels, but the 2018 total fertility rate is more than 2% lower than that in 2017 (CDC 2019). Moreover, the total fertility rate has fallen in every year but one since 2007. Furthermore, provisional estimates from the CDC provide no reason to believe the trend is about to reverse: by the third quarter of 2019, the fertility rate was 2.5% lower than the same period a year before (Driscoll et al. 2019).

The importance of these changes to fertility rates can't be fully appreciated without placing them in the context of the replacement rate. In the two decades leading up to 2007, the total fertility rate was always within 10% of this important mark, close enough to realistically make up the gap with immigration. By contrast, since 2012 the country has never gotten within 10% of replacement rate fertility. What's more, childbearing patterns are strongly correlated across geography. Total fertility rates are particularly low in the Northeast, where in 2018 no state exceeded 85% of the replacement rate and fell as low as 69% of replacement in Vermont. Still, while geographic differences are evident, the broader story is quite unified: in 2018, only South Dakota achieved replacement fertility.

Of course, births are the product of fertility rates and the number of women in childbearing years. It is possible for the number of births to increase even if fertility rates decline if the number of women rises sufficiently to offset falling fecundity. Something close to this happened in 2014. While the total fertility rate rose just one-quarter of 1% in that year, the number of births increased by nearly 1.5% due to rising numbers of young women (CDC 2013, 2019). This example is useful to consider because it illustrates how both the number of births and fertility rate are important when thinking about higher education's future.

In one sense, the number of births seems most critical. In 2032 and 2033, we can expect more young people in traditional-age prospective student pools because more were born 18 years prior. That these cohorts weren't generated by higher fertility rates won't make them any harder to recruit. On the other hand, the total fertility rate may speak to persistent attitudes toward childbearing that dictate long-term trends. While the larger number of babies born in 2014 foreshadows some demographic relief in the early 2030s, the fact that it was generated without meaningfully higher fertility rates should have been reason for pause. By 2015, it was clear that even though the number of births was a little higher, fertility rates remained on a downward trend. As a result, a decline in the number of births could be expected again at some point. As it happens, that point turned out to be 2015, and by 2018 the number of births had fallen to levels not seen since 1986. So, while birth numbers matter in the most immediate sense, fertility rates can describe attitudes toward childbearing that shape the future.

While Hispanics, non-Hispanic blacks, and non-Hispanic whites all experienced a decline in the total fertility rate during the Great Recession, the fall was disproportionately large among Hispanics. While Hispanic fertility exceeded the replacement rate by 35% in 2007, by 2016 their fertility fell just shy of this important benchmark. As a result, recent Hispanic fertility looks very similar to that of the US average prior to the financial crisis. However, while the fertility decline during the Great Recession was disproportionately concentrated among

Hispanics, since 2013 declining fertility has been more or less equally shared by all racial/ethnic groups.

Considering fertility by age also reveals important recent developments. From 1980 through the onset of the financial crisis, fertility in the country increased due to rising fertility among those in their 30s. During this same period, fertility among those aged 25 to 29, the most fertile age group for most of the past three decades, remained more or less steady, with gentle rises and falls reflecting the business cycle. Those in their young 20s were nearly as fertile as those in their late 20s until 2000, when childbearing among those between the ages of 20 and 24 began a steady decline. Perhaps unsurprisingly, during the Great Recession fertility decreased among all age groups, creating the large drop we have witnessed in total fertility. Since the onset of economic recovery, however, it appears we have entered a new era. While declines in fertility among 20-somethings have continued, since 2012 fertility among those in their 30s and early 40s has returned to its upward trend. As a result, in 2016 those aged 30 to 34 overtook those in their late 20s as the most fertile age group.

Of course, rising fertility among those in their 30s is simply an extension of a now decades-long trend. What is novel is the fertility trend seen among those in their 20s. After decades of high and stable fertility rates, we now see a decade of decline in this group despite a nonrecessionary economy. It appears that we are seeing a fundamental shift in fertility patterns across the life cycle consistent with delayed marriage. While some of the reduction in births during early adulthood is offset by births in the 30s and 40s, the latter rise is weaker than the former decline so that the net effect continues to drive total fertility downward. While fewer births today means smaller prospective student pools in the future, a trend toward older parenthood may lead to greater financial stability when children are of college-going age.

College Attendance Rates

Recent developments in college attendance rates provide a counterpoint to the demographic trends just discussed. Of particular note, since the early 2000s enrollment rates among Hispanic high school graduates have consistently increased—up more than 20% in just over a dozen years, reaching the national average in 2015 (National Center for Education Statistics [NCES] 2018, table 302.20).[9] Recall that college-going probabilities in the original HEDI forecasts were estimated based on experiences of students in the ELS who reached high school graduation in 2004. In that year, the Hispanic matriculation rate fell almost nine percentage points shy of the US average. Even as Hispanics have closed this gap, attendance rates among Asian Americans have continued ever higher, nearing or exceeding 90% in recent years. (Obviously, there is a limit to how far this trend can go.) Growth in attendance rates by the two fastest-growing race/ethnicity subgroups provides welcome relief to institutions foreseeing shrinking prospective student pools.

One might imagine that because Hispanics have traditionally had a disproportionately greater tendency to enroll in two-year schools, their recent increase in matriculation rates is driven by enrollment in two-year programs. (In 2017, according to the NCES [2018], table 306.20, 43% of Hispanic college attenders were in two-year programs. By comparison, only 27% of non-Hispanic enrollments were accounted for by these schools.) The data, however, point to a broad engagement by Hispanics that has involved institutions of all types. In recent years, the share of Hispanic enrollments at two-year institutions has steadily fallen, proportionately tracking changes seen in other race/ethnicity groups. (This trend away from two-year enrollment surely reflects economic recovery.) Indeed, from 2013 to 2017 the number of Hispanics enrolled at two-year schools has been flat, while enrollments at four-year schools jumped more than 25% due almost entirely to a nearly 40% increase in the number of Hispanic students enrolled at public four-year institutions.

In contrast to developments in college-going among Hispanics and Asian Americans, attendance rates for non-Hispanic whites and non-Hispanic blacks today are essentially the same as when the ELS was conducted. In what may be a worrisome trend for the future, even as Hispanics were closing the college attendance gap, the achievement gap for non-Hispanic blacks reemerged after being all but eliminated in 2010. While in 1990 non-Hispanic black high school graduates attended college at a rate more than 10 percentage points lower than that for the country as a whole, 20 years later the gap had fallen to less than three points (NCES 2018, table 302.20). Parity with the national average seemed imminent. Unfortunately, attendance rates in this part of the population have trended downward since 2010, and by 2017 the gap was again 10 percentage points—almost as large as it was in 1990. As a result, between 2010 and 2017 the number of non-Hispanic blacks enrolled in postsecondary institutions fell by more than 15%. These enrollment reductions were experienced at both two- and four-year schools and at institutions both publicly and privately controlled, though the effect was larger among two-year and private institutions. (During this period, public four-year colleges and universities experienced a 5% increase in enrollment by non-Hispanic blacks.) This pattern demands attention as we seek to reverse this worrisome trend. It also urges caution when celebrating gains in Hispanic attendance rates; we must work for next year's success even as we rejoice in past accomplishments.

Updating HEDI Projections

While none of the evolving trends explored previously suggest a wholesale reconsideration of the topline implications of the original HEDI forecasts, clearly it would be useful to learn how the most recent data shape the model's projections. First, with now-available waves of the ACS through 2017, HEDI forecasts can push into the mid-2030s to see how demographic forces may continue shaping higher education beyond the original forecast horizon of 2029. The addition of more years of population data won't likely lead to happier forecasts. After all, as this is written in the fall of 2019, students in the high school class of 2037 are already being born. From CDC fertility data, we already know that extending the forecast horizon by adding the latest birth cohorts only extends the period of low student numbers.

The second model revision provides greater reason for optimism. As noted earlier, the original HEDI projections were based on college attendance patterns observed among students reaching traditional college-going age in 2004. The revisions presented in the following chapters employ the Department of Education's latest longitudinal study, the 2009 HSLS, which follows a nationally representative sample of more than 23,000 students in 944 schools, each observed beginning in the fall of their ninth-grade year. These students are in the (expected) high school class of 2013 and have been subsequently surveyed to learn of their post–high school choices. By using the HSLS in place of the ELS when estimating the probabilities of college-going, the new forecasts reflect post–Great Recession patterns of postsecondary enrollment.

Cause for hope and caution are found in the chapters that follow. The next chapter reexplores projections presented in Grawe (2018) in light of the new data. While the larger story is still one of contraction, some temporary relief might be expected in the early 2030s, and the ultimate magnitude of the contraction is modestly smaller than in the original forecast. What is more, as later chapters describe, colleges and universities are actively engaging demographic change along multiple dimensions so that the demographic trends explored in this and subsequent chapters do not represent higher education's destiny.

TWO

Updated Projections of Higher Education Demand

A RMED WITH MORE RECENT DATA on college attendance patterns and Census data reflecting births through 2017, Higher
Education Demand Index (HEDI) projections can be revised and extended into the mid-2030s. This chapter focuses on revisions and exten-
sions of forecasts reported in Grawe (2018), disaggregating the prospective student pool into that for two-year colleges and three subsets
of four-year schools differentiated by their rankings in *US News &
World Report*'s lists of top national universities and liberal arts colleges. The first section examines national trends from 2018 through
2034. While this national perspective provides a panoramic view of
the future of higher education, few (if any) institutions attract a nationally representative application pool. To give a more local perspective, the subsequent section considers how these same trends are projected to evolve at the level of Census region and by metropolitan area
and nonmetropolitan portions of states. Next, the chapter reexplores
projected shifts in the composition of the college-going population
across dimensions of geography, race, and parent education. Finally,
the concluding section provides a detailed comparison of the updated

projections with those in Grawe (2018). (Appendix 2 compares updated projections with those of WICHE [2016].)

The National Perspective

According to the National Center for Education Statistics (NCES), approximately 70% of high school completers attend a postsecondary institution in the fall following graduation. Expanding the definition of attendance slightly to include all who enroll at some point in the years following graduation, attendance rates rise further. For example, among the 2009 ninth-graders in the High School Longitudinal Study (HSLS), 72% of all students and 75% of those with a high school credential had enrolled at a postsecondary institution by February 2013 (Radford et al. 2018). So, while in the middle of the last century it may have been easy to imagine changes in population composition that could lead to rising enrollment rates even if cohort sizes declined, today such a scenario is much less likely. The current near-ubiquitous rate of college attendance almost guarantees that the number of college attenders (defined in the broadest sense of postsecondary enrollment) will rise and fall with the population as a whole.

And indeed this is precisely the conclusion reached by HEDI predictions seen in figure 2.1, which shows the projected number of all 18-year-olds and college-bound 18-year-olds relative to their numbers in 2018. Between 2018 and 2025, both steadily rise by almost 5% before falling by more than 10% in the subsequent five years. In the early 2030s, the model anticipates a brief recovery—an echo of the short-lived increase in birth numbers around 2014—before continued decline. In all, comparing the numbers in 2018 and 2019 (hereafter, 2018–19) with those from 2033 and 2034 (2033–34), the number of projected college attenders reaching age 18 falls 5% compared with a 2% decline in the projected population of new young adults.[1] While the two time series exhibit significant similarities, the projection for college attenders shows less growth or more decline than that for the population as a whole. This pattern reflects the changing composition

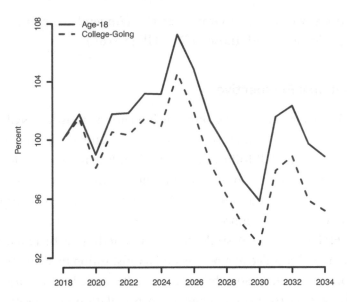

Figure 2.1. Projected Number of Age-18 and College-Going Persons Relative to 2018, 2018 to 2034. *Source:* Author's calculations based on data from the American Community Survey (2017), Centers for Disease Control and Prevention (2018a), 2009 High School Longitudinal Study (restricted and unrestricted), and the Panel Study of Income Dynamics (2011, 2015)

of the population toward subgroups with lower propensities to attend college.

While trends in overall college-going set an important context, the higher education market is extraordinarily diverse, and each institution type serves only a subset of the entire market. For instance, Radford et al. (2018) report that just under 40% of HSLS subjects who enrolled at a postsecondary institution began at a two-year college, and only 16% began at a private nonprofit four-year school. These lower, type-specific attendance rates make it possible for the number of students with markers suggesting attendance at a given institution type to deviate from broader population trends.

HEDI projections are disaggregated into four institution types in figure 2.2: two-year institutions, four-year institutions ranked by *US News & World Report* outside the top 100 national universities or national liberal arts colleges (hereafter "regional" institutions), four-

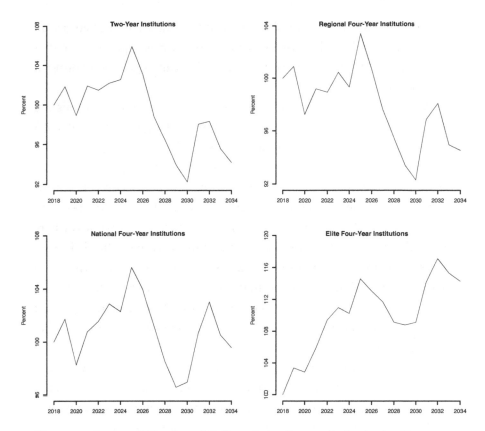

Figure 2.2. Projected Number of College-Going Persons by Institution Type Relative to 2018, 2018 to 2034. *Source:* Author's calculations based on data from the American Community Survey (2017), Centers for Disease Control and Prevention (2018a), 2009 High School Longitudinal Study (restricted and unrestricted), and the Panel Study of Income Dynamics (2011, 2015)

year schools ranked 51 to 100 on the *US News & World Report* lists ("national" institutions), and four-year schools ranked among the top 50 colleges or universities ("elite" institutions). (Note that because colleges and universities have separate rankings, there are approximately 100 national and 100 elite institutions according to this categorization.) Taken together, the projections reflect expected movements in the population of 18-year-olds as a whole—generally increasing through the mid-2020s with a subsequent decline that is briefly interrupted in the first half of the 2030s before continued decline. While the common patterns across subsectors make it evident that these submarkets are all part of a shared market for higher education, it is equally clear that some portions of the higher education market can expect more difficult paths than others.

While projections for two-year and regional four-year schools are similar—a modest rise through 2025 followed by a fall of about 10% in the subsequent decade that nets a loss of 5% to 6% over the entire time period—as we move from less to more selective types of four-year institutions the time series rotate in a more positive direction. The post-2025 decline among national schools is initially quite deep—over 8%—but the subsequent recovery leaves the market more or less where it stands today. And the market for the most selective schools is even more auspicious. A modest late 2020s reversal only briefly suspends a persistent rise that leaves the market up 13% from today's levels. (However, for both of these markets it should be remembered that CDC natality reports suggest that declines in cohort sizes continue beyond 2017.)

This comparatively better projection among selective schools is explained by three demographic trends that are explored in more detail at the end of this chapter. While the total population of young people in America is expected to contract over the next 15 years, some notable subgroups are nevertheless expected to grow: those in the Pacific West and South Atlantic, those claiming Asian descent, and those who have at least one parent who holds a bachelor's degree. All three of these demographic shifts represent growth in subgroups with stronger than average attachment to four-year colleges in general and selective four-year schools in particular. The resulting effect on projected student numbers exemplifies the fact that the composition of the prospective pool is as critical as its size.

Projections, Not Predictions

Recall, however, that HEDI forecasts are if-then projections and not predictions. All of the forecasts trace out an expected path if institutions and students continue behavioral patterns represented in the

HSLS data. That assumption can easily fail, temporarily or persistently. For example, business cycle variation creates strong, temporary shifts in demand for two-year colleges. When the economy booms and high school graduates easily secure good-paying jobs, two-year enrollments tend to decline (NCES 2017, table 303.25). And during recessionary periods, the opportunity cost of time at school falls, driving both traditional-aged and older students toward higher education. The college-going probabilities estimated in the HSLS reflect choices in the summer of 2013 through the winter of 2016, a period of modest economic growth, though in the shadow of the Great Recession. Whether 2034 is a time of robust growth or contraction may well determine whether actual two-year college enrollments at that time are higher or lower than those today. Due to temporary forces such as these, HEDI projections might better be understood as a forecast of the baseline around which actual enrollments fluctuate.

We can also imagine more fundamental, persistent changes to college-going that lead to a future that differs from the projections. For example, college attendance rates could rise in the coming decades, offsetting population decline. In fact, this is exactly how higher education managed to increase enrollments by 50% despite shrinking cohort sizes in the 1980s. Of course, that education boom was driven by a dramatic increase in the returns to college. According to the NCES (2004), in 1980 the difference in median earnings of young men with college diplomas and peers with only a high school degree was just 19%. By 2002, that gap had grown to 65%. Over the same years, the college earnings premium among women grew from 34% to 71%. In response, the share of high school graduates attending college rose from 50% in 1980 to 60% by 1990 (NCES 2018, table 302.10), and adult learners returned to higher education in record numbers (NCES 2018, table 303.40). Of course, as attendance rates have subsequently risen, it is more difficult to increase them today by an equal degree.

Just as students may make different choices in the future, institutions can and will adapt to a changing environment. Of particular note, while the model projects larger numbers of young people with demographic markers previously associated with attendance at highly selective schools, these schools need not expand their enrollment in proportion to the prospective student pool. While chapter 10 discusses examples of schools doing just that, others may respond to the expanding pool by decreasing acceptance rates. In this case, some students projected in the demand for elite schools may instead attend national or regional four-year schools. For the majority of higher education, the model projects fewer young people with demographic markers previously associated with attendance. As cases in chapters 6 and 8 illustrate, many institutions seek ways to expand access or otherwise attract students who might not have considered attendance in the past. This, too, would lead to deviations from the projections.

In sum, projections based on past behavior can give us a sense of the terrain ahead. But both higher education and its students can be expected to adapt as circumstances change.

Projections at the Regional and Local Level

While national trends point to important context, Strada and Gallup (2018b) provide evidence of the local nature of college demand: location is the most commonly cited reason (28% of respondents) for why students chose their institution of attendance—ahead of affordability, school reputation and fit, and preparation for a good job or career. While location is slightly more important among those who earned a two-year degree, Strada and Gallup find that it is the most common answer among those with four-year degrees as well. Because students generally desire to stay close to home (and perhaps benefit from the lower net tuition that follows this choice), more than 80% of first-time postsecondary students enroll in their home state (NCES 2018, table 309.10).

The local nature of enrollment requires geographically differentiated projections. Forecasted changes in higher education demand between 2018–19 and 2033–34 are mapped, by state and metropolitan area, in figure 2.3, while in figure 2.4, projected enrollments by Census region are plotted, summarizing the local patterns.[2] The panels of both figures present projections for the four institution types de-

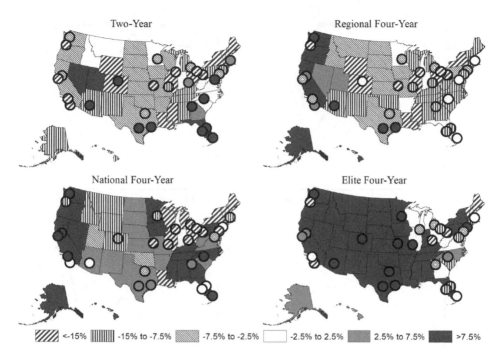

Two-Year

Regional Four-Year

National Four-Year

Elite Four-Year

///// <-15% ||||| -15% to -7.5%   \\\\\ -7.5% to -2.5%   ☐ -2.5% to 2.5%   ▨ 2.5% to 7.5%   ■ >7.5%

Figure 2.3. Projected Change in College-Going Persons by Institution Type, 2033–34 Relative to 2018–19. *Source:* Author's calculations based on data from the American Community Survey (2017), Centers for Disease Control and Prevention (2018a), 2009 High School Longitudinal Study (restricted and unrestricted), and the Panel Study of Income Dynamics (2011, 2015)

scribed in the previous section. Broadly speaking, the national patterns are paralleled in regional and local markets. Across all institution types, the 2025 peak in the 18-year-old population foreshadows relatively stronger (though not always positive) enrollment trends for the next few years before a marked downward move that is briefly interrupted in the early 2030s before the negative trend reemerges. In general, the West appears the most auspicious region for four-year institutions followed by the South. By contrast, the South is the strongest region for anticipated traditional-aged two-year college students. Across all institution types, the Northeast and Midwest foresee the greatest challenges.

Between 2018–19 and 2033–34, the numbers of students from the Midwest and Northeast are expected to fall by about 10% at two-year

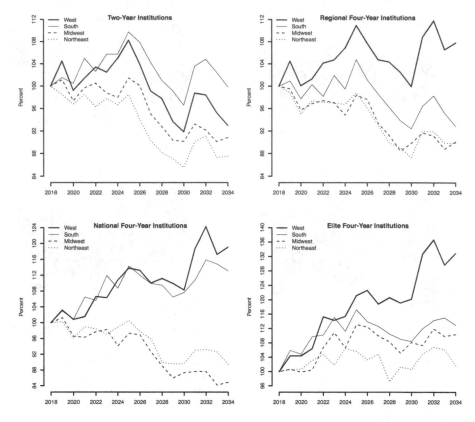

Figure 2.4. Projected Number of College-Going Persons by Institution Type and Region Relative to 2018, 2018 to 2034. *Source:* Author's calculations based on data from the American Community Survey (2017), Centers for Disease Control and Prevention (2018a), 2009 High School Longitudinal Study (restricted and unrestricted), and the Panel Study of Income Dynamics (2011, 2015)

and regional four-year schools. Most of this loss is expected in the years following 2025 as the consequences of lower births 18 years prior play out. Looking at the two-year market, only 1 of 9 and 2 of 16 local markets in the Midwest and Northeast, respectively, are projected to grow during this time period. In the Midwest and Northeast, local markets for regional four-year schools are similarly tight: only 1 of the latter and none of the former project more students in 2033–34 than in 2018–19.

The South and West offer mixed prospects for growth in the two-year and regional four-year markets. For two-year schools, the South offers opportunities while the West is down. By 2033–34, prospective two-year students are expected to hold about even in the South and fall by 6% in the West. In the South, about 60% of local markets anticipate growth in this market while less than one-third of local Western markets do so. Among regional four-year institutions, the predictions for the two regions are more or less reversed: from 2018–19 to 2033–34, regional four-year schools expect growth in the West (5%) and decline in the South (–6%). Almost 60% of local Western markets project growth in prospective student numbers for this subsector; less than one-quarter of local Southern markets foresee expansion. These patterns suggest some interesting divergence in the way the populations on the boundary between two-year and regional four-year schools are evolving in these regions.

Projections for national colleges and universities point to distinct regional variation. National demand is maintained between 2018–19 and 2033–34 by growth in the South (12%) and West (16%) that offsets decline in the Midwest (–16%) and Northeast (–9%). In both the South and West, growth is anticipated to be widespread, with about two-thirds of local markets showing net gains. Unfortunately, the declines in the Midwest and Northeast are also expected in nearly all local markets. Of course, while these schools have national names, most still draw a majority of students from within 200 miles of their campuses. Unless those patterns change, projections for national schools alone might suggest significant challenges for this sector in the Midwest and Northeast.

However, as noted previously, the prospects for national schools also depend on the evolving market for the most selective institutions. In this latter market, while growth in the West clearly outpaces that in the rest of the country, gains are expected in all regions. Insofar as elite schools do not choose to grow in line with the modeled expansion of prospective students, national schools will do better than projected. If forecasts for national and elite students are combined, from 2018–19 to 2033–34 the model projects contractions of only 9% in the Midwest and 5% in the Northeast. Because this combined market is projected to grow by 4% nationally, national schools in the Midwest and Northeast that can attract young people with demographic markers of elite attendance (perhaps particularly in the West) may yet avoid declining student numbers.

The Changing Composition of Students in Higher Education

By disaggregating projected data along dimensions of geography, race/ethnicity, and parent education, it is possible to consider how the distributions of prospective students in each of the market segments may shift over coming years. Changing geography of higher education demand is examined in figure 2.5. The two leftmost columns present the modeled share of young people reaching age 18 in various parts of the country—first in 2018–19 and then in 2033–34. A comparison shows a modest, continuing tilt away from the Northeast and Midwest toward the South and West. The change is not overly dramatic—a shift of less than two percentage points out of the former and into the latter. The subtlety of the change underscores the larger fact that all regions of the country have shared in reduced births.

Moving to the right in figure 2.5, the share of prospective students hailing from the Northeast and Midwest can be expected to fall in all subsectors of higher education. But the regional areas of expansion differ by institution type. The Southeast will become more relevant in the market for two-year schools. By contrast, the distribution of students likely bound to four-year schools is tilting toward the West and South Central. In fact, a smaller share of prospective elite students is expected from the Southeast (though this speaks more to a rising pool in the West rather than a decline in the Southeast).

Next, consider disaggregation by race/ethnicity. Census reports show what Frey (2018) describes as a "new 'minority white' generation." Specifically, Frey reports that in 2017 non-Hispanic whites made up less than half of each birth cohort under 9 years of age. The evolving distribution across race/ethnicity can be expected to affect higher education markets, as shown in figure 2.6. The leftmost columns show the shift among forecasted 18-year-olds in the population in 2018–19 and then in 2033–34. The share of non-Hispanic whites is expected to drop by

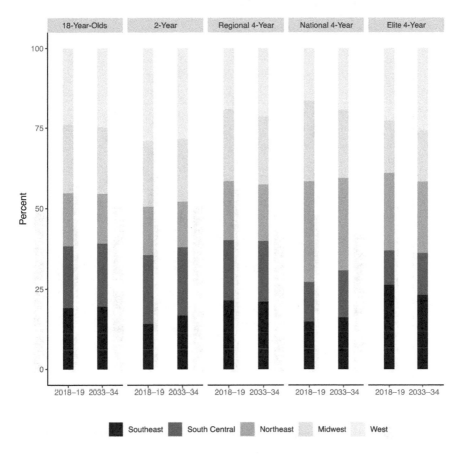

Figure 2.5. Geographic Distribution of Projected 18-Year-Olds and College Attenders, 2018–19 and 2033–34. *Source:* Author's calculations based on data from the American Community Survey (2017), Centers for Disease Control and Prevention (2018a), 2009 High School Longitudinal Study (restricted and unrestricted), and the Panel Study of Income Dynamics (2011, 2015)

five percentage points. This shift is larger than seen in Census counts of residents at any point in time because the HEDI incorporates expectations of additional immigration; young immigrants are relatively unlikely to be non-Hispanic whites. We can also anticipate a smaller share of non-Hispanic blacks. The lost share of non-Hispanic whites and non-Hispanic blacks in the population as a whole is largely accounted for by an increasing share of Hispanics.

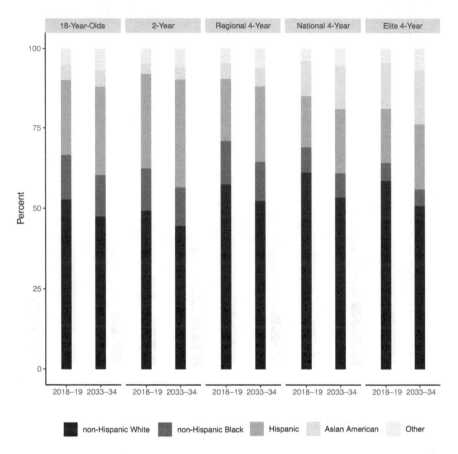

Figure 2.6. Racial/Ethnic Distribution of Projected 18-Year-Olds and College Attenders, 2018–19 and 2033–34. *Source:* Author's calculations based on data from the American Community Survey (2017), Centers for Disease Control and Prevention (2018a), 2009 High School Longitudinal Study (restricted and unrestricted), and the Panel Study of Income Dynamics (2011, 2015)

Moving rightward in the figure, the model suggests that prospective student pools for all institution types will be more diverse, though the diversification will be felt more keenly among four-year schools in general and selective four-year institutions in particular. Notably, the pool of students with demographic markers of attending elite schools will become substantially less white as the share of this group falls by eight percentage points. As a consequence, by the mid-2030s the pool of selective students will be nearly as diverse as that for less selective peers.

While all markets are becoming more diverse, the nature of diversification differs by institution type. Diversification of two-year schools and regional four-year colleges and universities, which serve a relatively representative group of Americans, naturally follows the population trends. At more selective institutions, the declining share of non-Hispanic whites in the pool is accounted for by rising shares of students indicating Asian and Other descent. (Note that Other includes those selecting two or more races.) Of course, whether these campuses actually follow the projected trends depends heavily on admissions choices, which in turn may be affected by the outcome of legal challenges recently brought by the Department of Justice.

Finally, we might explore the changing distribution of college students by parent education. By comparison of the two leftmost bars, a rising share of young people whose parents both hold a bachelor's degree is shown in figure 2.7. This increase is largely accounted for by a decrease in those with no parental bachelor's degree. And it isn't just the relative share of young people with educated parents that is rising: despite a falling population, the absolute number of such students is actually rising as well. Higher education's success in expanding access pays an intergenerational dividend as the children of our former students reach college age.

Moving right in the figure, it is perhaps unsurprising to see that this trend toward young people with educated parents is somewhat more pronounced among those likely to attend college (regardless of institution type). Some may be surprised to see that the movement away from first-generation student pools will be more pronounced at regional four-year colleges and universities than at more selective institutions. However, the nature of expanded access in the parent generation coupled with the relatively high share of first-generation students already at regional schools makes it all but unavoidable that these schools would see the largest reduction in first-generation share. Still, first-generation students will make up the plurality of students at regional four-year schools. Despite the direction of the trend, this will be an important group to serve. And if access initiatives form part of the response to declining prospective student pools, first-generation support may be even more important in the future.

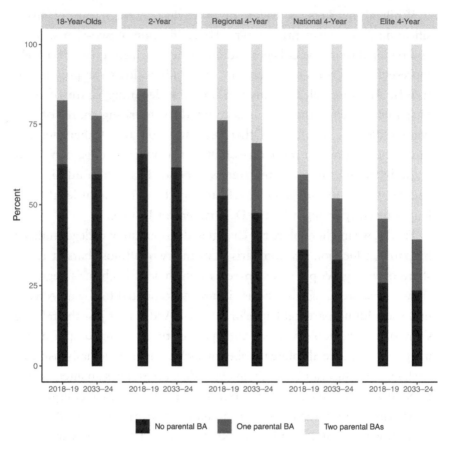

Figure 2.7. Parent-Education Distribution of Projected 18-Year-Olds and College Attenders, 2018–19 and 2033–34. *Source:* Author's calculations based on data from the American Community Survey (2017), Centers for Disease Control and Prevention (2018a), 2009 High School Longitudinal Study (restricted and unrestricted), and the Panel Study of Income Dynamics (2011, 2015)

Comparison with Original HEDI Forecasts

For the time period 2018 through 2029, the paths projected in Grawe (2018) can be compared with those here to see how the updates incorporated in the present work alter the anticipated future. Differences between the two forecasts are caused by two factors. First, as with any effort of this type, forecasts include a degree of error. Grawe (2018) explores the degree of that error by comparing projections based on data from the 2000 Census with realized observations of college-going reported by the Department of Education. In any given year, sampling variation in the American Community Survey (ACS) might lead to an especially high or low projection value. In addition to projection error, differences between the two forecasts may be caused by updated assumptions concerning migration, immigration, and college attendance patterns. Changes in these behaviors, after all, motivate present updates.

Looking at college-going in the broadest sense of attending any postsecondary institution, the two forecasts paint very similar pictures about the expected change in prospective enrollments over the coming decade—both in the modest rise between now and the mid-2020s and the subsequent decline.[3] Where the former study projected an increase of just less than 4% from 2018 through 2025, the present study sees growth of slightly more than 4%. Similarly, from 2025 to 2028 both projections see similar declines (9% in the former study and 8% in the present work).

Importantly, the two projections differ concerning the change from 2028 to 2029, the final year of the original forecast. Where the projection in Grawe (2018) points to a total decline of 15% off the 2025 peak, the present projection shows a fall of only 10%. This difference is due entirely to demographic differences between children less than 1 year old in the 2011 ACS as compared to those 6 years old in the 2017 ACS—it does not reflect differences in the probability of college-going. Taking the more recent iteration of the survey as closer to the truth, this means that the updated forecasts through 2029 are less pessimistic than those in Grawe (2018), though both projections point to significant decline. While it is possible this difference represents random noise inherent to sampling in a single year, it may also indicate a systematic issue regarding the model's treatment of infants—though, comparisons of other years of the ACS to the 2017 ACS don't suggest this is the case. Because this youngest generation sets the value of the projections at the forecast horizon, an undercount in this group can disproportionately affect interpretations. For this reason, projections presented in previous sections extend only to the year 2034, representing the cohort that is 1 year old in the 2017 ACS. (Forecasts of the number of college-going individuals in 2035 are 2% lower than those for 2034, which is consistent in direction and size with the continued fertility declines reported by the CDC for that cohort.)

With the exception of the forecast for 2029 just discussed, the updated and original projections also show general agreement when disaggregated by institutional submarket, as seen in figure 2.8. This is particularly true of the markets for regional and national four-year institutions where the original and updated forecasts for growth relative to 2018 are within a percentage point or two of each other for every year. The revised projections for two-year and elite institutions are somewhat more positive than in Grawe (2018) between 2018 and 2025. In the former group, where the original foresaw growth of just over 2% in this period, the updated forecasts show 6% growth. Similarly, while the earlier estimates suggested elite student numbers might grow by 10%, the updated model projects 15% growth. From 2025 to 2028, however, both models predict very similar declines for both groups (within one percentage point of each other).

What explains the slightly more optimistic near-term forecasts for two-year schools and elite four-year institutions? Broadly speaking, there are only two possible explanations. Variation between the projections presented here and in Grawe (2018) are either due to revised demographic trends that alter the numbers of young people—changes in migration, immigration, distribution across family income, for instance—or changing attendance rates within demographic groups. To distinguish between these alternative explanations, I applied the college-going probabilities estimated from the 2009 HSLS to the original 2011 ACS data used in Grawe (2018). The result is an alternate set of projections that capture what would have been generated with updated information on college-going behaviors but no change in demographic information. The resulting hypothetical forecast for the two-year college market is very similar to those in Grawe (2018). Less than one-quarter of the difference between the original and updated HEDI projections can be attributed to revised estimates of college-going probabilities. By contrast, 90% of the additional growth in the

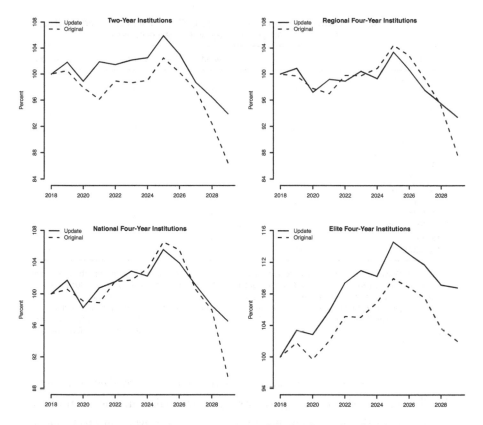

Figure 2.8. Comparison of HEDI Projection for Number of College-Going Persons Relative to 2018 in Grawe (2018) and Updated HEDI by Institution Type, 2018 to 2034. *Source:* Grawe (2018) forecast represents the author's calculations based on data from the American Community Survey (2011), Centers for Disease Control and Prevention (2012), 2004 Education Longitudinal Study (restricted and unrestricted), and the Panel Study of Income Dynamics (2005, 2009). Updated HEDI forecasts represent the author's calculations based on data from the American Community Survey (2017), Centers for Disease Control and Prevention (2018a), 2009 High School Longitudinal Study (restricted and unrestricted), and the Panel Study of Income Dynamics (2011, 2015).

number of potential elite students is accounted for by using the updated matriculation probabilities. This suggests that the more optimistic forecast for two-year schools between 2018 and 2025 is driven by updated demographic information while that for the elite four-year market is produced by revised information on college-going patterns captured in the HSLS.

Table 2.1. Projected Growth 2018–19 to 2027–28 in Original and Updated HEDI, by Institution Type and Census Region (in Percentages)

Outcome	West	Midwest	South	Northeast
Any Postsecondary				
Original	0	–9	–2	–6
Updated	–1	–7	–1	–9
Two-Year				
Original	–4	–10	–3	–6
Updated	–4	–7	2	–10
Regional Four-Year				
Original	4	–9	–2	–4
Updated	2	–7	–3	–8
National Four-Year				
Original	10	–9	1	–3
Updated	9	–10	8	–7
Elite Four-Year				
Original	12	–3	13	–4
Updated	18	9	9	1

Source: Grawe (2018) forecasts represent the author's calculations based on data from the American Community Survey (2011), Centers for Disease Control and Prevention (2012, 61(3)), 2004 Education Longitudinal Study (restricted and unrestricted), and the Panel Study of Income Dynamics (2005, 2009). Updated Higher Education Demand Index forecasts represent the author's calculations based on data from the American Community Survey (2017), Centers for Disease Control and Prevention (2018a), 2009 High School Longitudinal Study (restricted and unrestricted), and the Panel Study of Income Dynamics (2011, 2015).

Table 2.1 continues the comparison, disaggregated by Census region. While some markets are slightly stronger or weaker in one or another region under the updated projections, the two forecasts point to broadly similar stories. Specifically, the South and (especially) the West have more optimistic projections than do the Midwest and Northeast in all submarkets of higher education. And in all regions, future prospective student pools are more robust in selective markets than in open-access segments of higher education. One difference between the two projections that appears across nearly all types of institutions is that the Northeast looks weaker in the update than in the original projections. (The lone exception is the market for elite four-year institutions.)

As discussed in Grawe (2018), projection error naturally increases with geographic granularity because underlying ACS sample sizes per unit of analysis decrease. We might expect this to be particularly relevant when analyzing the national and elite four-year markets that attract a modest share of postsecondary students. To analyze the congruence between the original and updated projections at the level of the city/nonmetropolitan portion of states, I divide local forecasts for the period 2018–19 to 2027–28 in both the original and updated models using the same six categories as in Grawe (2018): –15%, –15% to under –7.5%, –7.5% to under –2.5%, –2.5% to under 2.5%, 2.5% to under 7.5%, and 7.5% or more. Table 2.2 reports the result.

Perhaps not surprisingly given the smaller ACS sample sizes in local markets, perfect agreement was observed only about 20% of the time for most institution types. This may serve as a reminder of projection error that argues for caution when interpreting data at a fine granularity. While it may be safer to consider projections at the Census region or division level, many institutions' markets straddle these arbitrary lines. Localized projections permit greater flexibility in defining regions. Moreover, as noted earlier, disagreements between the two projections may also represent updates to assumptions concerning migration, immigration, and college-going. Projections are not inviolable; changes in behavior rewrite the story. While perfect agreement is rare, agreement to within one category (e.g., categorizing a decline of more than 15% in one model and between –15% and –7.5% in the other) is achieved in almost two out of three cases even at the local level.

National and elite four-year institutions are outliers in the analysis of table 2.2. The lower degree of agreement in forecasts of the national market is consistent with the greater imprecision that follows from the small number of students attending such institutions. This same argument, however, would apply to the elite four-year market. In this case, the strong degree of agreement reflects the elite market's strength. The boundary of the upper category is set at 7.5%, so even if one projection foresees a "strong" market while the other anticipates a "very strong" market, both cases fall into the highest category.

Appendix 2 reports similar congruence when comparing HEDI projections for broad college attendance and WICHE's (2012) forecasts for high school graduates. For each year from 2018 through 2030, the two forecasts are very similar, suggesting the same change from 2018 levels within a percentage point or two. The WICHE series, however, suggests a smaller rebound in 2031 and 2032. Still, because the HEDI

Table 2.2. Congruence of Projected Growth Categories 2018–19 to 2027–28 in Original and Updated HEDI, by Institution Type and Census Region (in Percentages)

Outcome	Perfect Agreement	Deviation of No More Than One Category
Any Postsecondary	22	57
Two-Year	24	63
Regional Four-Year	21	63
National Four-Year	11	38
Elite Four-Year	54	60

Source: Grawe (2018) forecasts represent the author's calculations based on data from the American Community Survey (2011), Centers for Disease Control and Prevention (2012, 61(3)), 2004 Education Longitudinal Study (restricted and unrestricted), and the Panel Study of Income Dynamics (2005, 2009). Updated HEDI forecasts represent the author's calculations based on data from the American Community Survey (2017), Centers for Disease Control and Prevention (2018a), 2009 High School Longitudinal Study (restricted and unrestricted), and the Panel Study of Income Dynamics (2011, 2015).

Note: Growth rates were divided, as in Grawe (2018), into six categories: < −15%, −15% to under −7.5%, −7.5% to under −2.5%, −2.5% to under 2.5%, 2.5% to under 7.5%, and 7.5% or more.

foresees this rebound to be short-lived, the deviation does not last long. Similarities also extend to the regional level; however, the HEDI anticipates somewhat greater growth in the West than does WICHE. This variance appears to reflect differences in how the models account for interstate migration. In all, the similarities remind us that for large parts of higher education—two-year and regional four-year institutions, in particular—the messages from WICHE data on high school graduation cannot be ignored. Declines in high school graduates surely suggest declines in prospective student numbers for these markets. See appendix 2 for a complete discussion.

All in all, the updated forecasts show considerable continuity with the former HEDI projections. Both the original and updated forecasts see modest growth through the mid-2020s, before the birth dearth creates a significant and swift decline. Both the original and updated forecasts show generally greater growth and less decline among more selective forms of higher education. And particularly for the regional and national four-year markets, the expected change from 2018 to each year through 2028 are negligibly different. Still, the slightly greater near-term growth seen in markets for two-year and elite four-year institutions reinforces the value of utilizing more recent data to update information about both populations and college-going probabilities.

Observations Old and New

The picture painted by updated HEDI projections generally aligns with the findings in Grawe (2018), though the additional years of data provide some novel observations. To begin, what remains the same? Because both analyses rest on population counts that show a decline in births (a trend long in play in the Northeast and Midwest, and more recently experienced throughout the country), both reach similar conclusions about a decline in college-going numbers. If past attendance patterns persist, the northeastern quadrant of the country can expect a continuation of recent declines, and all of the country anticipates a sharper pullback in the mid-to late 2020s. The projection in Grawe (2018) presents a shaper decline among those reaching age 18 in 2029 than does the current analysis. However, because the latter foresees a continuation of contraction into the early 2030s, the ultimate decline is similar in magnitude.

Both analyses also predict less decline and more growth in the more selective subsectors of higher education than in other submarkets. This difference is driven by demographic shifts—geographically toward the Pacific West and South Atlantic, racially/ethnically toward those of Asian descent, and educationally toward young people whose parents hold bachelor's degrees. All three of these subgroups expect to grow in absolute numbers in the next 15 years despite a falling total population. (It should be noted, however, that the number of Asian American 18-year-olds is expected to peak in the early 2030s, suggesting that one engine of growth in the pool of potential students attending elite institutions may be decelerating.)

By incorporating the most recent Census data, it is possible to push the forecast horizon to the mid-2030s, which provides new insights. In particular, a short-lived rebound in births around 2014 can be expected to offer some reprieve. However, the subsequent decline in births makes that relief of modest duration. The observed decline in birth cohort size in each year from 2014 through 2017 (and subsequent CDC reports of decline through at least 2019) coupled with a persistently declining total fertility rate suggests that the outer edge of the current HEDI projections are not yet an ultimate bottom. As a result, prospective student pools may continue to shrink beyond the middle of the 2030s.

By disaggregating by institution type, the projections presented previously provide a more nuanced picture of higher education demand than population forecasts alone. But prospective students can be divided along other dimensions as well. How might demand for public institutions differ from that for private colleges and universities? How does the picture change if we focus on the first college of attendance? Do we see different trends among students who remain at a single institution for three years—or at least who persist in higher education for that long? After all, these students have a disproportionate effect on higher education's financial bottom line because they enroll in more coursework.

We might also want to know more about the role of immigration and migration in the HEDI projections. For example, to shed light on how some recent policy proposals would affect the pipeline of skilled labor required by industry, we might like to explore how the forecasts would change if immigration were reduced by half. Similarly, we might examine the importance of interstate migration to the regional variation observed in the projections. In addition to potential connections to policy, asking such questions serves as a check of the robustness of the model to changes in assumptions concerning immigration and migration. These variants are taken up in the next chapter.

THREE

New Lenses for Higher Education Demand

THE ANALYSIS IN chapter 2 reflects the fact that colleges and universities operate in a range of distinct markets differentiated by geography and student type. This chapter extends the prior work by exploring projections along several new dimensions. The first section applies a new lens to the HEDI projections, differentiating the submarkets for public, private nonprofit (hereafter "private"), and for-profit institutions. While too much can be made of the distinctions between these sectors (indeed, the premise of the second half of this book is that institutions can learn much from one another), differences in mission and resources naturally lead sectors to serve subparts of the higher education market. Do the projections of chapter 2 equally reflect the expected trends for these three subsectors, or are the numbers of young people with demographic markers consistent with public, private, and for-profit attendance following divergent paths?

Subsequent sections consider three divisions of prospective students based on their patterns of engagement with higher education. The first of these examines projections of first-time versus transfer enrollees. (Recall that the work in chapter 2 studies students who might ever attend an institution of a given type regardless of how or when they arrived at that outcome.) The next section divides students based on whether they were retained at their first institution of postsecondary attendance or persisted in higher education even if not at the same institution. Finally, projections for dual enrollments—enrollments in higher education taking place prior to high school graduation—are considered.

The final section of the chapter focuses on the importance of student movements. The model assumes that patterns of immigration and migration will continue as in the recent past. Public policy—at the national and state level—can upset these patterns, resulting in either more or fewer young people moving into or out of a geographic market. How might the future be affected if policy action or changes to the economic environment were to mute the rate of movement into and around the country? The results of this section can inform collaborative efforts within the higher education community, in partnership with industry that depends on a steady stream of skilled workers, to lobby for national and state policy reform.

Publics, Privates, and For-Profits

The study of prospective demand for public and private institutions in this section focuses on four-year institutions. Two-year schools are set aside because the market is dominated by the public sector. According to the National Center for Education Statistics (NCES 2018, table 303.25), of all two-year college enrollments in 2017, over 95% were at public institutions. As a result, there are too few nonpublic two-year enrollments in the HSLS to estimate probabilities of attendance at these institutions. Moreover, a large share (almost 80%) of enrollments at nonpublic two-year schools are at for-profit institutions (NCES 2018, table 303.25). For-profit enrollment is analyzed separately at the end of this section.

Within the class of four-year colleges and universities, no distinctions are made by selectivity due to similar sample size issues. Attendance at top-50 or top-100 colleges and universities is a rare event. When these enrollments are further parsed, distinguishing between public and private attendance, the latter enrollments become extremely uncommon. Among HSLS respondents, there are too few enrollments at private, selective institutions to estimate the probability of attendance using the models described in chapter 2 and appendix 1.

The projected path of prospective student numbers by Census region for public (top panel) and private (bottom panel) institutions is plotted in figure 3.1. The two plots show substantial similarities. In both, the aggregate picture for the country as a whole suggests declines of a bit more than 4% between 2018–19 and 2033–34. Moreover, both forecasts point to losses particularly in the Northeast and Midwest. While the private sector might experience somewhat larger total declines in these two regions driven by weakness prior to 2020, both figures exhibit stability for much of the time until 2025, after which student numbers drop off. Similarly, both public and private sectors see growth in the West, up 6% to 8% in 2033–34 relative to 2018–19 levels. This growth is somewhat stronger among private schools during the birth recovery of the early 2030s, however.

The forecasts for the South, however, stand out for their divergence. In the four-year sector as a whole, the number of prospective students in the South is expected to fall modestly by 5%, but this aggregate figure obscures meaningful differences across young people with demographic markers associated with interest in public and private institutions. While demographic shifts in the South increase the numbers of young people with anticipated private college attendance, they decrease those who appear likely to attend public schools. If private schools that recruit in the South do not expand seat counts in line with the growing prospective students, the loss felt at public institutions that recruit in this region could be lessened. The projected growth in the private sector is modest—about 3% over the entire period—but the divergence remains interesting. However, when considering this it is worth remembering that only about one-quarter of four-year enrollments in the South take place at private institutions (NCES 2018, table 304.60). By contrast, well over half of all four-year enrollments in the Northeast are private. As a result, the modest projected growth for private four-year enrollment in the South is growth off a small base.

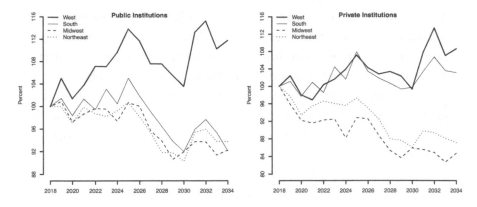

Figure 3.1. Projected Number of Public and Private College-Going Persons Relative to 2018 by Region, 2018 to 2034. *Source:* Author's calculations based on data from the American Community Survey (2017), Centers for Disease Control and Prevention (2018a), 2009 High School Longitudinal Study (restricted and unrestricted), and the Panel Study of Income Dynamics (2011, 2015)

Enrollments at for-profit institutions account for more than 5% of all higher education enrollments (NCES 2018, table 304.60). Of these, about 90% are recorded at four-year institutions. Regional variation in for-profit attendance is dramatic. In the Northeast, only 2% of enrollments take place at for-profit institutions as compared to 9% in the West. Since 2012–13, the for-profit sector has experienced a significant shake-up, and through 2017–18 the number of for-profit institutions fell by more than 30% (NCES 2018, table 317.10). For comparison, in the same period the number of nonprofit private institutions rose by 2%. This upheaval suggests caution when considering HEDI projections of for-profit attendance. After all, the model is predicated on the assumption that past behaviors continue into the future. Certainly, the decline in the number of available institutions represents the kind of break from the past that inherently undermines the model. Still, we can ask how the number of young people with demographic markers of attending these institutions will evolve into the future (if for no other reason than to identify students who might end up at a different kind of school).

The result, plotted in figure 3.2, is reminiscent of a mixture of the projected paths for enrollments at regional and national four-year col-

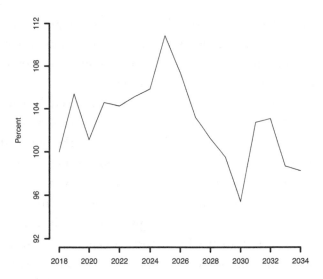

Figure 3.2. Projected Number of For-Profit College-Going Persons Relative to 2018, 2018 to 2034. *Source:* Author's calculations based on data from the American Community Survey (2017), Centers for Disease Control and Prevention (2018a), 2009 High School Longitudinal Study (restricted and unrestricted), and the Panel Study of Income Dynamics (2011, 2015)

leges and universities. From 2018–19 to the peak in 2024–25, projected enrollments rise by 5% before falling almost 10% through 2033–34 for a net decline of 4% relative to today. Of course, this only speaks to behaviors of traditional-aged students. Still, the projection for for-profits largely points to a bigger reality: whatever the differences in mission and practice across institutions, all clearly operate in a common market for higher education.

First-Time Matriculants and Transfer Students

The definition of attendance used in the projections of chapter 2 is broad: did the student attend an institution of this type at any point prior to February 2016? Because recruitment of first-time enrollees and transfer students often takes different forms and because some institutions are more reliant on either the former or the latter, it is useful to explore whether trends of students who *first* attend a particular institution type differ from those of students who *ever* attend such an institution. This section reports how the model's predictions are altered when we focus on those whose first college of attendance is of a given type versus those who make it to such an institution only after being at some other college or university.[1]

For both two-year and four-year markets, projected trends in first-time students look very similar to those for ever-attending students that are presented in chapter 2. This is true at both the national and regional level. In every region for both institution groups, the two growth projections are within one or two percentage points of each other; parsing out first-time attenders from the broader market of ever-attenders provides no additional insights. This result has an intuitive explanation. Every student who attends college is a first-time student somewhere, while only some students will be a transfer student. This fact leaves relatively little room for the baseline trends in chapter 2 to differ substantially from trends in first-time attending students. As a result, schools that primarily serve first-time students might focus on the baseline projections of chapter 2 without loss.

By contrast, because students who transfer are only a fraction of those who enroll in postsecondary education, anticipated trends for transfer students can and do differ from the projections in chapter 2. At the two-year level, the decline in the transfer student market between 2018–19 and 2033–34 is only half as large as that for the market of all two-year attenders—off 3% rather than 6%. While this difference is modest in absolute magnitude, drilling down shows that it is driven by larger differences by region. The relative advantage of the transfer market is driven almost entirely by much greater strength in the Northeast and West. In the former, while the market of ever-attenders is projected to fall 12%, the market for prospective transfer students only declines 5%. In the West, an 8% decline foreseen among ever-attenders is reduced to just 2% among the subset of students who arrive at a two-year school via transfer. While the transfer student picture is a bit stronger than that for all attenders in the two-year market, it is perhaps a little weaker in the four-year market—at least in the South. Nationally, a 5% decline in prospective ever-attending students expands marginally to a 7% decline among potential transfer students. However, in the South students with markers of transferring to a four-year institution decline by 9% as compared to a 5% loss in the market for four-year attendance as a whole.

Taken together, the projections for transfer and first-time students are very similar to those for ever attending. In no region and for neither institution class does this distinction reverse the projected direction of movements in the markets for higher education. Still, in a small number of regions, the model notes differences in how the submarket for prospective transfer students might be expected to evolve. This result serves as a reminder of the diversity of submarkets, which means that even in reasonably narrowly defined sectors we can expect some institutions to have better prospects than others.

Retention and Persistence

Of all students attracted to colleges and universities, those who reenroll over many terms and continue their studies account for a disproportionate share of all enrollments due to their repeat-customer status. This section explores the subset of students who have proven themselves persistent—at a particular institution or in higher education more broadly. The design of the HSLS imposes some limitations because the most recent observation is in February 2016, a little less than three years after the typical high school graduation date for students in the study. To capture a meaningful duration of persistence, I focus on students who entered their first postsecondary institution between June and November of 2013. In other words, these students headed off to college more or less directly following high school graduation. A student is said to be retained if in February 2016 they reported that they were still studying at or had received a degree from that same institution. Similarly, a student is said to have been persistent if in February 2016 they reported that they were still studying at or had received a degree from any institution.[2]

The model finds no meaningful difference between trends seen for retained or persistent students on the one hand and those who ever attend a postsecondary institution on the other. Nationally, while the number of prospective students for all institution types is projected to fall by 5% between 2018–2019 and 2033–2034, the anticipated numbers of retained and persistent students fall by 5% and 6%, respectively. When broken down by Census region, the difference in the projected decline/increase is never more than two percentage points. In other words, the model finds no evidence that the subset of students who stick with an institution or with higher education more broadly should be expected to evolve separately from the larger market that includes less persistent peers.

The retained and persistent students can be divided into two groups by the type of institution they first attended—a two-year or a four-year school. Recall from chapter 2 that the model projects a loss of 6% between 2018–2019 and 2033–2034 among students who ever attend a two-year school. Restricting the view to the kinds of students who begin at a two-year institution and retain or persist, the loss is almost twice as large. This difference is driven by declines in retained/persistent prospective students in the West and Northeast that are 1.5 to 2.5 times as large as the market for two-year students as a whole. By contrast, when looking specifically at retained/persistent students who begin at a four-year school, the model anticipates little difference in growth among this group and the four-year-attending market in general. At the regional level, the two groups are projected to have similar growth with the exception of the West, where retained and persistent students who start at four-year schools are expected to rise more quickly than the four-year market as a whole (with growth of around 10% as compared to 6%).

These results may intersect with those found in the previous section's analysis of transfer students. When looking at the two-year market, particularly in the West and Northeast, expectations are a bit better among the subset of students who transfer and noticeably worse among the subset of students who persist (whether at a single institution or at any institution). This set of findings suggests that the two-year-school projections from chapter 2 may not capture the whole story (at least in the West and Northeast). A growing share of the market opportunity in the two-year market is found among student groups who are less consistently attached to particular institutions and higher education as a whole. By contrast, the exact opposite can be said of expected trends for four-year schools. Particularly in the West, the four-year market is shifting toward the subset of students who are likely to repeatedly reenroll.

Dual Enrollment

For many institutions, dual enrollment—that is, enrollments in post-secondary coursework prior to completion of high school—accounts for an important piece of the enrollment picture, particularly at regional public institutions. According to experiences recorded in the HSLS, around one in six high school students enroll in a course at a postsecondary institution while still in high school. While dual enrollments sometimes represent an important source of enrollment revenue, the net effect on higher education is mixed. First, according to the HSLS, less than one-quarter of dual enrollees go on to enroll at the same postsecondary institution after high school graduation. Even in such cases, dual enrollments are potential substitutes for subsequent postsecondary enrollments because a student who earns credits while in high school may take fewer courses later. Indeed, that is the plan for many students. As a result, teaching dual enrollment students may not increase total enrollments at all. Finally, while tuition reimbursement for dual enrollees varies across states, some institutions receive less compensation for dual enrollment credit than they would get for the same credit if taken in a postsecondary setting. Of course, there is no guarantee that the dual-enrolled student would take those credits from the same institution if dual enrollment were not available. In all, the financial effects of dual enrollment are ambiguous and likely vary substantially from one institution to the next.

The NCES (2019a) reports that students engaged in dual enrollment are not representative of the country as a whole. Unsurprisingly, more students in cities dual enroll than do peers in rural areas—though rural students make up some of the enrollment gap through disproportionate use of online coursework. Moreover, the demographic profiles of dual-enrolled students echo those of students at four-year institutions: they are more likely to be white or Asian and their parents are more likely to hold a bachelor's. Given these and other characteristics associated with dual enrollment, how does the HEDI anticipate this submarket evolving over the next 15 years?

When compared to the projections of broad college-going in chapter 2, the national forecast for dual enrollment is only marginally stronger—a loss of only 3% versus 5%. But in the West and Northeast, the differences are more meaningful. In the former region, where the number of college-going students is expected to be essentially flat (down 1%), the projected number of dual enrollees continues to grow, up 4% between 2018–19 and 2033–34. In the Northeast, the dual enrollment market is also stronger than that for college-going as a whole: while the number of college-going students is expected to fall by 11%, projected dual enrollees fall by half as much. Combined with the forecasts in chapter 2, these results suggest that dual enrollment will continue to be a significant part of the enrollment picture at colleges and universities, and in the West and Northeast the share of enrollments that take place prior to high school graduation may increase somewhat.

Immigration and Migration

Enrollment lies at the intersection of prospective student bodies and matriculation rates. So, modeling the geography of higher education demand necessarily requires assumptions about the movements of young people—within the country through migration and into the country via immigration. HEDI projections assume that patterns of migration and immigration observed in the American Community Survey (ACS) will continue into the future, but what if those patterns change?

Immigration

According to the Census Bureau's 2016 Current Population Survey, 13.5% of US residents are foreign-born (and almost half of these are citizens).[3] The foreign-born are more prevalent among middle-aged Americans, making up almost one-quarter of residents aged 40 to 44. Not surprisingly, immigration with very young children is more difficult, and so a smaller share (4%) of those under the age of 20 were born outside of the country. Still, by the ages of 15 to 19, nonnatives account for more than 7.5% of the population, an important subpart of the market for higher education.

Levels of immigration can and do vary substantially across time. For example, in response to weakening perceptions of economic opportunity, from 2009 to 2013 the number of people becoming lawful permanent residents fell by 13% (Department of Homeland Security 2018c, table 1). (Immigration levels returned to 2009 levels by 2017.) Of course, policy reform can also alter immigration. While the Trump administration is currently supporting an immigration reform that reorganizes rather than reduces legal immigration, in the past it has supported proposals that would reduce legal immigration by as much as half (Baker 2017; Shear 2019).

Even absent legislation, some fear that administrative changes have already led to declining immigration (Tavernise 2019). They point to analysis of Census Bureau survey data by Frey (2019a), who finds that the net change in the US foreign-born population grew by only 200,000 between 2017 and 2018—a level of growth that is 50% to 70% lower than that in recent years. Frey further notes that the slowdown is accounted for by a reduction in the noncitizen population, particularly Latin Americans and Asians. Even with best practices, surveys (and specifically government surveys) suffer from nonresponse issues among undocumented populations, and many have voiced concerns that Trump administration policy positions may have made these statistical problems more pronounced. Still, Frey's findings point to the potential power of administrative changes in the implementation of existing law. Whether effected through such administrative channels or legislation, reductions to immigration can shape markets for higher education. To get a sense of the risk colleges and universities face in the area of immigration reform, this section studies the effects of a 50% reduction in immigration.

To better understand the meaning of the resulting forecasts, let me unpack how the model accounts for immigration by looking at a particular example. Setting aside a modest adjustment for mortality, one native-born 5-year-old observed in the ACS becomes one 18-year-old 13 years later. Foreign-born children, however, are different. That 5-year-old represents not only herself but also additional nonnative children of the same age and demographic characteristics who will be added to our population through immigration over the next 13 years. To account for this growth due to immigration, the HEDI compares the number of 5-year-olds to the number of 17-year-olds.[4] For example, if the latter are three times as large as the former, the model notes that each 5-year-old represents three young people by the time that birth cohort reaches the age of college-going. In the counterfactual case considered here, I ask what would happen if the level of immigration were halved. In this instance, rather than adding two children to this cohort, immigration would add only one.

It is important to note that this hypothetical reduction in immigration is felt equally across all demographic and geographic subgroups. This is in contrast to recent Trump administration proposals that are explicitly designed to reshape the makeup of the immigrant population. If we imagined a 50% reduction accomplished by a policy that simultaneously reflected the Trump administration's proposal to favor skilled workers, we would expect a somewhat different outcome than that presented here. In particular, I imagine that college attendance rates are higher among children of skilled immigrants. Even changes in immigration caused by economic forces are accompanied by changes in the composition of the immigrant population. For example, Sáenz (2015) finds that as the number of Mexican immigrants to the United States fell between the period 2003–2007 and 2008–2012, the population became older, more fluent in English, and more educated. Because the potential economic and policy factors that might reduce immigration are many and specific details are few, it is impossible to incorporate such nuance. Instead, I present the results of an across-the-board, 50% reduction in immigration and leave it to the reader to consider how potential shifts in the composition of immigrants under one proposal or another would nudge resulting projections either higher or lower.

At the broadest level, the effects of such a large reduction in immigration are obvious: fewer young people and fewer college enrollments. Where the baseline projection anticipates a 5% loss in postsecondary students between 2018–19 and 2033–34, if immigration rates were halved the loss would expand to 8%. Similarly, the loss anticipated between 2025–26 and 2033–34 increases from 7% in the baseline to 9% in the low-immigration case. The relative magnitude of losses due to reduced immigration would be felt nearly equally in the West, South, and Northeast regions of the country. By contrast, little effect would be experienced in the Midwest. Clearly, higher education has an interest in sustained immigration of young people—both to support enrollments and to fulfill its mission of meeting skilled workforce needs.

Not all parts of higher education would be equally affected, however. Perhaps because two-year schools serve a more representative swath of students, they would be less impacted by a change in policy like that imagined here; from 2025–25 to 2033–34, a 6% loss in the baseline model is only modestly amplified to a decline just over 7%. Four-year schools would be affected more noticeably, with selective schools experiencing a disproportionate share of the impact. Certainly, regional institutions would notice the missing immigrants: a baseline reduction of almost 6% becomes a loss of nearly 10%. Similarly, halving immigration would have a noticeable effect on the market for national and elite colleges, cutting growth by five or six percentage points.

Of course, halving the immigration rate might also alter the composition of the population. Effects on the distribution across race/ethnicity are discussed in the next chapter. Here I examine how lower immigration rates might be expected to affect the distribution by parents' educational attainment. The answer is little. Yes, reduced immigration would lead to fewer young people whose parents hold no bachelor's degree. But immigrants come from all kinds of parent education backgrounds, and so the number of 18-year-olds whose parents hold bachelor's degrees would simultaneously fall. The net result is little to no change in the anticipated distribution of young people by parent education. This is not only true for the population; even by institution type, the baseline and reduced-immigration forecasts show nearly identical changes to the share of young people whose parents have (or don't have) four-year degrees. The concern for higher education as we debate immigration reform may have more to do with the number of students we teach and prepare for the workplace than with the composition of that population.

Migration

Based on observations in the 2017 ACS, between 2016 and 2017 more than one in eight children moved from one home to another. Not surprisingly, most didn't move terribly far. Still, in just that year alone almost 2% of young people moved across state lines.[5] And of these state-movers, almost three-quarters crossed the borders of one of the nine Census divisions. In recent years, interstate migration has tended to move young people away from New England and the Pacific coast toward the South. No doubt a portion of this pattern is attributable to housing prices. For instance, one recent survey found that 53% of Californians (and 63% of millennials, the generation of today's young parents) were considering a move from the state (Edelman 2019). Talk is cheap, and anyone can consider just about anything. And if even half as many Californians left the state, the high housing costs that motivated such an exodus would be no more. But the point is clearly made: housing prices on the coasts are very high, an issue that is particularly salient to young people with children.

HEDI projections assume that recent migratory patterns will continue, an assumption that surely contributes to the difficult forecasts in the Northeast. Analysis of Current Population Survey data by Frey (2019b) shows that the share of Americans moving from one home to another has steadily fallen in the past 35 years from around 20% in 1983–84 to just 11% in 2015–16. So, in the broadest sense, Americans are less mobile today than in past years. However, Frey notes that the decline "is due to local moves rather than longer distance moves." Interstate migration has been more or less stable. This observation supports the HEDI assumption that interstate migration will continue at the same pace as in the past. But the decline in local mobility nevertheless reminds us that mobility rates are not set in stone. What if we relax the model's assumption and consider a decline in migration rates?

To get a sense of just how important migration is to the projections in the previous chapter, in this section we consider the following thought experiment. Suppose we measure the rates of migration between each of the geographic areas in the HEDI. Then suppose we cut those rates in half. For example, if 10% of a given birth cohort is projected to leave a state by age 18, in the hypothetical world only 5% leave. Of course, the state would also experience a proportionate reduction to in-migration. While such a change would likely follow from some systematic pattern, with no additional information to serve as a guide, suppose the reduction in migration resulted in a proportionate reduction in migrants moving to each of the other locations.

Such a change will have two effects. First and most obviously, it will change the location of young people around the country. Second, because Census geographic location influences the probabilities of college-going, changes to migration rates also affect the share of young people who attend college. However, this second effect is modest in magnitude. While migration is not trivial, moves across Census division lines are relatively uncommon and are often offset by others moving in the opposite direction. And so, reducing migration rates by half doesn't substantially alter the distribution of children across Census divisions. In all but the Mountain West and Middle Atlantic, the projected rate of growth of young people in the reduced-migration version of the model is within a percentage point or two of the baseline projections. In the Mountain West, halving migration rates would lower the growth in 18-year-olds from 10% to 6%, while in the Middle Atlantic a decline of 8% becomes a loss of only 5%. Similarly, reducing assumed rates of migration does not substantially change the expected share of young people living in the 28 largest metropolitan areas. Because the model allows college-going rates to vary by Census division and urban versus nonurban locations, this stability of the forecasts by Census division and urban status means that the national projections for students attending college in general or colleges of a particular type isn't meaningfully altered even if assumed migration rates are halved.

Just as projections of demand are largely unchanged at the level of Census division with only several modest exceptions, so too forecasts at the city/state level are generally unaffected. And the exceptions are relatively predictable. The number of prospective students in Alaska and Hawaii would be much greater if only parents didn't tend to move away from these states before their children reached age 18. Perhaps more importantly, a reduction in migration would shore up markets in Chicago and expensive coastal cities such as Los Angeles, San Diego, and New York (where recent out-migrations have contributed to lower numbers of young people) at the expense of in-migration hot spots of Charlotte, Denver, Phoenix, and San Antonio. Halving migration in these areas might affect growth projections by 7 to 10 percentage points. Looking at institution types individually, similar patterns emerge. Reduced migration would be good news for many coastal markets but less welcome to cities in the South and Mountain West. A very close reading shows that the effect of reduced immigration might be slightly more pronounced for more selective institutions. In all, the model's projections are relatively robust even in light of such a substantial change to assumptions concerning migration.

New Hopes and New Fears

By looking at HEDI forecasts from new perspectives—separating markets for public versus private versus for-profit institutions, distinguishing transfer students from first-time attenders, examining the impacts of assumptions surrounding immigration and migration—new layers of nuance emerge. Some of these new perspectives carry new concerns: in the four-year market, prospects for transfer students in the South appear weaker than those of the four-year market as a whole in this region, and, driven by weakness in the West and Northeast, students who are likely to retain or persist after beginning their careers at a two-year school are expected to decline more sharply than the two-year market as a whole. Other new observations suggest potential for greater opportunity: in the two-year market, growth in transfer students in the Northeast and West is expected to be stronger than that of two-year attenders as a whole, and private four-year enrollments might be expected to outpace four-year enrollments as a whole in the South.

While such nuance is important, the bigger picture supports the quip made by Bill Conley, vice president for enrollment management at Bucknell University, to the *Chronicle of Higher Education* (Lipka 2014): "If they weren't born, they're not going to go to college." With all of the subgroups compared in all of the submarkets in four regions of the country, most often findings point in the same direction as the projections in chapter 2. All institutions serving all subgroups of students are facing challenges that follow from the declining count of young people. Even policy reform designed to reduce migration is a zero-sum game across the country (though states obviously have an individual incentive to attract new families). Without steady or growing numbers of births, only increased immigration provides relief from pressures created by domestic contraction.

Before looking at how schools are proactively engaging the challenges of demographic change, the next chapter applies one more lens to the HEDI forecasts—race/ethnicity. Increased college attendance represents one of the obvious responses to declining student numbers. And addressing issues of access offers one path to that outcome. So, what can a deep dive into race/ethnicity tell us about coming changes?

FOUR

A Detailed Examination by Race

A S IMPORTANT AS the subgroups studied in the previous chapter are, perhaps no dimension of diversity receives more attention than that of race and ethnicity. Among Hispanics, recent convergence to the national mean in educational outcomes has been remarkable. As recently as the year 2000, postsecondary enrollment rates of Hispanic high school graduates lagged those of whites by more than 15 percentage points (NCES 2017, table 302.20). By 2016, that gap had been entirely eliminated. What makes this fact all the more impressive is that during the same period, Hispanics eliminated the gap in high school graduation. For those 15 to 24 years old, as recently as 1990 the dropout rate among Hispanics more than doubled the national average (NCES 2017, table 219.55). Progress has also been made in closing gaps in four-year college attendance. In 2000, only 42% of Hispanic enrollments were recorded at four-year institutions (NCES 2017, table 306.20), almost 20 points lower than the national average. While a gap remains, in subsequent years the number of Hispanics enrolled at four-year schools more than tripled, so that by 2016, 56% of Hispanic enrollments were accounted for by these schools. (The rise in four-year enrollments did not come at the cost of two-year matriculation, which almost doubled over the same period.) Private and public institutions participated nearly equally in this great convergence in Hispanic postsecondary education.

As encouraging as are the developments surrounding Hispanic engagement with higher education, recent trends in enrollments among non-Hispanic blacks have been disturbing. While almost 70% of 2009 black high school graduates enrolled in college the following fall, by 2016 the share of college-bound blacks fell to just over 55% (NCES 2017, table 302.20). And in absolute numbers, from 2010 to 2016, the number of blacks enrolled in college fell by more than 15% (NCES 2017, table 206.20). While the decline was particularly pronounced in two-year college enrollments, black enrollments at four-year schools were also down over 5%. Though the timing is consistent with countercyclical effects of a strengthening economy, increasing matriculation among Hispanics in this same period suggests other causes. Something distinct seems to be happening related to non-Hispanic blacks and higher education.

At the same time that enrollment rates have been evolving, immigration and fertility patterns have shifted. In each year from 2010 through 2017, Asian immigrants have outnumbered those from Central America (including Mexico and the Caribbean) (Department of Homeland Security 2018c, table 2). While the current American immigrant population is still significantly affected by immigration patterns from the late 1900s, Cohn and Caumont (2016) project that Asians will become the largest ethnic group among American immigrants around the year 2050. When these trends are combined with the decline seen in Hispanic fertility following the Great Recession, it becomes clear that the diversification of America extends beyond the Hispanic community.

Chapter 2 provided a glimpse into the consequences of these shifts. First, institutions of all types can anticipate more racially/ethnically diverse prospective student pools, and second, while the diversification of the population in the next 15 years will be driven by a rising share of Hispanic young people, among the subset of students with markers of attendance at selective institutions growth in Asian Americans will be more pronounced. This chapter unpacks and extends these observations to provide a more nuanced picture of coming changes.

Projections by Race/Ethnicity

To begin, consider the projected growth in population and college-going students by race/ethnicity and institution type presented in figure 4.1. The upper left panel plots the forecasted evolution of the population of 18-year-olds. Several features stand out. First, non-Hispanic whites and non-Hispanic blacks are already on a plateau or in decline; while declining birth rates following the Great Recession create a notable dip in the mid-2020s, the model does not anticipate significant demo-

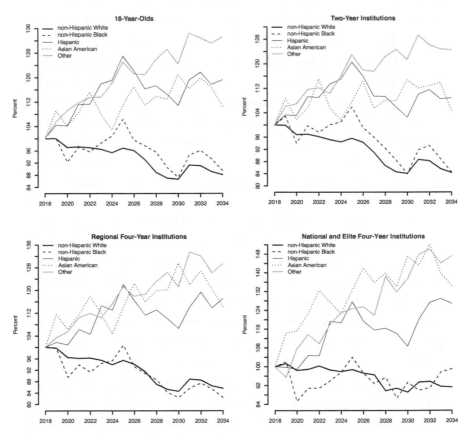

Figure 4.1. Projected Number of College-Going Persons by Institution Type and Race/Ethnicity Relative to 2018, 2018 to 2034. *Source:* Author's calculations based on data from the American Community Survey (2017), Centers for Disease Control and Prevention (2018a), 2009 High School Longitudinal Study (restricted and unrestricted), and the Panel Study of Income Dynamics (2011, 2015)

graphic strength for these groups at any time between now and the mid-2030s. These groups have had lower fertility and constitute a small part of the immigrant population, which means there is no engine for growth. By contrast, buoyed by higher fertility rates and/or immigration rates, Hispanics, Asians, and Others (which notably includes those of two or more races) are generally ascendant. The Great Recession creates a pronounced, mid-2020s correction in the Hispanic population via a disproportionate decline in fertility in this group. However, from 2030 on it appears Hispanics may regain a growth footing among the college-aged population. By contrast, recent growth among Asian Americans has been driven more by immigration than fertility, resulting in a steadier projected growth. Despite these different paths, both groups are projected to grow by about 15% between 2018–19 and 2033–34.

These population trends are echoed, with modification, in the remaining three panels of the figure, which trace out prospective college demand by institution type. The projections for two-year colleges (upper right panel) look very similar to those for the population of 18-year-olds as a whole. This fact reflects the role that two-year colleges have played in American higher education, serving a representative student body. Looking a little more closely, in all race/ethnicity subgroups it appears that growth among those with demographic markers of two-year attendance is a bit lower than in the population as a whole for all race/ethnic groups. These slightly muted growth paths reflect rising education levels among parents that predicts greater preference for four-year institutions if college-going patterns of the recent past persist.

Not surprisingly, demand for regional four-year institutions (lower left panel) also reflects the general trends within the population. However, compared with two-year demand, race/ethnicity groups show greater divergence in the four-year market. Declines among non-Hispanic whites are anticipated to be a little deeper for regional four-year schools than for two-year institutions, while projected growth in the Hispanic, Asian, and Other subgroups is a bit greater.

While the market for national and elite four-year institutions clearly reflects the same national trends, several notable differences emerge (lower right panel). First, while non-Hispanic whites with markers of attending such schools are expected to decline at a rate about equal to that of the population as a whole, the number of non-Hispanic blacks projected to be in the market for these schools ultimately holds steady despite a series of ups and downs. Perhaps more notably, Hispanic, Asian, and Other students with demographic markers of attending these schools are projected to grow more robustly than in the population as a whole. This is particularly true of the Asian subgroup, especially after the mid-2020s, when we will feel the effects of a steep decline in Hispanic fertility that occurred during and after the Great Recession. When combined with the steady decline among non-Hispanic whites, it is easy to see why and how the market for these selective schools is expected to experience the greatest degree of diversification.

Regional Variation in Diversification

While all parts of the country can anticipate a diversification of student pools for all institution types, some differences flow from distinct compositions of regional populations. The Midwest claims the least diversity with non-Hispanic whites, as projected by the model, making up almost 70% of the population of 18-year-olds in the classes of 2018 and 2019. By contrast, non-Hispanic whites comprise only 40% of the 2018–19 cohorts in the West. The South and Northeast lie in between, with non-Hispanic white shares of about 50% and 60%, respectively. Despite these differences, all four regions share an expectation of greater diversity in coming years. The greatest change is expected in the Northeast, where the non-Hispanic white share is expected to fall by almost 10 percentage points. The other three regions anticipate a decline of about five percentage points. By the time the high school classes of 2033 and 2034 graduate, the model projects that non-Hispanic whites will make up less than 50% of the class in all regions except the Midwest, where even at that late date non-Hispanic whites will make up an estimated 64% of 18-year-olds.

In the nation as a whole, increasing diversification of the population is driven by rising shares of both Hispanic and Asian Americans, offset slightly by a declining share of non-Hispanic blacks. Which regions account for these patterns? The rising shares of Hispanics and Asians can be seen almost throughout the country. The only exception is that the Asian American share in the West is projected to remain stable at 8%. Given that the West boasts the largest Asian share, this stability leads regions to become more similar in their Asian representation. By contrast, the declining share of non-Hispanic blacks is unique to the South; in other regions, the non-Hispanic black share remains constant. While these differences are notable, the overarching story is one of continued diversification throughout the country.

These regional population patterns play out in somewhat distinct ways across the several markets for higher education. The reason the markets for all institution types do not merely track the population is because racial/ethnic groups attend college at different rates. Asians lead all groups, with 85% of young people attending some college; by contrast, less than 65% of non-Hispanic blacks matriculate. These differences are not driven by two-year college attendance. In fact, two-year schools teach students of all races with nearly equal probability. This is only slightly less true of regional four-year institutions. For example, about 40% of HSLS Hispanics attended a two-year college, a rate only 33% higher than that of non-Hispanic blacks. By contrast, the relative differences in attendance by race/ethnicity are enormous in the market for selective institutions. Asian Americans are 570% more likely than non-Hispanic blacks to attend a national college or university, and the former are more than 11 times as likely to attend an elite school as the latter.

Given these attendance rates, projected patterns of diversification in the markets for two-year and regional four-year schools—both nationally and within each of the four regions—more or less follow population trends. The two-year market is perhaps slightly more diverse than the overall populations in the West and South, and the four-year market is slightly less diverse than the population in all regions (particularly in the West). But in general, the distributions of students attending these institutions track those of the population at large.

By contrast, the large race/ethnicity differences in selective school attendance rates result in meaningful divergence between diversity

trends on these campuses and in the population as a whole, both nationally and by region. Chapter 2 showed that the share of non-
Hispanic whites at both national and elite institutions is projected to
fall by about eight percentage points as both Asian and Hispanic shares
rise more or less in tandem. The degree of diversification in selective
higher education markets is projected to be greatest in the Northeast,
where the non-Hispanic white share will fall 10 percentage points. By
contrast, the Midwest looks to participate least in diversification with
the share of non-Hispanic whites in these pools falling by "only" four
or five percentage points. While diversification in these markets is forecasted to be driven more or less equally by rising shares of Hispanics
and Asians, in the West stable Asian populations mean a slightly different source of diversification. In that region, in addition to a three-
point rise in the Hispanic share, non-Hispanic blacks will gain one percentage point in selective school market share. By contrast, in every
region besides the West, non-Hispanic black share will fall. While a
one-point gain is, of course, very modest and perhaps reflects measurement error, the exception stands out in comparison with every other
region and submarket of higher education.

The Changing Demographic Makeup of Race/Ethnicity Groups

A deeper understanding of the drivers of diversification can be gained
by examining the model's projections for racial/ethnic groups' distributions across parent education and family income. As shown in chapter 2, the increase in educational attainment achieved in recent decades means that an increasing share of students can look to parental
models of a four-year degree. Between 2018–2019 and 2033–2034,
the share of 18-year-olds whose parents both hold a bachelor's degree
is projected to rise by four percentage points—a change of almost 25%.
Moreover, the model foresees similar movements in all submarkets of
higher education; whether looking at the market for two-year or selective four-year institutions, a larger share and absolute number of
students will be able to point to two parental bachelor's degrees.

While all race/ethnic groups are expected to share in this trend, not all do so equally. At one extreme, the share of "two bachelor's" (2BA) students among Asian American 18-year-olds is expected to increase substantially from less than 40% in 2018–2019 to almost 55% by 2033–2034. As a consequence, this racial/ethnic group that already leads the pack in terms of parental education will pull even further away from the national average. A larger share of non-Hispanic whites are also expected to be 2BA students, up seven percentage points from around 25% to not quite one-third. With relatively lower matriculation rates in years past, Hispanics and non-Hispanic blacks do not expect similarly large increases in the share of 2BA students—up only two or three percentage points. Of course, the recent surge in Hispanic matriculation will be reflected in a larger share of college-educated parents in decades to come—though this process will take time. Similarly, recent declines in college-going among non-Hispanic blacks will slow this important marker of demographic change in the future and signals an even greater challenge in achieving equitable education outcomes in future generations.

When broken down into markets for different segments of higher education, some nuance emerges. The shift toward more parent education among non-Hispanic whites is projected to be more or less equally experienced in all of the submarkets—whether you look at students with markers of two-year college attendance or elite four-year college attendance, the share of 2BA students increases by about eight percentage points between 2018–19 and 2033–34. Similarly, the shift toward 2BA status among non-Hispanic blacks is more or less equally experienced in all submarkets (though the magnitude of the shift is only a few percentage points). By contrast, among Hispanics, the shift toward 2BA status is disproportionately found in the subset of young people with markers of attending more selective schools. Among Hispanics projected to go to elite schools, the share who are 2BA rises by six percentage points—twice the increase found in the population as a whole or the market for two-year and regional four-year institutions. The reverse is true among Asians. While all institution types can expect to see a greater share of Asian students with 2BA backgrounds, the change is projected to be most pronounced within markets for two-year and regional four-year schools.

These shifts in the distributions across parent education help to explain the observed movements toward greater diversity in higher education markets. Not only do we see a rise in the share of Asian Americans as a whole, but this subgroup is simultaneously moving toward greater levels of parental education. It is little surprise, then, that the model foresees growth in the Asian share of four-year students, particularly at selective institutions. At the other edge of experience, among non-Hispanic blacks, the slow progress toward greater parental attachment to higher education coupled with low levels of immigration combine to create the shrinking black share foreseen for every institution type.

Similar analysis can be applied to the income distribution. Within each birth cohort, I divide the income distribution into four bins by position in the family income distribution: the bottom 50% ("lower income"), the next 21% ("lower-middle income"), the next 23% ("upper-middle income"), and the top 12% ("upper-income"). In the 2009 HSLS, these points in the income distribution were equivalent to family income of up to $55,000; $55,001 to $75,000; $75,001 to $115,000; and more than $115,000. Because this measure of income is relative, by definition there is no change in the income distribution within the population as a whole over time—for example, in every birth cohort, 12% of families are in the top 12% of the income distribution. But because the correlation between income and race can vary with time, the income distribution within a racial/ethnic subset of the population can change.

Given the size of the non-Hispanic white population, it is difficult to create meaningful shifts in the share of young people in each of these relative income groups. But minority populations can and do shift more noticeably. The model forecasts a sizable upward shift among Asian Americans so that the share found in the lower-income category falls from 44% to only 35%. It appears that this shift will be felt more clearly in the markets for two-year and regional four-year schools than among national or elite colleges and universities. In the market for these latter schools, the share of Asian Americans from low-income families will fall only four percentage points.

Hispanics might also expect to see a modest upward shift in family incomes. However, little change is projected for the subset of Hispanics with markers of attending two-year colleges; nearly all of the economic advancement among Hispanics is expected to show up in four-year submarkets. Among Hispanics with markers of attending regional, national, and elite four-year colleges, the projected shares who live in low-income families are expected to fall by five, seven, and nine percentage points, respectively. These projections point once more to the evolving nature of the Hispanic community. While it is true that Hispanics are disproportionately likely to be found among lower-income groups, as first-generation immigrants give way to the second (and third) generation, economic convergence moves the group toward higher income categories. This is particularly true in the subset of the community with demographic markers that predict selective college attendance, a force that supports enrollment growth in the market for selective higher education.

Taken together with previous results, these patterns add nuance to our understanding. The model projects a world in which selective schools experience more diversification than other institution types as both Hispanics and Asians make up a larger share of the prospective pool. But within this broader movement, the young people in these pools are expected to shift toward greater parental experience with education and (no doubt not coincidentally) higher income. By contrast, the expansion in the Hispanic share of students headed toward two-year schools won't be accompanied by substantial shifts in parent education or income. And while the model does not project that two-year schools should expect much change in the overall share of Asian students, the composition of these students will be shifting toward higher parent education and family income.

The Role of Immigration in Shaping Race/Ethnicity Trends

Immigration is an important channel by which the racial/ethnic makeup of our country is being transformed. According to the US Census Bureau, of the approximately 1.6 million 15-to-19-year-olds who are foreign-born, almost one-quarter came to the United States from Asia and more than half came from Latin America.[1] Less than 10% are European. Though race/ethnicity does not map perfectly onto region of origin, these data point to an immigrant population that is less non-Hispanic white than the US population as a whole. Moreover, this pattern has intensified in more recent waves of immigrants. Among those who arrived since the turn of the century, almost one-third came from Asia and less than 8% came from Europe. (Latin Americans make up a smaller share—only 49%—of immigrants who arrived after 2000, another reminder of the increasing peril of confounding immigration with Latin American immigration in twenty-first-century America.)

Given the racial composition of immigrants, it is interesting to explore how projections of racial/ethnic diversification might change if immigration were reduced along the lines of proposed policies considered in chapter 3. As in that chapter, the analysis here contemplates a 50% reduction in the rate of immigration applied equally to all immigrant demographic groups. Chapter 3 focused on how such a policy revision would affect the size of higher education markets. Here the question concerns the distribution of those students: were such policy reform enacted, how would HEDI predictions of the diversification of prospective college students be changed?

In the baseline, the number of Hispanic and Asian Americans reaching age 18 is forecasted to increase by 16% and 9%, respectively, between 2018–2019 and 2033–2034. In the hypothetical world, with less immigration the former group would grow by only 10% while the latter actually declines by 2%. However, these effects will not be equally felt on campuses of all types. In the two-year sector, halving immigration would marginally diminish growth in the number of Hispanic students from 7% to 5%. The same policy would have greater effects on Asian American students in this market, turning a 5% gain into a 3%

loss. These effects on the two-year market would be modest in comparison to what halving immigration would do to the market for four-year institutions—and particularly to the subset of that market outside the very top. Under the baseline, the numbers of Hispanic and Asian Americans in the market for a four-year education are each projected to rise by about 15% from 2018–19 to 2033–34 while that growth rate rises to almost 30% at national and elite colleges and universities. A policy that halved immigration would choke off much of that growth. The number of Hispanics and Asian Americans in the market for four-year schools would grow by only 4% and 2%, respectively. While growth would still be slightly greater in the market for national and elite institutions, what might currently be expected to be robust growth of more than 25% would dwindle to 12% for Hispanics and 18% for Asian Americans. Clearly, immigration contributes considerably to the foreseen diversification of higher education in general and at four-year institutions in particular.

Nevertheless, because the non-Hispanic white population is also in decline (largely due to low domestic fertility), even if diversification were slowed by a halving of immigration, the trends in racial/ethnic composition among the projected college-going groups would continue essentially unchanged from the baseline model: even with significantly reduced immigration, we can anticipate steady movement toward a more diverse America. For example, the baseline model predicts that the share of non-Hispanic white students attending two-year schools will fall by five percentage points from 2018–2019 to 2033–2034; in a world with halved immigration, the non-Hispanic white share would fall by 4%. In other words, even if the country were to implement a fairly radical reduction in immigration, higher education must prepare for a continuation of the diversification of our student bodies. Certainly, immigrants contribute to part of that diversity, but at this point in American history an increasingly diverse population is simply part of our national identity—with or without immigration. Of course, the thought experiment examined here considers a reduction in immigration that applies equally to all immigrant subgroups. Still, the lesson from this section is that immigration is only part of the country's diversification story—even a very aggressively tailored reform would be unlikely to stop the trend toward racial/ethnic diversity that is underway in America.

From Realization to Action

The findings presented in the chapters thus far clearly point to a changing world. The population is ebbing and shifting geographically as the forces of fertility, migration, and immigration reshape the prospective student pool. Moreover, the composition of the future student body is being transformed—and not in a simple fashion. For example, selective schools can expect greater diversification than open-access institutions, though they, too, will continue the trend toward a world with no race/ethnicity constituting a majority. Four-year colleges and universities that are heavily dependent on transfer students can expect this market to be softer than the higher education market as a whole. By contrast, the market for transfers into two-year schools will be stronger than the rest of the market. And the list of changes could go on. Realizing and accepting change, however, is only the first step in adaptation. The next chapters use examples drawn from throughout the country at institutions of all types to inspire the necessary response to this realization: planning and changed practice.

PART II THE RESPONSE OF HIGHER EDUCATION

FIVE

Strategies and Tactics for Tackling Disruptive Change

T HE NEXT DECADE will be a time of considerable change in higher education. Technology is opening up new ways of teaching and introducing new forms of competition, which some predict will amplify ever-present forces of innovative disruption (Christensen and Eyrling 2011). As healthcare and pension costs rise, federal and state budgets look to be even tighter, raising questions about future higher education allocations (McGuinness 2016b). Student conceptions and expectations of higher education appear in flux (Seemiller and Grace 2016). And now add a sizeable reduction in the number of available students. This could get interesting.

So, what is the best way to respond to the challenges that lie ahead? Surely, this is an ill-posed question. "All situations are contextual," observes Jon McGee, author of *Breakpoint* and former vice president for planning and strategy at the College of Saint Benedict and Saint John's University (MN). "The first thing you need to do before you [borrow a practice from another institution is to figure out] your unique context [and] culture." The opportunities afforded to one institution are not likely to match those offered to another. While this may seem obvious, Pam Eddinger, president of Bunker Hill Community

College (MA), notes that people often mistakenly look for *the* answer to pressing problems. "People think there's one particular model that is going to be the silver bullet," she notes, but big challenges don't yield to one-size-fits-all solutions. "This is iterative work," Eddinger continues. "[Solutions] will look slightly different depending on where you are, who you are, what state you are in; depending on funding and politics. Yet, the delusional silver bullet people want to have 'that one thing.' It doesn't work that way!"

Of course, this isn't to say that we learn nothing from the experiences of others. Consideration of the range of ways others are engaging demographic change inspires our own thinking as we consider how modified versions of those programs might fit with our own identities and contexts. Moreover, thinking beyond the limitations of our own context can lead to creative problem-solving that produces novel solutions. The examples in the chapters that follow are offered up in this spirit—not as "correct answers" but as possibilities and conversation starters.

Tactics and Strategies

Before turning to the examples, it is important to distinguish between tactics and strategies. McGee explains the difference using as an example conversation that follows a year in which admissions has missed an enrollment target. "There are two ways you can miss your goal," he observes. "First, your market practice isn't very good. You did something that might be good but not good enough." In other words, the institution has the right strategy and just needs to execute more effectively. The second, more serious reason an institution may struggle, he continues, is because "the market's just not buying what you are selling anymore. The former requires a change in tactic; the latter requires a change in strategy." This distinction is important for at least two reasons. First, tactical changes that fail to align with broader existing strategies are likely to fail. In the next chapter, we will see a range of recruiting activities being undertaken in response to demographic change. If we employ a tactic that effectively recruits new student groups without situating that work within a larger strategy that considers implications for financial aid, residential life, retention initiatives, academic programming, and more, we can expect to create many knock-on problems (and little long-term gain as those newly recruited groups figure out that we aren't serious about serving them).

McGee counsels leaders to approach the response to demographic change with an integrated perspective rather than focusing narrowly on a tactic here and a tactic there. "There is a hope piece" when you pick tactics without regard to the larger institutional context, McGee cautions; "you're hoping that all of these tactics add to something." The challenge is that many aspects of students' lives intersect on campus. Martin Sweidel, retired senior vice president for strategic initiatives at Goucher College (MD), notes that "students are whole people" who have a range of overlapping needs—academic, social, spiritual, and financial. Some educational models engage a wider range of these needs than others, he observes, but the broader point remains: tactical changes must be considered in light of a broader whole to be effective.

The second reason we must distinguish tactics from strategies is to keep ourselves honest about hard truths. For some institutions, the projections for demand in the previous chapters combined with healthy current circumstances suggest pressures that can be addressed with small changes to practice without fundamental change to identity. A tactical response might suffice. Other institutions should anticipate much greater disruption, demanding more fundamental change. McGee argues that attempts to address weakening demographics may be made harder by higher education's recent experience with persistent and robust enrollment growth. Decision processes developed in this more forgiving environment too often focus on modest proposals for new initiatives rather than on fundamental questions of greater urgency. In the context of enrollment, McGee explains: "It often comes down to [something like,] 'Just find me 12 students from China. There are 250 million [Chinese] people between these ages; surely 12 of them want to come here.'" But this piecemeal approach leads to unsteady leadership. "You lurch from tactic to tactic," warns McGee, and lose sight of larger, strategic questions at the core of the institution's identity.

An Example: Recruiting Adult Learners to Community Colleges

Pam Eddinger has experience leading through transformational change. In 2015, community colleges throughout the Massachusetts system experienced deep enrollment declines. Bunker Hill, the largest of the state's community colleges, has fared better than many, which Eddinger attributes to its location near gateway cities that attract adult immigrant populations, whose growth offsets declining domestic student pools. Still, the Massachusetts community college system as a whole has seen enrollment fall by more than 15%, she notes. This decline caused many to seek new student markets. With existing markets drying up, says Eddinger, "people began saying 'we need to bring back the adult students' in a very intentional way."

Prior experience as a provost and president in Southern California community colleges gives Eddinger invaluable perspective. "In Southern California at that time," she explains, "we [saw decreases] in enrollment to the tune of 4% to 5% per year," which precipitated deep budget cuts totaling 25% over four years. "It was devastating." Out of necessity, institutions developed plans to attract adult learners. "And we did," she says, "[but] we didn't think about what it meant to bring back older students and have them succeed. We shoved them into a two-year environment that mimicked a four-year environment and we didn't think about whether we had the right policies" to support the new student population. "None of that deep thinking was going on," she concludes. In the context of a 25% budget cut over four years, it is understandable how the conversation quickly turned to recruitment without pausing to think through everything else that would need to change to meet the needs of these new students. "We just knew we needed the numbers," Eddinger shares. "We got them in there, and it got us through those four years." Certainly, buying time for subsequent, in-depth strategic planning is not the worst outcome.

As similar conversations emerged in her new position in the Northeast, Eddinger pushed for a more holistic approach involving revisions to policies and programming across the campus to match the needs of the new recruitment pool. "Are we scheduling our classes at a time when these students can come for more than two classes at a time?" Eddinger asked. "What is it about our orientation process that demands that students be on campus twice before they can sign up for classes? How is financial aid working? If students are already receiving [Supplemental Nutritional Assistance Program], they have obligations for work hours as well as study hours. What does that do to their study patterns?" Eddinger stresses that the point isn't simply to think through a checklist. "It is a different way of thinking about what an adult community college looks like," she argues. (See Eddinger [2019] for a more complete description of how Bunker Hill is rethinking its work.)

A quick review of Bunker Hill's demographic profile makes the urgency of this work obvious. The college today serves a student body in which about two-thirds are adults, more than half are parents (and many of those are single parents), and three-quarters of them work, many of them full time. As a consequence, few students enroll full time, and most take four or five years to complete a two-year degree. Eddinger notes that the demand for education in this population is "more volatile because education is not at the center of their lives." If the institution cannot reduce or eliminate barriers, these students will simply walk away. But Bunker Hill's work is not motivated only by the unique challenges of a different student population. After all, new student groups also bring new capabilities and experiences. For example, Eddinger (2019) observes that "adult learners tend to be goal-oriented and focused, and generally carry prior work experience with them when they return to college." Tapping into these educational assets also requires that we rethink the way we operate.

The necessary institutional changes "are like tidal waves of transformation," she says. But not everyone enjoys tidal waves. Eddinger believes that "the hardest things to change are the hearts and minds of faculty, staff, and administrators." To support that change, she advocates for a program of deliberate professional development. "Unless we have had professional development along the way that invites us to think about equity work, a lot of educators are caught within the questions 'Why aren't you bringing me the right students? [and] What is wrong with students today?'" Such responses may be natural as longtime educators grapple with fundamentally disrupted markets. But Eddinger believes such views must be overcome for the institution to succeed on behalf of its students. "It's a mental fixedness," she contends. "Unless you are deeply reflective institutionally, you don't go to question [ingrained practices]."

While this example plays out in a two-year college context, the principles apply to four-year institutions as well. Campuses are complex systems with many intertwined offices and programs. It is usually impossible to make meaningful change in one area of the college without affecting many others. Regardless of institution type, strategic redirection draws many campus constituencies into difficult conversations that touch on institutional identities and often require carefully designed opportunities for professional development.

Commitment to Planning

These words of caution make clear the dangers in adopting new tactics without fitting them into the broader strategic vision. While holistic planning sounds obvious enough, many education leaders fear that too many colleges and universities have not actively engaged demographic change. One explanation for this inertia is that in much of the country, the challenges still lurk in the future. (Campuses in the Northeast and Upper Midwest don't suffer from this problem.) To be sure, some more persistent demographic trends such as the declining share of non-Hispanic whites have slowly evolved, requiring modest adaptation, but larger rethinking of the strategic mission of the institution hasn't been demanded by circumstances. James Galbally Jr., former associate dean at the University of Pennsylvania's School of Dental Medicine and current president of the Galbally Group, sees this as an application of the Tyranny of the Urgent. "There's a lot of activity going on attempting to solve *today's* problem," he observes. "It's not bad activity; it's just normal activity" that fails to address structural challenges that are relevant to the midterm health of the institution. The present challenge of leadership, then, is to draw campus attention to the ways the birth dearth will amplify demographic disruptions in the next decade so that choices can be made today that anticipate a new, less forgiving future. As Jay Simmons, former president of Simpson College (IA), puts it: "To maintain [institutional] health, we're going to have to change and make those changes now while we're healthy so that we can be more deliberate in how we go about it."

Attempts to lead a campus to change while the storm is yet miles away involve another layer of complexity: uncertainty.[1] As Yogi Berra is said to have observed: "It's tough to make predictions, especially about the future." While we can be sure that demographics are changing, many uncertainties remain—in future patterns of college-going, families' willingness to pay, competitors' behaviors, cost structures, job markets, macroeconomic conditions, alumni support, and more. In addition to encouraging a campus to confront the changing environment, leadership must make a series of difficult assumptions. This critical process of assumption-making requires deliberate bets about an uncertain future, often paid for in tangible and certain present sacrifices.

If agreeing to fundamental, sacrificial change is hard in times of plenty, it can be nearly impossible when decisions are put off until the moment of crisis. "People think about [the demographics of their market] episodically," argues McGee. "And, of course, they think most about them when they miss their goal, but maybe then they are not thinking carefully. Often times, they are panicking." In the context of a tuition-dependent institution, the urgency of a missed enrollment target can seemingly demand immediate tactical change without the luxury of time to consider larger strategic questions. If the limits of time lead to a tactical-strategic mismatch, the result can be more failure, leading to yet another round of crisis-driven tactical conversations and leaving little space to discuss and settle on strategic adjustment.

To avoid falling into this unvirtuous cycle, in 2018 former president José Antonio Bowen of Goucher College (MD) convened a Goucher 2025 strategy committee, made up of faculty and staff, to generate better choices for the challenges foreseen in the decade ahead. He tapped Martin Sweidel to lead the effort. Sweidel explains the Goucher 2025 charge "to reanimate the space for continuous big thinking and innovation" and "build relationships and shared vision across campus." As a "blue sky" initiative, the committee was to develop and initiate a process capable of transcending the status quo. The work, Sweidel explains, was to focus "more on the issues that involve future students than those affecting those currently on campus."

Early on, Sweidel's team determined that the work would be better accomplished by multiple small groups of volunteers, with members chosen from across various campus "silos" instead of the typical large body designed to give equal representation to all stakeholders. Each group was to come up with answers to two questions: "(1) How might we increase demand for a Goucher education? and (2) How might we deliver an even better Goucher experience at a lower cost?" In doing so, each group was led through a facilitated process to generate a compelling list of "what if we . . ." responses to both of these questions. Ultimately, six groups presented their answers at a spring 2019 board meeting. "In the small groups, I found new voices speaking out and mindsets evolving," reports Sweidel. "It was fun."

If this or a similar process can break through the constraints of unhelpful, historical assumptions, institutions will have the chance to consider a wider range of options and think through how the institution and culture might need to change to meet student needs in the next decade. "Adaptation and becoming more agile requires letting go of some fundamental assumptions," Sweidel contends. "Often stakeholders are not even consciously aware of those assumptions, hence I prefer calling the struggle that often ensues 'immunity to change' rather than 'resistance.'" The present context seems far more auspicious for substantive programmatic and institutional change than waiting until the late 2020s, after several years of low enrollment and the resulting budgetary fallout.

Where the Examples Come From

For at least two reasons, the stories shared in the following chapters are not derived from a representative sample of institutions. First, studying a representative set of schools is probably infeasible, and even defining a representative sample in higher education would be a major challenge. Second, comprehensive coverage of any single category of response could easily fill a book. (For just one example, see Kirp's [2019] survey of retention initiatives.) But most importantly, my goal is not to describe representative campus activities as much as to capture sharp examples of a wide range of activities being implemented. Because action is often driven by unusual circumstance, it isn't even clear that we would benefit most from a truly representative sample of institutions.

That said, it is clear that institutional characteristics of geography, size, and mission offer both opportunities and limitations that influence possible responses to demographic pressures. And so, reflecting the range of activities naturally elicits examples from a diverse set of schools. The chapters that follow include examples and observations from leaders at two-year and four-year institutions, public flagships and small privates, those drawing on very local markets and those with a national brand, schools with open admission and others that are highly selective, minority-serving institutions, single-sex institutions, religiously affiliated colleges, and more. While readers may not find a school "exactly like theirs," I believe the examples hold potential lessons for most contexts.

If it is true that institutions under stress are likelier than most to enact change, then a corollary follows. Some of the institutions highlighted in the chapters to follow show signs of significant duress. Some have drawn an incoming class far short of their target. Others have run deficits as enrollments have trended down. Some have announced program eliminations or faculty and staff layoffs. Most have experienced significant increases in their discount rates. (The National Association of College and University Business Officers' 2018 report suggests that most private colleges fit that description!) Readers may have the impulse to ignore examples from these institutions, arguing that missed enrollment targets or painful program cuts are prima facie evidence of poor policy making.

Inclusion of these examples underscores several alternative perspectives. First, even failing institutions may provide positive models in parts of their operations. For example, a school may miss their enrollment target in the aggregate despite having effectively carried out a program designed to improve retention—or even succeeded in increasing yield in a critical subgroup within their recruitment pool. Second, some proactive reforms can look like failure or retrenchment in the short run. For example, restructuring academic programs, while painful, may be necessary for long-run sustainability. Precisely because reprioritization is painful, it is rarely done absent significant external pressures. If implemented correctly, the result can be a stronger institution than could have been achieved without facing challenges. Finally, circumstance plays a disconcertingly large role in institutional success. Institutions that have been dealt a difficult hand may show significant signs of stress despite insightful, forward-looking leadership based on sound data and reasonable assumptions. For these reasons and more, the examples in the following chapters are not restricted to schools with growing enrollments, modest discount rates, and expanding budget surpluses.

Accountability: A Final Ingredient for Effective Change

As I completed the interviews that underlie the examples of the following chapters, I found myself thinking often of the 100,000 Lives Campaign undertaken by the Institute for Healthcare Improvement (IHI). Recognizing that large numbers of hospital patients have died preventable deaths because evidence-based protocols are not ubiquitous, the IHI challenged hospitals to adopt a short list of known best practices—such as infection prevention procedures and elevating the bedhead for ventilated patients to avoid pneumonia—and to document the subsequent change in hospital deaths with the goal of documenting a total of 100,000 lives saved in 18 months from January 2005 through June 2006. At the initiative's onset, IHI staff hoped to engage more than 2,000 hospitals (Berwick et al. 2006).

To communicate the urgency felt by campaign organizers, IHI adopted the slogan "Some is not a number. Soon is not a time." The attitude evident in the motto seems critical for the completion of any meaningful goal. If 98,000 lives were saved by June 2006, however laudable the outcome, the 100,000 Lives Campaign would have fallen short of its goal. As it happens, by the June 2006 deadline, the IHI had recruited more than 3,100 hospitals and documented 122,342 lives saved (IHI 2006). In contemplating what made the 100,000 Lives Campaign a powerful force for change, I wonder if the most important ingredient was the explicitness of the goal. Having a hard target, grounded in realistic expectations, against which the organization would be measured, created an incentive to do what was necessary to achieve the project's objective. As the campaign's slogan suggests, it seems likely that little would have been accomplished if organizers had merely encouraged the healthcare community to "save some lives sometime soon."

As the nation draws nearer to years in which each high school cohort will be smaller than the one before—a reality already known in much of the Northeast and parts of the Midwest—we can be assured that the demographic challenges we face will be anything but fuzzy. Contractions in student pools and compositional shifts toward groups underrepresented on campuses will be all too quantifiable. We can mitigate the disruption caused by these changes through a range of actions explored in the chapters that follow, from increasing access and inclusivity, to retaining the students we already recruit, to developing new programs that attract new students and more. As we think through our tactical options, viewed through a strategic lens, accountability can be a source for healthy urgency: Some is not a number. Soon is not a time.

SIX

Recruitment and Financial Aid Policies

W HEN CONFRONTING a demographic decline, many turn to the offices of admissions and financial aid, looking for ways to recruit more broadly or increase yield. If the problem is conceived as too few prospective students entering the admissions "funnel," then the solution appears to be recruitment practices that branch out into previously untapped student groups—whether across geography, culture, age, or some other dimension. On the other hand, the declining prospective student pools can be reframed as a problem of yield. In that case, solutions may look like revised financial aid practices that convert more accepted students into matriculations. These admissions-focused responses often proceed with an implicit hope that they might address enrollment challenges without changing the way the institution works in any other part of the campus.

Perhaps the directness of these arguments explains their popularity: if the problem is not enough students, the solution is to recruit more students or increase yield. NACUBO's 2018 tuition discounting study reports that recruitment strategies were the most common approach to increasing net tuition revenue, a tactic employed by three-quarters of private colleges in the study. Moreover, related financial aid strategies were the third most cited approach to net tuition revenue generation, named by two-thirds of schools in the sample.

While one important goal of expanded recruitment efforts is to generate sufficient net revenue, most institutions also view these initiatives as critically connected to how they communicate institutional values to audiences of students, alumni, trustees, and donors. For example, Wheaton College (MA) president Dennis Hanno recalls the Wheaton Refugee Scholarship, which was created in response to President Trump's January 2017 executive order banning entry for citizens of Iran, Libya, North Korea, Somalia, Syria, Venezuela, and Yemen. The scholarship would pay all costs of attendance for a student without US citizenship or permanent residency status (though, refugees legally in the country were eligible) who had fled the violence of war. Preference was given to those who had lived in one of the countries listed on the travel ban. The impact was as sudden as it was large. With help from extensive media coverage, Hanno notes that the single scholarship generated eight million online impressions. International student applications for admission in the fall of 2017 jumped by more than 50%, from around 1,100 to over 1,800. Applicants from Yemen alone totaled more than 200 after numbering just one the prior year. But application bumps were not limited to the travel ban countries. Applications from citizens of Egypt, Jordan, Kenya, Pakistan, Turkey, and the United Arab Emirates also posted notable gains. While this application activity held the potential to reinforce Wheaton's position with international students, the Refugee Scholarship was ultimately a means "to communicate our values," says Hanno. While Wheaton's Refugee Scholarship may be an unusual example, it captures the capacity to communicate an institution's brand through efforts designed primarily to expand access in one dimension or another.

While recruitment and financial aid strategies might be common responses to demographic change, risks and limitations are inherent to this path through the difficulties of a shrinking prospective student pool. Most new recruitment efforts target college-bound students. During periods of growing student numbers, this is not necessarily a problem. As more and more students make their way toward higher education, it is possible for all institutions to maintain or expand cohort sizes while recruiting the same kinds of students year after year. But in a period of declining numbers of students, this form of recruitment takes on the nature of a zero-sum game: for one institution to recruit a "new" student, another must lose an enrollee. However easy it may have been in past years to establish footholds in new segments of the college-bound market, in leaner times we must expect greater competition from peers who face similar challenges filling the class.

Of course, recruitment initiatives don't have to be zero-sum in nature. When new efforts draw in students who would otherwise not have attended college, the aggregate pool is expanded. In this sense, as a response to demographic decline, programs that increase access are of much greater value to the system because they address the underlying challenge rather than moving it from one campus to another. But the work of expanding access is admittedly hard. In fact, the expansion in access that higher education has achieved over recent decades just means there are ever-fewer untapped student markets, making it even harder to imagine significantly offsetting population decline through higher matriculation rates. Our past success limits our future potential.

In opening this chapter with words of caution, I do not intend to argue against recruitment as a means of mitigating the effects of demographic change. Even if we accept that we will need to look beyond recruitment efforts to navigate paths through the demographic challenges ahead, we may find those efforts to be of critical value. Such efforts nudge institutions and higher education as a whole toward fulfilling more completely our missions of access and workforce preparation. Whether through the competition that follows from pursuing students with a high probability of college attendance or the collective rethinking necessary to reach otherwise underserved student groups, higher education is forced to become stronger. So, even if recruitment alone is an insufficient response, in appropriate times and circumstances and paired with campus initiatives that extend beyond the admissions office, efforts like those described in this chapter may be a part of a broad response to the changes that lie ahead.

Taking a Ride Down the Demand Curve: Pricing and Financial Aid Policies

While we might think theoretically about new or expanded recruitment efforts independent of financial aid, in the real world these two parts of the admissions office are intimately related. In general, demand curves slope downward; we can increase quantity demanded by decreasing price. In particular, any efforts to expand recruitment in previously underserved communities are disproportionately likely to involve recruiting students from families with limited means to pay. Enrolling such new students requires that we overcome two related financial aid challenges: one based in reality and the other in perception.

The problem of reality is that quality higher education is an expensive product. Despite recent efforts to revolutionize the educational model via online courses with large enrollments that decrease average costs, we have not as yet found a consistently effective method for teaching that dramatically reduces the number of faculty and staff members per student. Course management systems, smartboards, lecture capture, and the like offer the potential to increase learning outcomes when used effectively, but these advances are nothing compared to productivity advances we have seen in manufacturing industries like steel, where from 1980 to 2014 the number of worker hours required to produce a ton of steel fell from an average of 10.1 to just 1.9 (American Iron and Steel Institute 2015). Baumol and Bowen (1966) note that industries with relatively modest technological change, such as healthcare and education, suffer from a "cost disease": advances in other industries lead to higher wages throughout the economy, which push costs relatively higher in the lower-innovation industries.

An extensive scholarly literature studies the effects of need and merit-based aid on college attendance and graduation. (Deming and Dynarski [2010], Dynarski and Scott-Clayton [2013], and Page and Scott-Clayton [2016] provide useful reviews of that work.) In general, the evidence is consistent with economic theory. By lowering the price, scholarship support encourages attendance and increases the likelihood of degree attainment. Administrative details matter, however, and can lead to offsetting behavior that mutes desired impacts. For instance, positive effects of the federal Pell Grant program have been mitigated by associated reductions in institutional aid (Turner 2014). Another example: Cohodes and Goodman (2014) find that a Massachusetts merit scholarship program led to increased enrollment at in-state public institutions at the expense of decreased enrollment at other colleges. Moreover, because this shift in attendance moved students away from institutions with higher graduation rates, the authors find that the initiative actually decreased the number of college graduates. Taken together, the evidence is clear that financial aid expansion at an institutional level can increase enrollments at that school, though much of this effect represents a shift from other schools. The effects of state or federal grant programs are more difficult to summarize because they depend substantially on participation rules and how institutions respond to greater external aid.

While studies demonstrate that the actual cost of higher education matters, even generous aid offers can be stymied by a second challenge: the *perception* of financial inaccessibility. Despite investments in web pages with detailed information on financial aid, testimonials from prior aid recipients, government-mandated net price calculators, simplified private net price estimators, and more, prospective students and their families still struggle to understand college pricing. Nienhusser and Oshio (2017), for example, estimate that 80% of high school students overestimate tuition and fees charged by four-year public institutions in their state; almost two-thirds overestimate private tuition and fees. Moreover, the typical perception errors the authors find are not small—about $10,000 and $5,800 for public and private options, respectively. As worrisome as these average findings are, the authors find even more reason for concern as we think about buffering enrollment losses by better serving underrepresented communities: black and Hispanic students were particularly prone to overestimating tuition. And these results don't begin to explore misperceptions resulting from financial aid awards.

To address both the real cost of college and to reduce barriers associated with perceived price, many colleges have experimented with changes to pricing and aid policies. While some of these programs target particular populations, others take an across-the-board approach.

Targeted Programs

In recent years, public and private institutions have made news with offers of free tuition to students from families with lower family income. Whether it be Princeton's full scholarship to families earning less than $65,000 or New York State's Excelsior Scholarship offering free tuition to full-time students from families with incomes below $110,000, these programs are often framed as access initiatives, expensive but worth the price. While enrolling low-income students doesn't yield as much net fee income as attracting higher-income peers, it is still possible for scholarship programs targeting lower-income students to contribute to the financial health of the institution.

Robert Massa explains the approach taken by Drew University (NJ), where the state's tuition assistance grant (TAG) to students attending private colleges is almost $13,000.[1] "If I have a full Pell-eligible student and a full TAG-eligible student," he points out, "they're bringing in almost $19,000 [in net fee income]." As a result, it's possible to generate significant income even while pursuing socioeconomic diversity. (According to the university's 2017 fact book, 33% of Drew students are Pell-eligible, 23% are the first in their family to attend college, and 37% are domestic non-white students.) Of course, by definition, this recruitment tactic creates less geographic diversity, a fact that required campus conversation. "Faculty said 'We have to become more national,'" explains Massa. "We're not going to do that because in order for us to get the kind of diversity that we need," the New Jersey students who bring the financial support of the TAG are critical.

Simpson College has found a similar approach to be successful despite a TAG in Iowa that is only half as large. Launched in November 2017 in response to recent declines in enrollment by students with family incomes below $65,000, the Simpson Promise offers Pell-eligible Iowa residents free tuition to on-campus, first-year students who apply for federal financial aid. (In subsequent years, the family is responsible only for incremental tuition increases.) Former Simpson president Jay Simmons argues that the zero-dollar tuition "takes away all of the mystery of how grants and scholarships work" for students of low-income families. Early returns point to success. "In the fall of 2017, we had 48 students who would have been eligible for the Simpson Promise had it been available. . . . In the fall of 2018, the entering class included 152 students who are participating in the Simpson Promise," says Simmons. While making higher education accessible to Pell-eligible students is a social good, Simmons notes that the program also makes fiscal sense for Simpson. In the context of excess capacity, the combination of federal aid, state TAG funds, and room and board coming from more than 100 additional students is a critical part of Simpson's efforts to address the budgetary challenges created by prior enrollment declines.

Tuition Resets

While the Great Recession made a serious dent in most financial time series, published tuition and fees continued upward. Over the past decade, inflation-adjusted tuition and fees have risen 26% and 21%, respectively, at public and private four-year institutions (Ma et al. 2018). By contrast, the Bureau of Labor Statistics reports that inflation-adjusted median family incomes are up only 3.1% in the same decade. Consequently, we are collectively pursuing the high-fee/high-aid model in ever more aggressive forms. The National Association of College and University Business Officers (NACUBO) (2018) reports that average discount rates at private schools have increased by about one point per year with discounts for first-time, full-time, first-year students exceeding 52% as institutional grants are offered to 90% of students. As a consequence, NACUBO reports that recent growth in net fee income per student has been volatile and generally falls short of inflation whether measured by the Consumer Price Index or the Higher Education Price Index. As more leaders question the sustainability of such a model, one in five schools would consider a tuition reset (Chronicle of Higher Education 2017).

Presently, the number of schools substantially cutting tuition remains quite small; only 20 private schools ranked by *US News & World Report* posted lower tuition and fees in 2018–19 than five years before (Powell 2018). Among them is Drew University. Robert Massa, retired senior vice president for enrollment management and institutional planning, shares the context and consequences of Drew's decision to cut tuition by 20%, reducing the comprehensive fee from $62,864 in 2017–18 to $53,608 a year later.[2] When Massa arrived at Drew in the fall of 2014, the college had just enrolled 302 students, well short of the targeted 375—and even further removed from the 495 enrolled just four years before (Drew University 2017)—with a discount rate of 57%. Given such a large miss, Massa explains that "it was really, really important to get the critical mass up." The urgency of the situation left few options but discounting, and in one year the discount rate jumped to 67% in an effort that attracted 350 students the next year, still well short of capacity. The following year, with fewer than 5% of students paying the full price and significant under-enrollment, Drew was emboldened to enact the more aggressive 20% tuition reset. The result was dramatic as the university enrolled 420 new students. Despite a lower fee (that very few had actually paid), higher volume meant substantially higher net revenue—50% higher than four years before.

Of course, tuition resets don't always work out this well. Lapovsky (2015) reviews the short- and long-term success of resets at 8 institutions (out of a set of more than 30 private colleges completing substantial resets in the prior 20 years). The resets, which reduced tuition between 8% and 43%, consistently produced immediate increases in enrollment (with only one exception, which lost 42% of its students the next year, a result of "poor execution" according to administrators at the school). Moreover, enrollment gains were relatively persistent in subsequent years—in one case, gains were maintained over a 19-year span. Year-over-year total net tuition revenue increased between 11% and 19% at five institutions posting gains; two others reported losses of 1% and 9%.

Interestingly, the size of the net tuition bump in Lapovsky's sample was not well-correlated with the size of the reset but rather tracked enrollment changes. This is consistent with Massa's observations about the limited circumstances under which resets have potential. First, to capitalize on the splash of a reset, it is important to develop innovative programming that can be sold to new prospects (in Drew's case, "sync[ing] career preparation with academic programs"). "We marketed the heck out of it," says Massa, first launching a campaign "about Drew's strengths and where we were growing" about a month before the reset announcement, which was made at the National Association for College Admission Counseling conference. But much more obvious and basic conditions are also critical: excess capacity and very small numbers of students paying the full fee—both conditions that described Drew in 2014.

Kenneth Redd, senior director of research and policy analysis at NACUBO, adds one more important limiting context: "One school tries something different and other schools watch and they say . . . 'Let's try and do the same.' After a while the effects . . . start to peter out."[3] In the context of tuition resets, the resulting price competition is an example of the classic prisoners' dilemma game. When others' high prices are held constant, a resetter may tell tales of great success, but if we enter a period of widespread discounting, the results will almost surely be much less positive. As former provost of Lafayette College (PA) Abu Rizvi notes, while colleges may be able to balance their books despite extensive discounting today, "you look ahead and see the lines diverge between family incomes and our costs. It's hard to feel complacent." W. Joseph King, president of Lyon College (AR) and author of books on higher education governance, puts the question more directly: "Are we going to beat each other to death with this game [of tuition discounting]?"

Alternative Models of Student Loan Repayment

From an economist's point of view (and that of many prospective students and their families, according to Strada and Gallup [2018a]), education expenditures are an investment. Similar to a corporation installing new factory equipment, you pay up front to acquire an asset (knowledge) that increases future productivity. But there is one critical dissimilarity—you can't collateralize your "human capital." If a business fails to make payments on a loan for a physical asset, the bank can repossess the asset and so mitigate losses. Not so for human capital. As a result, many economists argue that we see too little investment in education, with many young people denied access even though the return on that investment is significantly higher than market interest rates. In other words, while many pundits take as given that student loan totals are too large, economists such as Avery and Turner (2012) wonder if students do not borrow enough.

Because private capital markets are prone to failure in the area of higher education, economists have advocated for a range of public policy responses: publicly funded pre-K–12 schooling, state subsidies for public universities, federal and state college grants to lower-income students, government-subsidized (and guaranteed) student loans, and more. In each of these instances, the government is filling a hole that the private sector is presumed to be unable to fill.

Recently, several financial aid offices have created a new financial aid option—income sharing agreements (ISAs)—that seeks to address the market failure through a combination of altruism and the profit motive. Purdue's (IN) Back a Boiler program, the first ISA at a major university, is one of the more prominent examples. Unlike a loan, the ISA does not necessarily require full repayment of the funds granted to the student. Rather, the student commits to repay a fraction of future income during a 10-year repayment period, where the repayment share depends on the amount of ISA funding and the student's major. For example, in the Purdue program an economics major in the class of 2021 accepting $15,000 in ISA funds would pay 5.55% of income while an English major would pay 7.45%. In both cases, the expected ISA repayments would be similar to those of a PLUS loan and less than those for a typical private loan (Purdue University 2019). Of course, not all students will earn the average for their field, and so the ISA effectively shifts some of the earnings risk from the student to the ISA-granting institution.

Given the nature of ISAs, some institutions may find them to be a poor fit. First, in some cases they are layered on top of subsidized student loans so that students are making ISA repayments on top of loan repayments. Of course, if a student uses the ISA as a substitute for PLUS or private loans, this may not represent a new burden. While critics such as Reed (2015), citing the inability to shed ISA agreements in bankruptcy, compares ISAs to indentured servitude, parallel arguments can and have been made concerning student loans (Vigo 2017). Second, because the institution has no control over students' subsequent work choices, ISAs carry some financial risk for the institution. Finally, as the previous example illustrates, the ISA explicitly offers different rates depending on a student's major, a practice that may run contrary to institutional values.

To designers, this final criticism is a feature rather than a bug. Current student loans also require the average English major to repay a larger share of income than an average economics major. But in the case of an ISA, because average income levels also vary by major, the English student can also expect to repay a smaller total—about $26,000 as compared to more than $33,000 paid by the economics major—due to the higher earnings of the latter. Traditional student loans are not so forgiving to students who take on careers with lower compensation. Moreover, the ISA provides a healthy dose of real-life data about earning prospects in various fields that students may find useful as they make their choices, information that PLUS loan providers keep to themselves.

Shifting the Demand Curve: Expansion into New Markets

In confronting declining student numbers through recruitment, many consider expanding their geographic footprint into new markets. The imagery often sounds like the recent diversification experienced at St. Olaf College (MN).* When Michael Kyle, vice president for enrollment and college relations, arrived on campus in 2004 he was con-

---

*For full disclosure, St. Olaf is my undergraduate alma mater.

cerned by the narrow regional representation among enrolled students. "You can't have a national reputation without having a national student body," he contends. "It's not just that St. Olaf is more diverse—the high schools [we recruit from] are more diverse," he argues. "[Students] who are serious expect that and want that." The effort to expand recruitment pools began as most such projects do. The college expanded search names, started a modest alumni relations engagement program, and leveraged good publicity from inclusion in Pope's (2000) *Colleges That Change Lives* to create toeholds in targeted markets outside the Midwest. With concerted effort, the college did become more geographically diverse. Where 57% of students hailed from Minnesota in 2005, only 42% did so in 2018. And while cultural diversity was not the primary initial goal, Kyle says this dimension of diversity naturally followed. The share of entering cohorts who were domestic multicultural rose from 9% in 2005 to 22% in 2019 (St. Olaf, n.d.). More recently, Kyle says, continued racial/ethnic diversity has been explicitly targeted in a strategic plan that aims to increase the share of domestic multicultural students by 1% per year. From fall 2014 through fall 2018, the college made good on this goal.

To schools intending to navigate demographic change by seeking new markets, all of this might sound terrific, but the gains of diversity have not come without cost. "When you make those kinds of commitments," Kyle explains, "your discount rate is going to go up and your net revenue is going to be flat or is going to go down." While these costs are nontrivial, Kyle believes that "the longer-term play is that the kids and the families are going to be willing to pay more if, in fact, the place is not only academically rigorous but is also committed to being diverse." While the campus is now less dependent on the in-state market, Kyle notes: "We don't have incredible stability" in new markets; "we could have 45 [students] from California or we could have 27." So, in addition to lower net fee income, the college faces some new enrollment management risks. After a decade of mostly flat net fee income, some indicators suggest the college may have established financial stability within its more diverse recruitment pool: for three years in a row, they have increased net revenue per domestic intercultural student.

St. Olaf's story underscores the fact that shifts in recruitment do not come free. They come with risks and costs, and even a decade after implementation, gains may not be assured. In the transition, as the costs are felt on campus, leaders will need to explain and reexplain the necessity of the investment to the institution's mission. And this is the cost when things work out well. Many institutions serve regional markets and are unlikely to be able to generate significant relief by carving out a new geographic market. McGee (2015) suggests 500 miles as the "outer limit of travel for most domestic students" (32). For many institutions, the relevant market is much smaller. Grawe (2018) estimates that half of two-year college attenders traveled less than 15 miles from high school to college; among regional four-year college attenders, the median distance rises only to 60 miles. Acknowledging these caveats, some colleges are finding ways to connect with new markets.

Putting Standardized Measures of Performance in Broader Perspective

In some sense, expanding access is as simple as saying yes to more students. Of course, a much more challenging and relevant question is how to say yes to more of the right students. Admissions teams already work tirelessly to identify those likely to succeed at their respective institutions. Despite this effort, admissions staff members often suspect they've systematically missed students whose measured performance presents a distorted picture, warped by missing contextual information that could reshape the response to an application file. In particular, students whose achievements far surpass those of neighborhood or high school peers may possess attitudes and skills missed by typical metrics. "Our job in admissions is not just to reward performance; we're also supposed to be identifying talent," explains Joy St. John, dean of admission and financial aid at Wellesley College. "And sometimes we don't have good information on a prospective student's talent because of limited resources within the student's school community." Arm an admissions officer with better information about the student's neighborhood, and a "no" may become a resounding "yes."

Piloted by 15 schools in 2017–18, the College Board's Environmental Context Dashboard (ECD) (recently rebranded as Landscape) is a new tool that attempts to provide exactly this kind of information. The system merges student data including standardized test scores and high school coursework with environmental information about students' neighborhoods. In addition to school-level data on SAT performance, AP offerings and enrollment, and AP exam-taking rates and scores, the dashboard presents neighborhood measures of adversity related to crime, family stability, housing, income, educational attainment, and more.[4]

Of course, there is nothing new in principle about contextualizing applications, particularly at small liberal arts colleges. For years, admissions counselors have specialized in geographic regions and schools so that they can bring this kind of information into admissions decisions. However, even offices with the healthiest budgets cannot afford such expertise for every applicant's school. This limitation is increasingly relevant as colleges seek to expand into previously underserved areas; the ECD supports broader recruitment efforts by mimicking (even if only imperfectly) what has previously been done with human assets. ECD information is particularly useful when reading applications from relatively new markets according to St. John. "We're seeing more applicants from markets where it's not part of their college counseling culture to have a lot of students apply outside of their state system," she explains. "Schools don't always know what information to send us [in the school profile], what information would be helpful in the selective college process." By automatically sharing that context with admissions readers, the ECD effectively levels the playing field for students hailing from schools with less experience sending students to selective institutions.

The Supreme Court's attitude toward direct consideration of race/ethnicity in the admissions process suggests increasing benefits to careful consideration of student context. In *Grutter v. Bollinger* (2003), Justice Sandra Day O'Connor, writing for the five-justice majority, affirmed the limited use of information about race and ethnicity in admissions to remediate historical and legal prejudice. However, the ruling also notes that "race-conscious admissions policies must be limited in time," before opining that "we expect that 25 years from now, the use of racial preferences will no longer be necessary." Indeed, at the time of the 2003 ruling, three states—California, Florida, and Washington—outlawed race-based affirmative action at public colleges and universities, and the court explicitly counseled higher education to "draw on the most promising aspects of these race-neutral alternatives as they develop." Since the 2003 ruling, the number of states with race-neutral admissions policies has expanded to include Arizona, Georgia, Michigan, New Hampshire, Oklahoma, and Nebraska so that today approximately one-third of high school students reside in a state with prohibitions on race preference in college admissions (Potter 2014). In light of this expansion, it is easy to imagine the court setting aside affirmative action before the year 2028.

Working at a public institution in Florida, John Barnhill, associate vice president for enrollment management at Florida State University, has been living in that race-neutral admissions future for almost 20 years. In 1999, Governor Jeb Bush instituted the One Florida Initiative, ending by executive order any race-based consideration in admissions decisions. In the ensuing years, Florida State has taken numerous steps to comply with the race-neutral requirement while recruiting a class with diversity that serves the educational goals of the institution. Barnhill explains, "We started experimenting with all kinds of different things, and they're all kind of the same thing. There's really not much new under the sun . . . whether that's visiting high schools with a higher minority population or creating a stronger bridge program or even partnering with schools with higher minority populations, looking for first-generation [or] low socio-economic [populations]." So, when the ECD pilot program opened up, while Barnhill was excited to try the new tool, it was adopted as an addition to a well-developed suite of strategies designed to draw a diverse student pool.

Understandably cautious in the pilot implementation, Barnhill initially used the ECD in selecting 400 admitted students for Florida State's summer bridge program. After applying the tool to the 2,000 or so program applicants, Barnhill says that "the tool was wildly successful." With consistent information on the context of student performance, those selecting bridge program participants "felt that they made the best decisions that they'd ever made." Encouraged by the outcome of this pilot implementation, Barnhill made a more aggressive decision. At the tail end of the admissions process—after a majority of decisions had been all but finalized, though acceptance letters had not gone out—he asked his staff to reevaluate, using the ECD, the files of all applicants who were on the bubble with very high disadvantage scores. After taking into account the additional context information, his staff decided to offer admission to more than 1,000 applicants, most of whom had been slated for rejection. Out of this group, about 400 additional students attended Florida State. Compared to the 4,060 first-year students who entered in fall 2017, this is a large effect. The resulting entering class was notably more diverse along the dimension of race/ethnicity (41% were domestic multicultural as compared to 38% the previous year) and posted higher test scores. Barnhill is appropriately cautious in his interpretation. "There are many moving parts in admissions," he notes, and so it is difficult to pin down the contribution of any one change in practice. In addition, future evaluations of student persistence will be important. Still, Barnhill is excited by the potential and has implemented the ECD in all admissions decisions for future years.

Because the ECD makes it easier to identify the student whose performance reflects the aid and support of extensive neighborhood resources, some have noted that, should the use of the tool spread across institutions, parents would have an incentive to move into school districts with fewer advantages. St. John chuckles at this idea. "That's great if we can end housing segregation with this tool! I'm all for it!" By her reckoning, such thoughts are exactly why the ECD is a useful tool. "That's the point," she says. "We have such segregated education now that we have to be thoughtful about it when we make our admissions decisions. . . . [The ECD] holds us accountable; we can't pretend we don't know [that neighborhood segregation shapes the appearance of college readiness] because we have that information."

New Programs as Recruitment Tools

New programs can help target specific demographic groups for both recruitment and retention. King aptly captures the philosophy behind this approach: encourage students to engage with a campus group or activity that creates connection to the wider campus—what King calls "the core affinity." While this general goal is hardly new, King sees campuses like Lyon doing more to make this process deliberate in light of increasing demographic pressures. At Lyon, one recent example of this work is the creation of a Reserve Officers' Training Corps (ROTC) program beginning in fall 2019. "ROTC really helps out our first-gen families who have an affinity for the military" says King.

President H. Scott Bierman saw a similar opportunity when he arrived at Beloit College (WI) in 2009. He was struck by the modest number of students enrolled from suburban Chicago, just an hour away. Drawing on the rapid rate of growth, particularly in the Midwest, in high school lacrosse programs, the college invested in adding the sport to its athletic offerings. The associated up-front cost was substantial. In addition to hiring coaches and funding an operating budget, the school required a new field to play on and equipment. Looking back, Bierman is very happy to have taken that risk. The men's team very quickly recruited upward of 20 students per year. "The economics of that are stunningly good," says Bierman. Indeed, in terms of net tuition revenue generated, he says, lacrosse quickly rose to the top of all of Beloit's sports teams. While high school lacrosse players do tend to come from families with greater capacity to pay for college, the team still maintained a healthy income distribution. "It wasn't like you had a lacrosse program with just a bunch of rich kids," Bierman explains.

Bierman acknowledges the good fortune of recruiting a pair of "rock star" inaugural coaches. Early success on the field predictably led them to new jobs. In addition, over time "we didn't have the shiny penny of a new program," says Biermann, and so returns unsurprisingly declined a bit over time. Despite this reversion to the mean in recruitment numbers, Bierman says the investment has easily paid off. Initial success paid for all of the field and equipment, and continuing recruits generate sufficient income to more than pay for ongoing costs. Of course, it might not have turned out this way. Up-front costs may never be repaid if new program investments focus on programmatic spaces with little recruitment or retention gains or if the implementation fails to make good on potential that does exist. (Chapter 8 provides many more examples of new program creation, particularly in the academic sphere.) But when done well, new programs can be a recruitment tool.

Sometimes the payoffs from new programs come from unexpected corners. Champlain College (VT) has augmented its on-campus offerings in Burlington, with extensive online programming. A large part of the online portfolio serves nontraditional students who are offered free coursework by their employers as a job benefit through Champlain's online truED platform. (The federal government is a large client.) While the goal of the truED program was to diversify into online and nontraditional markets, Lisa Bunders, vice president of enrollment management, reports an unexpected side benefit. Online coursework is raising Champlain's brand awareness in the nontraditional market, and that awareness is bleeding over to the children of truED students. "We're seeing funnel development in areas that we hadn't before and that largely can be attributed to some of the truED marketing that we're doing in those markets," says Bunders. As a result, the campus has developed several new pipelines for traditional students in the South Atlantic, far from its northern Vermont home. While the context of Champlain's work is somewhat unique, it points to the generalizable principle that the recruitment benefits from new programs often extend beyond the primary audience.

Thinking Outside the Box and Inside the Cell

While correspondence courses have long been offered to inmates, new face-to-face programs have recently become available. Rebecca Silbert is senior fellow and director of the Renewing Communities initiative at the Opportunity Institute, which works with community colleges to provide courses to inmates in California prisons. In the four years following passage of a 2014 law allowing community colleges to collect apportionment for credits taught to inmates, she says the program has seen the number of face-to-face prison enrollments at the state's community colleges increase from 0 to over 9,000. Despite the short time frame, the practice is now widespread, providing a community college connection at 33 of the state's 35 prisons.

It is too early to measure the ultimate effects of the program on degree attainment, recidivism, or the wide range of outcomes one might hope to affect with a prison education program. But tentative, initial evaluations give reason to hope for success. "We see overwhelmingly positive results," says Silbert. "There are waiting lists for more college. And every single time—and I do mean 100% of the time—I go into a prison classroom, a student raises his or her hand and asks 'When can I get the BA?'" Moreover, Silbert concludes that the program "has transformed the students' belief in what they can achieve." (While practicalities of funding need to be worked out, Silbert's recent work has included talks with California State University schools interested in meeting this demand.) Silbert believes that the potential to increase educational attainment among the incarcerated is only the beginning. As prisoners talk with their children about the value of their learning experience, "the intergenerational and ripple effect of higher education is enormous."

While education of the incarcerated is an end in itself, for many students the purpose is to prepare for life after prison. Silbert sees success in this dimension as students become engaged in their educational future: "Overwhelmingly [incarcerated students] say 'if I don't finish here, I'm going to finish on the outside.'" With only four years of experience, we have limited data on the realization of this goal following release. Moreover, privacy rights limit the ability to track formerly incarcerated students. But Silbert can point to dramatic growth in student clubs that support those who have had experience in the judicial system. "Five years ago, there were about 5 campuses that had a student club or campus program; now we're somewhere between 30 and 40 depending on how you count," she shares. "They're out there tabling next to the chess club and the hip-hop group."

If the potential for prison education seems clear, so, too, are some of the challenges. "Where we lose students is in the handoff [from prison to the community college campus] upon release," explains Silbert. Family reintegration, stable housing, and basics like food must come first. "We have students who are really fired up to continue while they are on the inside," says Silbert, "and then other things are just overwhelming." In addition, teaching in prison is uniquely challenging. For example, suppose in the eleventh week of the term "you show up [to teach] and the prison says 'we went on lock-down and confiscated all of your materials.' Now what?" Silbert asks. Or suppose a professor is sick. "On campus you might reschedule that class for the next day," she observes, "but you don't get to do that in prison." Even organizing an end-of-term tutor session, something that is trivial in the on-campus setting, is difficult in the prison context. "The challenges for the teacher and the student are greater than anyone imagines."

Finally, the ethics of power must be considered when contemplating outreach to students in prison. Silbert notes that some argue that it is "unethical to target students in prison because they do not have sufficient choice or capacity. . . . Anyone motivated by the desire to find new students is inherently suspect." Even those who ultimately conclude prison college programs provide net benefits can acknowledge problematic incentives inevitably created by a captive audience with no alternative educational options. (Not only might prisoners have no choice in institution, but they often have no choice of professor.) In particular, Silbert cautions against the financial motivation to make choices that compromise quality for the sake of cost, particularly when institutions consider distance modalities instead of face-to-face teaching. "It doesn't serve students," says Silbert, "but it's appealing to Departments of Corrections and some college administrators because it is easier and cheaper." Even the best-intentioned providers must surely face this issue head-on because every institution routinely tackles questions of cost reduction. So, how can an institution engaging the prison population test whether its interests are appropriately focused? For Silbert, the answer is straightforward. "It is incumbent upon the institution to ask: Is what we are doing student-centered?"

Moving beyond Recruitment

At a recent conference on strategic enrollment management, I participated in an open discussion session focused on work by the National Student Clearinghouse Research Center that outlined coming demographic challenges. The first three participants to speak all voiced their sense that while the aggregate data point to real problems for many, their institution will be just fine because their feeder schools expect continued growth in student numbers. The attitude behind these remarks seems naïve. While it is possible that some schools are blessed with robust markets, it must then follow that others face even deeper contractions than average. Moreover, it seems unlikely that struggling institutions will carry on per usual and suffer deep enrollment declines, leaving untouched more fortunate peers' better recruitment pools. As demand contracts and competitive pressures increase, all institutions will be pushed to consider innovations in recruitment.

But if thinking too little about recruitment is dangerous, so, too, is thinking about it too much. At the 2018 College Board Forum, a group of rising admissions and financial aid leaders were informally polled as to their institutions' responses to coming demographic change. Were they preparing for tighter budgets, looking to increase enrollment by widening access, or did they plan to redouble efforts to out-recruit the competition. The vast majority indicated the final option. Clearly, as a mathematical truism, it isn't possible for everyone to out-compete everyone else.

Still, might recruitment efforts offset shrinking prospective student pools by expanding access? To a degree, but we must be realistic. For example, to maintain enrollments while the number of young people falls by 15%, college-going rates for all race/ethnicity subgroups would need to increase by 12 percentage points. It took us about 25 years to raise the attendance rate from around 60% to our current 70% figure. And with the attendance rate for Asian Americans already above 87%, we should not expect the next 12 points to be easily won. A more realistic goal might be to raise all groups' attendance rates to at least the level of non-Hispanic whites (70.5%). The "trouble" is that Hispanics already have met this mark. Increasing the nonwhite, non-Hispanic attendance rate, while noble and worth pursuing, would only offset one-third of the population decline. The bottom line is that to avoid demographically induced contractions will almost surely require engagement beyond the admissions office. The next chapters discuss examples of such initiatives.

SEVEN

Retention Initiatives

To BORROW A PHRASE from the private sector, by adopting new strategies to increase retention rates, colleges and universities have the opportunity to do well by doing good. With more students returning to campus each term, smaller new-student cohorts sustain the same overall enrollment levels and so benefit the institution's financial health. Obviously, from the student perspective, anything that avoids costly transitions between institutions and speeds persistence to degree completion is of tremendous personal and financial value. Finally, society benefits when improvements in teaching, advising, student support, and bureaucratic processes allow us to embody more fully our collective mission to provide an educated society.

Some have pushed back on the idea that demographic change provides a reason to attend to retention. We've been working on retention for years, they say, and some institutions have markedly improved performance. With so much effort expended on the problem, what more can be gained? Two answers come to mind. First, financial and time investments into retention initiatives are undertaken with at least some consideration of costs and benefits. As an economist, I say this without a hint of criticism; counting the costs is an essential step in any planning exercise. But the cost-benefit analysis must change with the environment. In an era of declining student numbers, perhaps the cheapest student to recruit is already on campus. As a result, it may make sense to revisit previously rejected retention efforts that seemed too costly in decades of growth.

Second, while some institutions have made impressive gains in retention rates, national data show that much remains to be accomplished. The National Student Clearinghouse Research Center (2019a) reports only modest recent improvement in first-year retention and persistence. In 2018, only 62% of students returned to the institution at which they began studies the year before, and more than one in four failed to enroll at any institution in the second year. (Both retention and persistence rates are approximately 10 points higher when the sample is restricted to full-time students.) Despite obvious room for improvement, retention and persistence rates have increased only modestly, by about three percentage points when compared with the cohort entering college in 2009.

Degree completion rates at both two- and four-year institutions also provide little reason to declare victory. Among students entering two-year institutions in 1989–90, by 1994 only 38% had earned any degree and only 6% had acquired a bachelor's (NCES 2000, table 311). Students entering similar institutions in 2003–04 were slightly less likely to have earned a degree by 2009 (35% had done so) but more likely to have earned a bachelor's (11%) (NCES 2017, table 326.40). (Note that the later measurement allowed an additional year for degree completion.) Evidence of improved retention outcomes is only slightly stronger among students beginning their studies at four-year institutions. Of those entering in 1989–90, 60% held some degree five years later and 53% had earned a bachelor's (NCES 2000, table 311). The share of entrants in the 2003–04 cohort holding a degree six years later increased slightly to 64%, and 58% had earned a bachelor's (NCES 2017, table 326.40). Whether these figures suggest real improvements or only the fact that slow degree completion has led us to now measure six- rather than five-year graduation rates is unclear. What is obviously true is that a large share of our entering students still do not persist to completion.

While the greatest loss is experienced by the individual student who suffers the psychological and financial costs of transfer or failure to complete (and often carries student loans that serve as a monthly reminder of these setbacks), the costs for institutions are high as well. Consider a school with a first-year retention rate of 75% and a six-year graduation rate of 60% (accomplished with only 10% losses in the transitions from sophomore to junior and junior to senior years). These retention and graduation rates are better than the national averages, and so the school might count itself successful. However, because of nonretention, at any point in time the school only enrolls about three-quarters the number of students who would be enrolled if all students persisted to degree completion. Put another way, the admissions department is recruiting one-third more students than it would need to achieve the same total enrollment level in a world with no attrition.

Obviously, we can't expect to retain every student. Some students learn new things about themselves and so choose to transfer. Others actively plan to transfer to a more aspirational school after shoring up their academic record at a prior institution. Still others have serious medical setbacks that make departure the best option. So, let's not set the bar quite so high. Instead, suppose our hypothetical college reduces year-over-year attrition rates by half so that the first-year retention rate stands at 87.5% and the graduation rate rises to 78.5%. While such a goal is ambitious, the payoff is enormous. The number of total enrollments would increase by 15%, holding the number of incoming students constant. For many institutions, this gain would offset the demographic losses projected in earlier chapters. Of course, retention programs often operate by eliminating unnecessary credits, reducing the enrollment gain. Moreover, when one institution retains a student, another may experience the loss of a transfer student. So, we should not expect enrollment gains proportionate to persistent improvements at any individual institution or for higher education as a whole. Still, attrition reduction clearly holds significant potential to mitigate enrollments lost due to demographic decline.

From Access to Student Success

Retention efforts are likely to become more challenging—and more critical—in coming years as institutions diversify recruitment pools to offset declining prospective student numbers. New student groups come with new needs that require the campus to find new ways to support student success. Abu Rizvi, former provost at Lafayette College (PA), sees clearly the challenges that institutions face as demographics transform the student pool. One advantage of recruiting locally, he says, was that "there was a certain kind of homogeneity to the student population. And when you don't have that . . . , then there needs to be attention to student transition, student support, different kinds of curriculum, different [pedagogical] approaches. And that also costs." This inconvenient truth creates an essential connection between admissions innovations described in the last chapter and retention efforts described here. Failing to make this connection poses two threats. Most directly, recruitment without attention to student needs is unlikely to yield intended enrollment numbers as attrition erodes recruitment gains. More importantly, changes to recruitment patterns that proceed without attention to student success threaten the institutional mission.

Jon McGee, author of *Breakpoint* and former vice president for planning and strategy at the College of Saint Benedict and Saint John's University (MN), was part of a team that oversaw significant diversification at those institutions. Since 2005, the schools have more than tripled the numbers of students of color, from less than 4% of the campus to almost 20% today. While the numbers suggest successful diversification, McGee and his colleagues recognized important work remained. "Just because we enroll a more diverse student body hardly means that we are automatically more inclusive," he notes. Measured by retention and graduation rates, St. John's/St. Ben's has been successful in adapting to these new student groups and supporting their success. For example, retention rate gaps between whites and students of color have closed to within a few percentage points in most years. However, McGee notes, "standard statistics that measure success—graduation rates, retention rates, student enrollment numbers—are all nice, but they don't tell you about the kinds of experiences students really have." To help bring this important work to its full completion, the campuses implemented a campus climate survey. Even while highlighting elements of success, the results reminded McGee of the ongoing work required to fulfill the promise of his institutions. "There are many students—especially students of color," he notes, "who indicate that this isn't the most comfortable place for them to be." And so, McGee and his colleagues press on.

As higher education grapples with smaller yet more diverse prospective student cohorts, Michael Kyle, vice president for enrollment and college relations at St. Olaf College (MN), expects that "retention is going to be a bigger issue at every school." In an era of plentiful prospective students, institutions may be lulled into satisfaction with "good enough" student support. And, with relatively fewer options, students may even accept "good enough." However, as the supply of students declines and higher education becomes more of a buyer's market, it is easy to imagine that unresolved issues of inclusion might lead to emerging retention and recruitment gaps. As Kyle puts it, "The next big challenge is full participation in the gamut of campus activity." And so, even for institutions with strong retention and graduation rates across demographic groups, now may be an ideal time to look closely at threats to academic attainment and social belonging to ensure that all students thrive.

Collective Ownership for Student Success

Many education leaders who are tasked with setting goals for increased retention emphasize the need to create a widespread culture of ownership around the issue. Martin Sweidel, retired senior vice president for strategic initiatives at Goucher College (MD), puts it this way. Suppose we consider an ideally recruited student—one for whom the institutional match is terrific. "They make that choice, and you've done everything to understand them—who they are, meet them where they are, address their concerns, relieve their anxiety, help them realize that this is the right choice for them," Sweidel lays out. "They make that choice, and then they run into transactional experiences that don't align with [their expectations]. Or," he continues, "that transformation that they paid for is not happening for them for whatever reason." The bottom-line question is: "Who is reenrolling them?" Sweidel's focus on reenrollment is significant. Outside the offices of enrollment management, too many think of recruitment as a one-time event that takes place around May 1. For students, however, enrollment is an ongoing, repeated event. Each term presents multiple interactions that can determine whether they can envision a path to success—at the present institution or somewhere else. When retention is seen through the lens of "reenrollment," it becomes clear that the entire campus is responsible for bringing in next year's (or next term's) class.

When thinking about the many people who determine a student's successful reenrollment, some may immediately think of faculty, staff in student support services, directors of international or minority student programs, and others whose job descriptions engage them directly with student learning in the curricular and cocurricular spheres. Indeed, such roles are very important. But Sweidel pushes us to think more broadly, more holistically. "[Students] don't separate their cognitive interests from their relationship interests from their physical interests from their spiritual interests from their financial interests," he observes. As a result, for the integrated student, the experience of our institutions doesn't break down along organizational lines, and it is certainly not limited to faculty and student affairs staff. Students make meaningful relationships with student work supervisors, financial aid counselors, custodial staff in their dorm, and all other employee groups on campus. In this light, the question might better be posed as "Who isn't reenrolling our students?"

Jay Simmons, former president of Simpson College, has seen how creating a broad ownership of retention pays dividends. While the college has taken more traditional approaches—appointing a faculty member to the role of full-time retention coordinator, researching predictors of persistence, expanding student support services, and augmenting training for academic advisors—the institution has adopted an all-hands approach to reenrollment. Simmons explains, "Once we get through the registration period, we start an all-out campus push to make sure that every student who has not registered for the succeeding semester is contacted. . . . So, we'll have everyone from the residence hall advisors to the student development staff as well as academic personnel making contact with students who have not registered."

Wheaton College (MA) has gone even further to emphasize the collective responsibility to make connections with students vulnerable to attrition. President Dennis Hanno has issued a challenge to the campus: When the college achieves a 90% first-year retention rate, all employees will receive a 1% pay increase. With every employee from professors to dorm staff to campus security incentivized to hit the goal, the campus has drawn very close to the mark. While campus success will obviously produce budgetary costs, Hanno is not concerned because "each percentage point in retention is worth about $500,000." Like Simpson, Wheaton's retention efforts include other institutional reforms, such as a new advising model. What I find notable about Wheaton's example is the value of "running the numbers." Increasing retention isn't vaguely "helpful to the budget"; it has an explicit valuation that sharpens thinking and opens doors to new ways of understanding the feasibility of novel and creative retention efforts. Susquehanna College (PA) has routinized this connection between retention and compensation. President Jonathan Green explains that the college's annual budget process includes "variable compensation" that allows for one-time bonuses depending on realized net tuition revenue. Calculated each semester, bonuses of up to 3% are paid when the campus hits predetermined targets. Green believes the potential for bonus pay "incentivizes everyone to focus on recruiting and retention."

A labor economist might observe that incentive pay may be disliked by employees, especially when pay is tied to outcomes beyond the control of one individual. That risk is certainly relevant to these retention initiatives. Because the actions of a single employee cannot determine whether the college hits a retention target, some may begrudge the added variance in their paychecks. That may be true for some employees, but in this case the compensation programs seek to accomplish more than merely incentivizing behavior: they are designed to communicate institutional values and core principles underlying the long-term viability of the institution. As Green explains, in addition to nudging every employee to consider how their work intersects with the student experience, the bonus program "has helped all of our campus colleagues better understand our business model."

Creating a Sense of Belonging

When first engaging with issues of retention, many immediately think about the importance of academic preparation. But research suggests that sense of belonging plays an equally critical role. In his seminal contribution, Vincent Tinto (1987) notes that "eventual persistence requires that [students] make the transition to college and become incorporated into its ongoing social and intellectual life. A sizeable proportion of very early institutional departures mirrors the inability of new students to make the adjustment to the new world of the college" (135–136). For example, according to the Center for Community College Student Engagement (CCCSE) (2019), through intentional cultural development, tribal colleges and universities (TCUs) have succeeded in creating a sense of belonging among 90% of their students, even as early as the first three weeks of the term. This high level of connection appears to lead TCU students to seek out student support services and engaged learning opportunities such as civic engagement at rates higher than Native American students attending non-TCUs (CCCSE 2019). This might explain how TCUs account for 14% of associate's degrees earned by American Indian/Alaska Native students, even though they claim just 9% of enrollments by this group (NCES 2019b).

In recent decades, understanding of retention has grown and developed, and it is clear that we are losing too many promising students because they don't establish a sense of belonging in their academic communities. (Strayhorn [2018] provides a useful review and entry point into this literature.) Certainly, belonging can intersect with issues of academic success; struggling students may well question their place on campus. Institutions' academic support initiatives are taken up in the next section, but first consider programs that target belonging directly.

Encouraging Early Engagement

Given high attrition rates within the first year, campuses are working to engage students immediately. The PICK ONE! program, developed at the University of Iowa, aims to cement student connections to the campus very early in students' first terms. The idea is simple. Each entering student is encouraged to join at least one student organization or campus activity. To help students find a good fit, a website offers suggestions in a range of categories including academic groups, intramural and sports clubs, and volunteer organizations.[1] The concept, which normalizes the transition to college and lowers the bar for getting connected, has been adopted at other campuses.

The University of Wisconsin–Stout implemented the program as part of a recent strategic plan. As at other institutions, Stout students who are more engaged with the campus are more likely to be retained, explains assistant chancellor Meridith Wentz. "While we have a lot of opportunities for engagement at the end of student careers," she notes, there were fewer intentional offerings for underclass students. In addition to options in clubs and athletics, Wentz says the university funded opportunities to work with faculty members on modest projects (for a $500 stipend). "It's not a lot of hours," she says of these collaborations with faculty, because research notes that excessive work hours can lead to attrition. But the faculty-connected projects are "meaningful experiences relevant to students' academic work" and create an opportunity for deep faculty-student mentoring.

Amy McGovern, associate director of housing, led the committee that implemented the PICK ONE! initiative at Stout. She sees benefits from the program, particularly for student groups at risk for low sense of belonging. The program resources make it easier for faculty and staff working with less engaged students to identify paths to involve those students, she explains. "The thoughtful organization of content creates a pathway for connection that cuts across campus departments." In its first year, the program increased the fraction of students participating in at least one on-campus activity by more than two percentage points. Unfortunately, the program's effects on retention are clouded by other simultaneous changes creating retention headwinds: significant budget cuts, resulting attrition of experienced faculty and staff, and a wholesale reorganization of the university's colleges. McGovern believes that increased student connection mitigated what would have been larger retention declines during the transition and is optimistic that recent retention gains seen in the fall 2018 cohort reflects the program's effect. Despite its potentially wide-reaching impact, program costs are quite modest, notes Wentz. The initiative largely leverages existing activities that require no additional financial or time commitment. "Other than a few modest costs for promotional materials, the program didn't add costs," she says.

Based on this success, Jason Nicholas, director of institutional research and analysis, subsequently brought the program to Northern Michigan University (NMU). NMU plans to roll the program out as part of a broader retention initiative in the fall of 2020. Nicholas notes how the simplicity of the PICK ONE! program facilitates consistent messaging throughout campus that encourages students to get connected. As he explains, faculty and staff are encouraged to support the initiative through conversational nudges. "Because every student is supposed to have selected an activity, 'What's your PICK ONE?' is an easy conversation starter with new students."

Incentivizing Persistent Engagement

Degree "guarantees" attempt to create a comprehensive system of incentives for ongoing engagement. For example, DePauw University's (IN) Gold Commitment promises that if students don't secure employment or graduate school admission within six months of graduation, the university will offer a free term of classes or arrange for an entry-level position through its alumni network.[2] However, to qualify, students are required to maintain good academic standing, participate in career center programming, and take advantage of multiple opportunities for engaged learning. As a result, students who fulfill their side of the bargain are typically highly engaged, which bodes well for a wide range of student success measures from retention through graduation to job placement and alumni engagement.

Morningside College (IA) has adopted a similar Guarantee.[3] In an interesting innovation, the college has leveraged the potential of the Guarantee by emphasizing it in the context of their new X Path program, designed for students who come to college undecided on a major. President John Reynders notes the importance of this subgroup, saying: "Exploring students [that is, those without a planned major,] are the third-largest group of prospective students who are interested in Morningside." William Deeds, retired provost who oversaw the program's creation, describes how X Path engages students even before they arrive on campus through online tools such as a prematriculation strengths assessment. Then a one-on-one career advisor meeting—in a virtual setting over the summer or in person in the fall—initiates a wrap-around program of advising, self-exploration with assessment tools, alumni mentoring, and externship experience that guides students toward a major. "It's all about connecting them to the College," explains Deeds.

And that connection is of particular importance for these exploring students. Lacking an academic home, they miss out on the benefits of a peer cohort working through common gateway sequences and departmental programming that draws them into the college life. This is where Morningside sees the power of the Guarantee. Through its requirements of campus engagement, the Guarantee incentivizes students to get involved, even though they don't have a declared major that might require similar activities. In addition to its benefits for student engagement, Terri Curry, vice president for student life and enrollment, regularly witnesses the recruitment power of the Guarantee combined with X Path. "[Parents] are concerned about sending a student to college without a major in mind," she relates. "The Guarantee is something they really hang on to." But as much as the recruitment benefit is real, Curry emphasizes the benefit to student success is the primary goal, by encouraging students toward activities that promote their long-term welfare.

Leveraging Student Work

Too often, both students and colleges view student work as merely a part of a financial aid package. Rutgers University (NJ) is trying to change that, placing student work at the center of a new pilot program designed to increase retention. Elena Ragusa, director of strategic initiatives in the Division of Enrollment Management, explains that the program is built on research showing that participation in student work can increase retention because it "shifts student peer groups and gives students more opportunities for mentors." The new program aims to capitalize on these connections. While the New Brunswick campus's first-year retention rate sits above 90%, Ragusa notes that holding on to just 70 additional students increases that measure of student success by one point.

At Rutgers, student employment is a critical component of college financing. About 28% of the class is Pell-eligible. In addition to paying for college, some Rutgers students also provide financial support to their families. Unfortunately, limited university financial aid funds leads to gapping and a scarcity in student work positions, which in turn drives many students to off-campus employers. As a result, the institution has observed that many students maintain employment relationships—typically in the retail sector—developed prior to enrollment. While such positions can be great learning opportunities, the lack of connection to the university inherently creates limitations. For one, a student who asks for reduced hours in December to accommodate end-of-term assignments is much less likely to find a listening ear in a retail position than in a campus student work assignment. What's more, when a student experiences an academic setback, their supervisor has little to offer beyond generic advice and sympathy. By contrast, a campus work supervisor is aware of the array of programs available to help students overcome obstacles: through institutional knowledge and connection, the on-campus job becomes another strand in the campus network that supports student success. "If [the student] can find a person who can help them navigate a problem they can't handle on their own, they are more likely to stick around," Ragusa concludes.

The program to be piloted in 2019–20 will target 70 students identified in the financial aid process as having substantial need, being first-generation to college, and not being involved in any other support programming on campus, such as Rutgers's Educational Opportunity Fund program. This target group has been found to be most at risk for early attrition. The recreation center, libraries, and student centers—the three largest student employers on campus—have earmarked positions for participants, guaranteeing on-campus employment for 10 to 12 hours per week. To foster relationships, the initiative also builds in regular meetings between students and their work supervisors who have received professional development training about needs and experiences of first-generation students and have been given a guide book that outlines campus resources. At each meeting, supervisors will complete a "pulse check"—a short set of questions about the student's experience at work, interpersonal relationships, and connections to the campus. In other words, the work supervisor becomes another member on the student's advising team.

In addition to developing relationships with supervisors, the program will create a peer network through cohort programming beginning with a kick-off retreat in August. Over the course of the year, the Department of Leadership and Experiential Learning will conduct three further meetings to guide students in what Ragusa describes as a "day of reflection, connecting their work experience to their academic experience, helping them to make meaning about what they are doing and how that helps them with long-term plans and career interests."

While the program does not explicitly target subgroups based on race or sex, Ragusa sees particular potential to improve retention among African American and Hispanic males, two groups that have experienced lower rates of student success. She notes that these two groups "happen to be highest financial need, most likely to reject their work study offers, and most likely to indicate that they are working off campus." If the program better connects a modest number of students to the university, these students become positive models for many more peers. "That domino effect could be the difference maker" in generating large gains in retention and persistence, says Ragusa.

While the pilot project is modest by design, its ultimate implications could be much larger. Most directly, Ragusa notes that program success would inform broader campus deliberations about whether "financial aid for students—especially work study dollars—need to be a really significant investment." In addition, the process of designing the pilot is already reshaping how the Division of Enrollment Management is approaching all student work, "reframing [language around work awards] from just work study to talk about the added opportunities, skills, and connections" all students can gain from this rite of most college careers. By informing best practices and even the conception of student work across campus, the pilot has potential for substantial impact. "We're viewing this as an intervention not only for our students and not only for the system," says Ragusa, "but also for our on-campus employers."

Identifying Students at Risk

David Robinson, professor of statistics at St. Cloud State University, began thinking about the connections between retention and student belonging in response to a project developed for one of his undergraduate courses. As part of an assignment drawing on institutional data, Robinson asked his students to explore material from a subset of questions from a Mapworks survey. Somewhat aware of the scholarly discussion around belonging, Robinson included responses to survey questions related to this topic. In the data examined by students, "belonging was so strongly related to retention I could hardly believe it," says Robinson. But more than that, Robinson and his students found that, because belonging is uncorrelated with GPA, measures of social belonging could identify a new class of at-risk student. Robinson explains, "GPA is a very strong predictor [of attrition]; if a student is flunking out, it's very clear they won't succeed. Belonging is important in a different way, a hidden way. The student [who lacks connection to the campus] looks just fine" yet may be on a fast track to dropping out.

Excited by the potential to use existing data to improve the experiences of at-risk students, Robinson reached out to Glenn Davis, then interim dean of the college, and two additional colleagues to form a research team and turn his students' initial finding into an institutional tool. As described in Davis et al. (2019), the group refined the original list of questions into a 10-item Social Belonging Index (SBI) that is an even stronger predictor of attrition than is GPA. While 99% of fall-term, first-year students with high (top-quartile) senses of social belonging reenroll in the spring, only 82% of low (bottom-quartile) social belonging peers do so. Clearly, students who are disengaged from campus are at risk for attrition. In addition to its predictive power, Davis points to the SBI's value in campus conversations. The research-driven index "gives us a way to make [belonging] visible institutionally," he says. And that visibility is being channeled into action.

The SBI survey is now administered to all fall-term, first-year students. "Students who are performing well academically but have a low sense of belonging are [identified] to faculty members," explains Davis. How faculty reach out to those students is up to the individual faculty member. Some seek opportunities to compliment course performance while others might engage students around department activities or short-term research opportunities. In his own case, Robinson took a low-stakes approach: a conversation over a cup of coffee. "We had a great conversation," he says—the beginning of a connected relationship that may be the difference between student persistence and attrition. Individual efforts are leveraged in professional development workshops that encourage faculty to find opportunities to share with their students about their own transition to college or to facilitate study groups that generate even more connections to campus.

Efforts don't stop with the faculty. Residential life staff, who Davis notes "have potential to see the students more than anyone else on campus," are also connected with the SBI data. Ultimately, says Davis, the goal is to "get students connected to people who can help them thrive." For the initiative to achieve its potential, the university recognizes the need to tap into the entire campus. And that will inevitably require the campus to address some deep-seated perspectives about who "owns" the retention problem. "Hopefully this work is about changing a culture, and that takes time," says Davis.

Supporting Diverse Students: An Example from Mental Health Services

Efforts to create supportive learning environments for underrepresented groups are, of course, underway at nearly all colleges and universities as we are decades into persistent trends toward more diversity on campuses of all types. Insofar as expanded access is part of the solution to dwindling prospective student numbers, these trends will surely continue. Scripps College (CA) has identified an interesting intersection of this trend with the rising demand for mental health services. Scripps president Lara Tiedens explains that for many students "mental health issues are often intertwined in their social identities." Unfortunately, like many other colleges, the modest scale of her institution makes it impossible to employ a mental health staff that perfectly mirrors the diversity of the student body; the number of full-time staff is simply too small to represent all student subgroups. The resulting consequences for students' sense of belonging (and mental health support) are easy to see.

Scripps's solution has been to expand mental health services through an off-campus referral network rather than focusing solely on expanding FTE in the on-campus clinic. The college has built relationships with a team of local therapists, prioritizing professionals who increase provider diversity. When students meet with therapists in the referral network, the college agrees to pay a portion of the fee. Because Scripps students make up only part of each therapist's practice, for the cost of a single, new, on-campus therapist the college is able to markedly increase the diversity of its associated network. This approach to expanding mental health services results in greater opportunities for students to find support services that meet their needs and enhance sense of belonging.

Financial Aid Incentives

The effects of significant financial aid "gapping" extend beyond lower yield prior to matriculation, increasing the risk of attrition. As a result, the size and structure of financial aid awards play important roles in supporting the broader mission of the college. "We're not admitting students so that they can come, take classes, and leave," notes Robert Massa, retired vice president for enrollment management and institutional planning at Drew University.[4] "Access doesn't mean anything if they don't graduate." Research on recipients of the Gates Millennium scholarship (GMS) confirms Massa's experience-informed perception. Boatman and Long (2016) find that when compared to peers who just missed qualifying for Gates Millennium Scholars awards, program participants were more likely to engage with peers on academic work outside the classroom, serve in the community, and join in cocurricular activities. These choices are undoubtedly made easier by financial aid that relieves pressure to work long hours. Moreover, these same markers of student engagement are routinely cited as predictors of student learning and persistence.

Mary Wagner, assistant vice president for enrollment management at the University of South Carolina (U of SC), sees the same connections in the Gamecock Guarantee program. Targeting first-generation students with family income at or below 150% of the poverty line, the Guarantee's primary goal is to expand access to students from families with lower socioeconomic status. The program promises to cover undergraduate tuition and fees, and students with other grant or scholarship awards may even apply the $4,500 annual award toward room and board, books, or other related expenses. As a consequence of the generous aid award, those graduating in four years leave with average student loan debts below $15,500; those graduating in five or six years leave owing less than $24,000 (U of SC 2018).

Given the long-established connection between socioeconomic status and academic performance, it is not surprising that some Gamecock Guarantee students present lower academic profiles, in terms of test scores, than the average U of SC admitted student. However, these students earn grades comparable to their peers during their initial terms at U of SC. Moreover, Wagner notes, "With the support that we provide them, their retention and graduation rates are at or, in some cases, above the overall retention rates for the regular freshman cohort." Indeed, despite an average family income of only $18,000, Guarantee participants have achieved a 90% first-year retention rate, two points higher than that for the institution as a whole (U of SC 2018). Similarly, the six-year graduation rate among participants stands at 71%, just two points lower than the university average. "We know that the support works," concludes Wagner.[5]

While financial aid professionals might think the connection between aid and persistence is obvious, the scholarly literature has actually been mixed. (See Clotfelter et al. [2017] for a good overview of existing studies.) Dynarski and Scott-Clayton (2013) argue that studies may find no impact of financial aid because the effects depend critically on details of program implementation. For example, Clotfelter et al. (2017) find that an aid program in North Carolina had no effect until the financial assistance was complemented by a program of nonfinancial support. Perhaps for this reason, the widely acclaimed Accelerated Study in Associate Programs (ASAP) at the City University of New York takes a comprehensive approach. While a waiver of tuition and mandatory fees may be the hook for many ASAP students, enhanced support services, priority registration, and a dedicated program advisor likely account for extraordinary persistence gains. Strumbos et al. (2018) find that 52% of participants in the wrap-around program completed associate's degrees, a success rate twice as high as matched peers outside the program.

If the takeaway from these studies is that the effectiveness of aid programs depends on changes in the student environment, then an alternative to expansions in institution-provided support might be added incentives for students to seek out existing resources. Dynarski and Scott-Clayton (2013) conclude that performance-based scholarships (PBSs) do, in fact, achieve greater persistence gains than do grants without conditions. This theory motivates recent expansion of programs that use targeted aid awards in hopes of accomplishing more with fewer resources. EAB (2016) summarizes several recent experiments designed to incentivize student behaviors that support success. For example, through its Fly in 4 program, Temple University (PA) offered high-need students an addition $4,000 in grant aid if they completed 30 credits per year, registered by the priority course registration deadline, met each term with an advisor, and implemented a four-year degree plan. As compared with peers with only slightly less need, 5% more program participants were retained from fall to spring semester. While Temple's example follows the traditional path of packaging programs for incoming students, Seattle University instead offered similar performance-based incentives to at-risk first-year students and achieved a 5% gain in first-year (fall-to-fall) retention. Indiana State chose to focus on summer enrollment. Noting research that suggests that students who complete summer credits are more successful, the university offered six free credits plus $300 for books to students on track to complete 24 credits by spring term. Recorded retention gains nearly matched those seen in the Temple scholarship program.

Scholarly evaluations of PBS programs suggest modest potential effects. For instance, in a California-based randomized control trial, Barrow and Rouse (2018) find that PBS students put more time into their academic work. In addition, in community college randomized control trials in Arizona, Florida, New Orleans, Ohio, and New York City participants were found to have earned one to three additional credits in their first year (Patel et al. 2013). However, this advantage evaporated by the end of the scholarship (Monaghan et al. 2018). Year-to-year retention rates were sometimes found to be impressively higher (nine points higher in New Orleans), but in about half of the trials no effect was found (Monaghan et al. 2018). Echoing Dynarski and Scott-Clayton's (2013) focus on implementation, Monaghan et al.

(2018) conclude that PBS programs can improve retention to a modest degree but appear more effective when implemented in concert with academic and advising support.

Student Support

I doubt Nancy Griffin, vice president for enrollment management at the University of Southern Maine (USM), would be surprised by studies that emphasize the importance of personalized student support. Located in the far northeast, USM is situated at ground zero for declining birth rates. Griffin connects the state's demographic challenge directly to the university's mission. "On any given day there are about 31 births and 41 deaths. Our workforce needs are through the roof," she observes. "There is an urgency in our state to make sure that we're credentialing and preparing people for the workforce." Indeed, WICHE (2016) estimates that the number of high school graduates in the state is 15% lower today than at the 2008 peak, with an additional decline of 15% expected over the next 15 years. Early on in that decline, the university struggled to navigate demographic headwinds (no doubt coupled with consequences of recovery from the Great Recession), and undergraduate enrollment fell by 20% from 2009 through 2015. In 2013–14, declining enrollments precipitated program cuts and layoffs including 51 faculty and 119 staff—a reduction of more than 15% of those employed at USM (Gardner 2018). Since then, Griffin has led a successful effort that has increased enrollment by almost 5% driven by an eight-point rise in first-year retention off of a low of 62.5% in 2015. As a result, the university has enjoyed budget relief despite continued demographic decline (Gardner 2018). Key to USM's ability to overcome: intensive, student-focused advising.

In the context of budgetary shortfalls, USM's enrollment management work was afforded no new staff. The job was to improve performance by better use of existing resources. Griffin determined that prior efforts to improve efficiency through technological automation too often overlooked the individual. "There was this acceptance that in the automation some students will fall through the cracks, and that was okay." A new approach reflected a different philosophy that paid greater attention to each student as an individual. A shored-up advising system engaged students in the summer prior to matriculation with a 90-minute academic advising session. Meaningful changes followed from modest efforts. For example, by discussing disability services prior to matriculation, the university was able to identify and support more students in need of accommodation right from day one. "We had a 38% increase in the number of students that were registered with our Disability Services Office before the first day of class that first year," explains Griffin. And students whose employment plans reflected unrealistic expectations that threatened academic success were guided to more sustainable work and financing choices long before trouble with course grades emerged. Griffin stresses that the changes were not extraordinary. Rather, the system simply paid keen attention to well-established best practices like those advocated for by Complete College America.

This is not to suggest that technology can't be an effective tool supporting personalized retention work. Kirp (2019) argues, for instance, that by "using online tools, students can create roadmaps that show them the most direct path to a degree" (19), avoiding disorganized course plans that slow progress toward graduation and create financial barriers to persistence. He points to Georgia State University's use of text message nudges to keep admitted students on track or connect them with an advisor if they need assistance. Following the implementation of the text system in 2017, Kirp reports that summer melt fell by more than 20%. As useful as technology may be, Kirp also points to the importance of the human connection advocated by Griffin. His conclusion that "the power of the personal is the make-or-break factor" (63) appears prescient in light of more recent studies that find little effect from (often technology-supported) nudge initiatives implemented on a large scale (Bird et al. 2019; Gurantz et al. 2019; Oreopoulos and Petronijevic 2019; Page et al. 2019). In discussing the explanation for these programs' failures when applied at scale, Bird et al. (2019) conclude that "it seems like the relationship between the student and the sources of the nudge matters" (21).

Griffin's mantra, "Student Focused Every Day," extends the individualized perspective to decisions throughout the university. For example, where the times and locations of course offerings had previously been driven by department and faculty preferences, USM now assigns classes on their two campuses after an analysis of students' location needs. Rather than students traveling to professors, the new system often has professors traveling to students. As a consequence, students face fewer degree conflicts driven by inaccessible courses.

At the same time that the university was using retention efforts to grapple with declining enrollments, they simultaneously changed admissions standards—but not in the direction you might expect of a campus struggling to generate net tuition revenue. Rather than expanding admission to students whose capacity for success was questionable, Griffin explains, her team looked more carefully at applicants to be sure that admission invitations were extended only to those who would find success at USM. Students who were not presently prepared for success weren't told "no," however. Griffin says the university instead communicated that "you will be admitted to the University of Southern Maine, but it may not be today." Through coordination between USM and local community colleges, students are given active advice on the coursework needed to bring them back to USM in the near future.

In this context of student-focused advising and admission predicated on capacity to succeed, the university of around 6,300 undergraduates increased its financial aid budget by about $10 million. But even in student aid awards, the student focus is evident. Griffin observed that too many students in the past had approached tuition financing with a very short-term perspective that led to plans incompatible with a four-year investment. In response, the financial aid department added financial literacy programming to help students formulate more reasonable plans that would actually lead to a degree.

Listening to Griffin, improving retention appears straightforward. "Stop hiring consultants and go back to the basics," she advises. "What we've lost [in our automated approach] is the ability to really get to know that student and help that student progress." In this view, Griffin echoes Kirp (2019), who argues that "the good news about the dropout scandal is that we know what must be done to end it" (33). According to Griffin, individualized academic support and advising that address the needs of one student at a time have been the key to USM's recent retention gains. Despite real progress, though, work remains. Retention and graduation rates at the university still fall short of the national average. With demographic decline already well underway, Griffin has no trouble finding motivation or seeing the importance of bringing this work to completion: "We're working for the future of Maine."

From Statistics to Personal Experience

One common thread running through the previous examples is the motivational power of data. For example, recent regulatory reforms that simply require Pell-receiving schools to report Pell-eligible students' retention and graduation rates have sparked important conversations. Whistle and Hiler (2018) find that at more than 200 institutions, the Pell-student graduation rate falls short of 25%. Statistics like this motivate action. But too often the same statistics lead to inertia. For instance, Whistle and Hiler (2018) also find that "after six years, only 49% of first-time, full-time Pell recipients earned a Bachelor's degree at the institution where they started." An institution managing to graduate 65% of students in this group might be tempted to celebrate relative success despite low absolute performance.

For data to inspire change, things often need to get a little personal. The examples in this chapter make this principle evident as well. For some, the marketplace makes retention personal. Failure to attend to student success ultimately undermines institutional viability—particularly now that we've left the era of ever-larger high school graduating classes. For others, the student experience gets personal. An 85% retention rate turns into a 15% attrition rate. One in seven students arriving on campus in the fall won't even return for a second year. For most students, this is a mini-tragedy of sorts. Some will transfer and succeed elsewhere, but national graduation statistics remind us that for too many the hopes and aspirations of the first-year student transform into feelings of inadequacy and debt entrapment. This picture is difficult to look at.

Once it gets personal, "we've never done things that way" ceases to be an argument for the status quo and becomes an argument for accountable experimentation. The next chapter examines how institutions are disrupting their programming across campus—even touching sacred cows of the classroom and curriculum—to enhance the student experience and respond to changing demographics.

EIGHT

Program Reforms

IT GOES WITHOUT SAYING THAT ADMISSIONS and enrollment management staff need to be at the top of their game as we navigate demographic changes ahead. However, for many institutions the decline in prospective student numbers will be too large to manage without engaging the rest of the campus, including the academic program, as appropriate. For some faculties, such conversations raise understandable concerns. If academic programs and faculties have been built with student learning goals at the forefront, do changes to the nature or delivery of academic content that are prompted by enrollment pressure place form over substance? Of course, too often it isn't clear that current practice is best practice. In many cases, path dependency and the vagaries of history explain much of how programs are structured rather than careful, rational design. In such cases, reform may simultaneously bolster student demand while improving the academic experience. What is more, Jon McGee, author of *Breakpoint* and former vice president for planning and strategy at the College of Saint Benedict and Saint John's University (MN), argues that openness to curricular change can be empowering to faculty at institutions at risk for enrollment decline. At some point, he says, faculty realize "we *can* adapt—which gets you past 'I'm just stuck in the book of Lamentations.'"[1]

Martin Sweidel, retired senior vice president for strategic initiatives at Goucher College (MD), reasons that faculty buy-in is essential, not just helpful. Ultimately, the quality and nature of the academic program is what we are offering, he observes. In the context of his work leading a blue sky committee at Goucher, Sweidel acknowledges that discussion of enrollment management and strategic marketing and recruitment choices would be inevitable. "But," he continues, "ultimately it's got to be about what it is we're offering that's distinctive and at the same time meets the need of prospective students—really genuinely meets it—so that they are willing to make [Goucher] their choice."

Indeed, while the academy in general and faculty in particular are often painted as resistant to change, this stereotype is often inapt. Indeed, the best individual faculty are constantly adapting. Citing the twentieth-century creation of community colleges and federal loan guarantees, Alexander (2020) argues that "while academia is at times conservative . . . , the sector is capable of generating new forms" (218). On a more local scale, Marcus's (2018) analysis of IPEDS data finds that institutions collectively added more than 41,000 degree programs from 2012 to 2018—an increase of 21%. Surely this evidence undermines contentions that faculty are inherently conservative and unwilling to consider pedagogical innovation. This chapter looks at examples of campuses that are reinventing parts of their curriculum—through curricular innovation and student support—to answer Sweidel's provocative challenge to offer a distinctive, high-quality educational experience.

The Curriculum
What We Teach: General Education

General education reform is widespread, and for good reason given the retention rates described in chapter 7. In a column questioning the value of the algebra requirement, Andrew Hacker shares his perspective at the City University of New York (CUNY), where at the time of his writing in 2012, "57 percent of its students didn't pass its mandated algebra course." In a faculty report, Hacker's colleagues concluded that failure in the mathematics sequence "affects retention more than any other academic factor." National statistics show that these challenges are not unique to CUNY. Around 60% of students at public two-year schools and one-third of those at public four-year institutions enroll in remedial math courses (NCES 2016). Six years after college entry, only 50% of students complete all of the required math courses. Not surprisingly, those who do not complete remedial requirements are about twice as likely to drop out as those who are successful. What makes these dropouts particularly tragic is that the math courses that impede degree completion are weakly connected to students' desired programs, says Connie Richardson, leader of the curriculum development team at the University of Texas at Austin's Dana Center Mathematics Pathways program.

In response to these worrisome figures, scholars at the Carnegie Foundation for the Advancement of Teaching have developed new math curricula intended to align with students' academic and career plans. The resulting Quantway and Statway courses emphasize quantitative reasoning and empirical analysis closely connected to a wide range of disciplines. Building on Carnegie's efforts, the Dana Center now works with states and institutions to implement mathematics pathways. At its core, the pathways approach recognizes that degree programs and careers have different mathematical needs even as all students need quantitative reasoning skills. The center partners with institutions to offer an array of course sequences such that every student engages in material that is aligned to academic and career goals. Consistent with the Strada-Gallup research described later in this chapter, Richardson sees retention benefits flowing from pathways' alignment with student goals. "If they see how their content is relevant to their program and their future goals, they are more likely to prioritize that work and persist through struggle."

In addition to creating greater appeal to students, this alignment can better prepare students for the work that lies ahead. Richardson explains that many students in traditional algebra-centric pathways spend considerable time on material they will never apply in future studies. As a consequence, "they're not getting the math content that they do need," she argues. "For many students, statistics would be much more relevant in their field." In other words, pathways work is not about "dumbing down" the content. Rather, its goal is to engage students with the mathematics content that is well-suited for their education paths.

Of course, adopting a pathways approach will not obviate remediation. But when remediation is necessary, the Dana Center advocates for a similar alignment with student learning goals. Where possible, it is accelerated with approaches such as corequisite remediation, in which students simultaneously enroll in college-level work and a complementary support course that provides just-in-time remediation. In addition to citing evidence that this approach increases the rate at which students earn college-level math credit, Richardson points out that "time and money are the enemy for students completing college; if we can accelerate them, there are going to be increased success rates." This approach addresses one of the most distressing problems in higher education, that students are "leaving school with more debt than anything else."

Interim findings from an MDRC evaluation suggest that accelerated math pathways increase student success in completing college mathematics courses (Rutschow 2018). As compared to peers in traditional remedial sequences, students in the mathematics pathways were 50% more likely to have passed a college-level math class by the end of three semesters. As promising as these results are, Richardson sees ongoing opportunities to further reduce inter- and intra-institutional barriers to amplify the potential of the pathways model. Even in states that require transferability between institutions, receiving schools often have narrowly defined prerequisites for upper-division courses such that students earn transfer credit but still have to retake courses to meet major requirements. "Getting institutions to cooperate on the regional level is one of the things we really focus on," Richardson says. Whether collaborating with individual institutions or in partnership with entire systems, the Dana Center has worked in nearly every state in the nation to expand the math pathways model. As these efforts expand to include more institutions, we might expect barriers to success to be reduced as algebraic alternatives gain wider understanding and acceptance throughout higher education.

What We Teach: Major Programs

In addition to reforming general education to promote student success, colleges are creating new and revised major programs that speak more clearly to student objectives. Lisa Bunders, vice president of enrollment management at Champlain College (VT), argues that at the most basic level, the goal must be to avoid "commodity programs"—offerings that, to students at least, are indistinguishable from those at any of a number of competing institutions. For example, Bunders points to Champlain's business school and notes a less expensive competitor, the University of Vermont, literally just blocks down the street. To differentiate itself from the competition, Champlain's business school has partnered with the Center for Appreciative Inquiry, which is located within the school and offers national workshops on the Appreciative Inquiry–based management approach advocated by Cooperrider (1986).

In many cases, institutions are finding differentiation at the intersection of existing fields. One popular option called CS + X pairs computer science with another field, often drawn from the humanities or another discipline grappling with lower enrollments. For example, the University of Illinois combines computer science with anthropology, linguistics, and music; Lewis University (IL) offers pairings with history, music, and theology; and Stanford (CA), through 2019, promoted joint programs with 14 humanities departments. It is easy to see important intersections between computer science and all of these fields, not to mention how highlighting those connections might attract digitally native prospective students—and even reverse recent enrollment trends that have left computer science departments scrambling for faculty as much as humanities departments are scrambling for students. Humanities departments might embrace such crosscutting programming "as a way to bring in students who are drawn to such disciplines but feel they need computing skills for their careers" (Ruff 2016). Of course, realizing this potential hinges, in part, on the level of commitment. For example, Leighton's (2019) account of the discontinuation of Stanford's program notes that enrollments in the new majors were limited, perhaps in part because students felt they bore "too much of the responsibility to identify connections between the fields."

This doesn't mean similar programs won't succeed elsewhere, but success may depend on institutional context and implementation. Lafayette College, for example, recently identified interdisciplinary areas in which to deepen offerings and provide new academic programs, including those associated with the liberal arts college's historic strength in engineering. Established more than 150 years ago, the engineering department accounts for more than 18% of the college's graduates. Former provost Abu Rizvi explains the new programs have been launched coincident with a plan for college-wide enrollment growth that supports a proportional increase in faculty lines allowing for new appointments in: data science and digital scholarship; design, media, and the arts; and environmental studies. While scale is often cited as necessary to support interdisciplinary programs, Rizvi actually sees advantages in the college's relatively modest size. "The possibility of interdisciplinary programs that cross between the traditional liberal arts and engineering are more possible here because engineering isn't siloed in a separate college or school," he argues.

While new programs are hardly assured success and must work within institutional contexts, Randall Deike, Cleveland State University's senior vice president for enrollment management and student success, believes that movement toward the intersections of disciplines is necessary. "Until we start thinking about curricular reform in terms of developing [*Robotproof* skills], I think we're missing the boat," he contends. "Institutions are almost completely vertical and we need to be a lot more horizontal." Ultimately, he concludes, "the institutions that are able to effect that kind of change in the experience that students are having are the ones that are going to win."

In discussions of program delivery, it rarely takes long for the topic of technology—in general and through online education in particular— to arise. While early hopes for massive cost restructuring have not been realized, many campuses look to use online delivery to meet the needs of twenty-first-century students, reaching new student groups in the process. Jeff Morgan, associate provost for education innovation and technology at the University of Houston (TX), leads an online teaching program that reaches deep into the curriculum. In spring 2018, 60% of students at Houston took at least one online or hybrid class, and 30% of core-level hours were taught online. Morgan doesn't see the online platform as a radical pedagogical departure so much as a specific instance of seeking the best teaching tools and methods. Still, current demographic trends fuel Houston's drive to innovate. "The landscape of higher education is changing at such a rapid pace," he observes. As demographic change creates pressure elsewhere in the country, "we'll have competition for students in [the Houston] area like we've never seen before," Morgan predicts. "If we aren't out in front of this, we will pay the consequences for it."

In addition to allowing some students to take classes that were otherwise inaccessible, Morgan sees pedagogical improvements that flow from online learning environments—particularly for students with weaker attachments to higher education. For instance, he believes the degree of anonymity afforded by online learning generates greater and better participation by some student groups. In particular, Morgan believes that first-generation students are more likely to benefit from online discussions where they are freed from inhibitions that limit engaged learning practices—feelings of insecurity around asking a "dumb question" or aversion to publicly responding to questions when uncertain of the answer. As the demographic landscape of Houston has shifted and the university's mission has become more connected to serving first-generation students, Morgan sees the online platform as a particularly timely tool that enhances the institution's ability to recruit, retain, and support students.

While Dunwoody College of Technology (MN) serves a clientele very distinct from those attending the University of Houston, president Richard Wagner sees similar potential for online teaching tools that dramatically reduce the barriers of time and place that impede adult learners. In Dunwoody's electronics technician program, for instance, Wagner wonders, "What would it look like if we could put the entire didactic portion of the program online? Students can watch a lecture, do the homework, and then come to a campus, which is an open lab, at any time to demonstrate that they have mastered a competency." These competencies could be bundled into courses, and courses could be bundled into degrees such that students demonstrate their qualification with minimal time spent in a traditional classroom setting.

It is easy to articulate potential problems with a competency-based reform of higher education. For example, might such a movement heighten incentives to teach to narrowly defined content at the expense of deeper understanding? On the other hand, it is equally evident how realizing this vision in appropriate contexts might expand access particularly among adult learner populations who need to balance work, family, and education while upgrading workplace skills.

Of course, online instruction is not a panacea, particularly in cases in which budgetary motivations take a more prominent role in driving the initiative. Guthrie (2019) warns against a particularly "dystopian" vision of a future in which we create a "two-tiered [education] system":

> In this negative projection one can envision a very small number of well-endowed institutions that cater to the wealthy, well-prepared class as well as a small number of carefully picked representatives from various groups. These students would receive a world-class education, while most students would be at risk of receiving a much lower quality education that is overly-reliant on poorly built computerized teaching systems or online learning courseware that does not provide the kind of encouragement and motivation that is required to help students through the many challenges encountered when learning. Following this path could well lead to a self-perpetuating system across generations where a

small elite group benefits from a compounding level of social capital, while most students are left out, leading to a widening of social, political, cultural, and financial gulfs.

These words carry weight because budget-conscious forms of online education, often designed to reduce faculty and staff time inputs, often undermine student engagement and educational effectiveness. However, acknowledging the potential for educational harm falls well short of equating technological innovations like hybrid and online instruction with lower quality. Just as with its face-to-face counterpart, the quality of instruction depends on a myriad of teaching decisions. Ultimately, students, parents, and employers will likely offer a tangible assessment of program quality.

While technology-centered reform might be sexy, many institutions are discussing some old-fashioned, analog questions. For example, Morgan, the excited champion of online solutions, is equally enthusiastic when describing significant advantages Houston has gained by creating three centralized testing centers "with the capacity to give about 340 proctored exams per hour." The idea is simple and distinctly disconnected from the digital frontier: students take exams on a self-scheduled basis outside of class, thus freeing contact time for high-value, engaged, student-professor interactions.

In a typical course with two or three midterms and a final, moving test-taking out of the classroom and into the domain of "homework" can mean as much as 10% more contact time. While all students stand to gain, Morgan believes the benefits may be particularly important to students who struggle to learn on their own because additional contact time gives them a little more space to understand challenging material with the help of the professor. In this way, the centers support goals for student retention and success. At a school of Houston's size, the potential gains are enormous. "We gave about 200,000 proctored exams last year," says Morgan, which he described as "just a drop in the bucket of all exams given" at the university of 45,000 students.

Wagner similarly underscores the importance of analog revisions to Dunwoody's curriculum design. For example, he notes that a midcareer, displaced worker can't dedicate four or even two years to retraining. Wagner describes that adult learner's perspective: "I'm mid-life, and I need access to an education that gets me in the field quickly at a good-paying wage in a job that has some upward potential." Dunwoody's recently developed Right Skills Now for Manufacturing initiative begins with a one-semester course for computer-numeric controlled machine operators. This single course provides the credential needed to land a job in a well-paid, undersupplied sector, even as it serves as an entry point into three two-year, associate's degree programs that are taught through night classes. With this design, the program quickly returns adult learners to the labor force with good pay while simultaneously preparing them for future education.

The theme of work-friendly curricula is echoed by Ross Gittell, chancellor of the Community College System of New Hampshire. "With many adults, you're looking at up-skilling for current workplaces and positions as opposed to identifying new careers," he says, "providing the worker with an opportunity to move into a higher-level position with the same employer." For Gittell and his colleagues, that means reconsidering practices copied from traditional bachelor's degree programs and designed for students not working full time and without significant family responsibilities. This includes some minor and more major changes to the academic calendar. For example, with minor change and drawing on research of adult students' preferences, Gittell believes that many adult learners would rather take two eight-week classes than enroll in two concurrent courses over a 16-week term. By reconfiguring the rhythm of the term in this way, Gittell hopes that colleges in his system can help this important student group better manage the stresses that emerge when academic work is combined with employment and family life. "With the split academic semester, you don't have two finals at the same time, two midterms at the same time," he explains.

Wagner sees potential for even more radical departure from traditional academic delivery as higher education establishes partnerships with industry. Because many firms are struggling to find qualified workers—a problem that will become more pronounced as low-birth cohorts reach working age—Wagner has witnessed companies being "willing to form uncomfortable partnerships with competitors to create a bigger pool of skilled labor." Partnering with industry groups will likely require further changes to academic rhythms, changes that may create discomfort in parts of campus. But failing to work with industry may lead to even greater discomfort. Already we have seen growing numbers of corporations developing competing postsecondary programs (Fain 2019), a trend that could pick up speed if higher education is unwilling to explore partnerships. While not dismissing the tensions, Wagner focuses on the potential, concluding that "there's a great opportunity if we can be flexible enough to meet industry's needs."

Student Support In and Out of the Classroom

Changes to the curriculum, facilitated by technology, increasingly blur the boundary that defines the classroom. Through guided pathways, corequisite remediation, and advising content woven into instructional time, institutions are looking for ways to improve outcomes by integrating the student experience. For example, Gittell cites the first and second of these strategies as key to recent improvements in student success at New Hampshire community colleges. As explained by Bailey et al. (2015), "guided pathways" replace the traditional buffet of class offerings with an explicitly articulated sequence of courses that lead to a degree. While limiting student choice, the plans provide clarity and incentivize early credit completion, which has been shown to increase retention and persistence. In a sense, guided pathways serve as an institutionalized form of student advising that helps students identify a path to their goals. "We want to get [students here] with a purpose and a path to get there," Gittell explains.

Providing a guided pathway, however, involves much more than merely communicating a course sequence. As Bailey et al. (2015) describe, successful guided pathways require new ways of operating for both the institution and the faculty member—"a systematic redesign of the student experience" (2). The course sequence is combined with an integrated articulation of student learning goals that creates coherence across courses. In addition, professors leverage the clear structure of the program, assessing students in light of the broader program rather than in the isolated course context. The more holistic approach to the entire course sequence encourages students to develop metacognition skills as they see how an individual course fits into the learning objectives of the program and aligns with their future life goals.

Of course, even clarity of vision like that aspired to by guided pathways cannot overcome gaps that appear when a course calls on skills or experiences that a student did not successfully develop in prior educational experiences. Following the same arguments made by Dana Center staff in the context of mathematics pathways, advocates for guided pathways propose corequisite remediation to provide just-in-time student support while maintaining forward progress toward a degree. Following this approach, Gittell reports tremendous progress at New Hampshire community colleges, where they have "doubled first-level college course completion in English and math—from one-third to two-thirds completion." These improvements laid the foundation for greater degree completion—the ultimate goal. "We had a record number of graduations this year," Gittell notes. Of course, higher levels of persistence lead to more enrolled credit hours, a win-win for the institution and its students.

While this example demonstrates how student support is blended with the curriculum to increase success among existing student groups, work at Morningside College (IA) shows how the same support model can be leveraged to expand access to new student groups. The newly launched Education Enhancement Program (EEP) is designed to attract and support socially or economically disadvantaged students whose prior educational experiences leave them on the margin of Morningside's prospective student pool. Terri Curry, vice president for student life/enrollment, explains that "these students have looked at Morningside in the past; we [in the admissions decision process] haven't looked at them." Through the EEP, Morningside intends to make itself student ready for this subset of prospective learners, who bring many talents but also need additional mentoring and support.

The program, which combines a summer bridge experience with a scripted fall semester, offers conditional admission to participants with the promise of unconditional admission upon completion of a successful first semester. In this way, the EEP mirrors four-year institutions' conditional-admission collaborations with two-year schools (see chapter 11) but do so entirely within a single institution. Advising is woven into the curriculum to provide students with basic information about navigating campus and preparing for college success. Students are registered for fewer credits in carefully selected courses with the idea that participants are being given every opportunity to set their Morningside careers on a foundation of success. To further increase focus on academic progress, those admitted to the EEP are not permitted to be involved in campus "talent groups" such as varsity athletics and college-sponsored music groups. Recently retired provost William Deeds, who designed the program, explains that this choice also makes clear to everyone that the purpose of the program is to expand student success rather than to provide a recruiting loophole for campus organizations. "We do think they are likely to be successful," says Deeds, "and we provide them the support to make that happen." But to realize this potential, Morningside is also acknowledging that effectively expanding access to new student groups requires a willingness to consider new methods of pedagogy and support.

Connecting to Life after College

Recent work by Strada and Gallup (2018a, 2018b) unsurprisingly shows that students view higher education as a stepping-stone to lives and careers that follow. For instance, when asked to identify the "main reason for choosing [your] level of education," the top answer, representing 58% of respondents, was "good job or career"—far outpacing the second-place "learning and knowledge," which drew another 23% (Strada and Gallup 2018b). Even when deciding on the specific institution to attend, almost 20% of respondents cited "good job or career" as the "main reason" for their choice—about four times as many as those citing "learning and knowledge." Clearly, for students education is an investment in life after college.

And students may be wise in emphasizing this connection. Strada and Gallup (2018a) find that alumni who experience their postsecondary studies as relevant to their lives and careers are much more likely to see their educations as "high quality" and "worth the cost." In fact, perception of relevance is a better predictor of perceived quality and value than demographic characteristics, income, field or level of study, cost of attendance, graduation rates, and student loan default rates. Unfortunately, "only 26% of working U.S. adults with college experience strongly agree that their education is relevant to their work and day-to-day life" (Strada and Gallup 2018a, 3). While the Strada and Gallup results reflect past generations of students, Seemiller and Grace (2016) argue that Generation Z is even more eager to make connections between education and "the real world." Having witnessed the challenges that their parents faced in the Great Recession and increasingly prone to questioning the cost and value of higher education, these students are "highly concerned about gaining meaningful employment after graduation" (214).

Internships or co-ops, of course, represent one way to connect the curriculum to career. Colleges with signature internship or co-op programs require that all students complete one or more of these experiences before graduation. With more than 100 years of experience in co-op education, Drexel University (PA) is a leader in this field, partnering with more than 1,600 employers around the world. In addition to a four-year degree program with one required six-month co-op, Drexel students are also offered a five-year option incorporating three six-month co-op experiences. Students are supported through the Steinbright Career Development Center, where they experience an extensive infrastructure connecting them with vetted co-op partners. Students participate in an intensive interview process to secure their co-op, 85% of which are paid, and benefit from 10 or 20 professional interviews before their end-of-college job search.

Randall Deike advocates nationally for the power of the co-op model, drawing on his long experience leading Drexel's program.

Because of co-op experience, he sees students who are better prepared for career engagement after college. "Students go away as college students and come back with six months of professional experience that really helps them think through what comes next," he says. But even more than that, Deike argues, students use their co-op experiences to learn about themselves—what they bring to the table and where they need to grow. "They are incredibly self-aware from a professional perspective," he observes. Impressive co-op-related employment statistics bear this out: citing a survey of Drexel alumni nine months following graduation, Deike reports that 60% of graduates have a job offer originating from a co-op experience.

Listening to Deike talk about the benefits, establishing a co-op program can feel like an obvious choice—until he starts talking about the costs required to do it well. "It's a big investment," he warns. The infrastructure to support the stewardship and development of co-op partners, and the university-specific interview process, is significant. Relationships with co-op partners must be maintained, culling partners who fail to create an effective experience and keeping the total number low enough that all partners get matched with a student over the course of several years. In addition, Drexel makes sure that students are prepared for the experience through the first-year course CO-OP 101, which teaches interview skills, résumé construction, professional communication, and modern issues of the workplace. Perhaps most notably, even as the university communicates its needs to co-op partners, it also solicits feedback about how to reform the curriculum. Deike believes the willingness to revise curricular content will be of increasing importance in the future. "Curricular reform is going to be critical as roles change," he contends. "We have an inside connection [through co-op partners] that really helps us to better understand and be better prepared in developing the curriculum of the future." This feedback loop inevitably raises long-recognized questions about control of the curriculum, but Deike maintains that by wrestling with these questions Drexel has maintained a rigorous curriculum enhanced by professional experience.

Unsurprisingly, co-op education supports recruitment. "The focus on return on investment has never been stronger" in his 35 years of experience, says Deike. Drexel's co-op leadership may partially explain how the university has grown by 12% since 2010 in a northeastern market that has been challenging for so many. Deike notes that Drexel is not alone in its success. He points to Northeastern (MA), another school with a signature co-op program, which has seen enrollment grow by 15% in the same period. While Drexel and Northeastern are larger, national schools, regional schools with signature co-op programs also seem to be bucking the sliding trend in the northeast. At Endicott College (MA), for example, the number of full-time undergraduates is up more than 30%. But Deike cautions against the idea that the co-op alone draws students. Like anything else, it requires broader investment. "[In the past, Drexel] talked about co-op as the only differentiator for the university," he says. "Basically, our message was, 'Come to Drexel. Get a job.' We completely undermined the academic component of the experience." Deike believes that their success in the market has only come through a more holistic story: "a strong curriculum enhanced by the professional experience [of co-op] in a city that is incredibly vibrant."

When discussing programmatic revision to highlight the connections between undergraduate work and subsequent careers, some conflate relevance with specific fields of study, particularly STEM fields and quantitative social sciences. Implicitly and explicitly, studies in the arts and humanities, core components of the American model of a liberal arts education, are too often caricatured as frivolous and extraneous to life after college. H. Scott Bierman, president of Beloit College (WI), rejects this view entirely. "I completely and utterly deny the conflict between caring about a student's career development and a liberal arts education," he says. "It's a false dichotomy."

One reason people may falsely believe that majors in the humanities are somehow at odds with career preparation is because they hold incorrect views of the correlation between college major and career choice. In reality, humanities majors take up a wide range of vocations.

For example, according to the American Academy of the Arts and Sciences (AAAS), 16% of humanities majors with a terminal bachelor's degree work in management, exactly the same share as that for undergraduates as a whole (AAAS, n.d.). Similarly, 10% of humanities majors work in business and financial operations, the same share as that for all undergraduates. While average earnings are slightly lower and unemployment rates marginally higher among humanities majors, the fact is that humanists work in many fields and report strong job satisfaction (AAAS 2018). And so workplace connection is as important to this part of the academy as to any other.

Scripps College's (CA) Public Humanities clinics demonstrate the connection between humanities work and the world's practical problems. Scripps has long been recognized for its humanities orientation. For instance, all Scripps students complete a three-course humanities sequence in their first two years. "[Work in the humanities] is a huge part of the culture here," says president Lara Tiedens. Established through the most recent strategic planning process, the new Public Humanities clinics draw on this deep commitment to and reputation in the humanities. The program concept has been modeled on sister-school Harvey Mudd's clinics around live business problems. Faculty develop senior-level courses that engage students in humanities clinics in broad problems such as education, poverty, health, or homelessness. In the clinics, students are asked to use their academic experience to generate humanities-specific solutions to these pressing challenges. For example, Tiedens points out that environmental issues are too often viewed as the bailiwick of the sciences. "If you start from the perspective of the human experience and basic human concerns about life," she wonders, "how does that help to understand the problem—what the causes are and what different types of solutions might be?" In a world in which scientific advance enables increasingly dystopian technological "progress," we can only hope that higher education leads society to recognize the critical role that the humanities should play in today's pressing problems.

Through its new Channels program, Beloit College is similarly emphasizing the complementarity between liberal arts studies and successful careers. And while commitment to mission is at the heart of the initiative, the work is also done in the context of enrollment pressure. With an enrollment target around 330, from 2015 to 2017 Beloit welcomed an average of more than 365 students each year. Then, in 2018 and 2019 new student numbers hit a wall, falling to just over 260. Like other schools, part of the response to these challenges has been to underscore the relevance of Beloit's academics to fulfilling careers. However, where for some institutions this means a move toward preprofessional work, president Bierman argues that a focus on success in the world calls for a reaffirmation of the liberal arts institution's values. He points to the four student learning outcomes identified in the college's 2019 strategic plan: effective communication, productive collaboration, creative problem-solving, and intellectual and professional agility. "We know these are being taught in classrooms," Bierman says. The question is "how we are intentional about connecting them to careers and lives after college through a developmental process."

The Channels curriculum begins with a required first-year course co-led by faculty and staff and designed to introduce students to metacognitive skills that frame education as a process that leads to the future. In addition, ongoing, credit-bearing advising with faculty, staff, and student peers encourages students throughout the first two years to apply these lessons to their own educational journey. As students progress into the second year and beyond, they are encouraged to declare a topical channel such as business and entrepreneurship, health and healing, justice and rights, and sustainability. Rather than organizing these paths around majors, students from all majors will choose the channel of greatest interest to them. Once in a channel, Bierman explains, students will be mentored by a team of faculty, staff, peers, alumni, parents, and community members to discern how engagement with student groups, work study, off-campus study, speaker programs, networking events, and internships can support student aspirations. Within each channel, tracks to specific professions will be supported, but every channel serves all students regardless of major.

Inaugural channels have been built around existing programs with long-standing budget support and demonstrated success. As one example,

Bierman points to the Weissberg Program in Human Rights, which, over two decades, has established a strong track record of launching Beloit students into human rights careers. As a result, creation of the first channels called for organization of existing assets rather than creation of new programming, which made it possible to quickly reach critical mass. While the programming in early channels is not entirely new, these programs of historical strength "now have a pride of place within the College that was lacking before," explains Bierman. The ultimate goal for the initiative extends beyond the initial channel offerings, but Bierman notes valuable momentum gained from building out from existing areas of strength both in terms of student engagement and fund-raising success that will be critical for program expansion.

The inclusion of internships clearly reflects principles of co-op programs described earlier. However, Bierman observes that Beloit's context requires more than mere mimicry given its rural location. Rather than copying programs that have thrived in large urban centers, Beloit is capitalizing on "the opportunities of a small town." For example, Bierman points to educated-workforce needs in the town of 35,000. While Beloiters might not find a position at a Fortune 500 company nearby, they can have a disproportionate impact in local positions. (Bierman also notes that some students will need to find internships away from campus.)

While the Beloit program differs from co-op programs in some design elements, both models require significant investment. Bierman says the college is "financially recognizing the faculty and staff time commitment required." It is inconceivable that the program could meet its goals if it were simply layered on top of existing commitments. Ultimately, Bierman recognizes the initiative as a professional development program that demands institutional support as faculty and staff work one-on-one with students to help them integrate their liberal arts experiences of all kinds with successful careers.

The Alternative to Proactive Change

Despite the challenges we face and the practical difficulties of change, Dunwoody's Wagner is enthusiastic about our future. "It's an exciting time to be in higher ed right now," he says. "We need every type of institution we have. For institutions like Dunwoody, there are real opportunities to help solve some of the skills gaps [we see in the job market]. And when we solve those problems," he continues, "we help end cyclical poverty and build social capital in areas that really need it." That is a moving vision that points to the collective societal mission colleges and universities share in preparing the next generation of leaders and workers. But even those who are roused by such a vision can see that many movements toward proactive change contain seeds of conflict as various stakeholders consider the consequences of reimagining our future. Given the many competing objectives present on any campus and across the alumni community, we can expect most paths forward to generate at least modest resistance.

In such moments, Randy Deike cautions that we remember that leadership "is not about consensus; it's about momentum."[2] Waiting for near-unanimous agreement too often places institutions on a reactionary footing in which many proactive approaches are no longer viable by the time consensus is achieved. "If the only time you are willing to change is the point when you are standing on the abyss," argues McGee, "that's a problem."

While we don't want to wait until we reach a cliff before changing direction, it might yet be useful to look at examples of schools that have been made to confront cuts—whether modest reprioritization, deeper retrenchments, or, in the most dire of cases, closure and consolidation. For some, consideration of such difficult decisions provides motivation to reopen conversations about a change that had seemed unacceptably large until placed into this greater context. Others may have already determined that trimming is inevitably a part of any successful path forward, and for them examples of downsizing offer perspective on the way forward. For both of these cases, the next chapter offers examples of reduction.

NINE

Reorganization, Rightsizing, and Other Names for Retrenchment

THIS CHAPTER WILL likely be viewed as the least popular for many readers. The plethora of euphemisms for significant budget cutting—reorganization, rightsizing, downsizing, restructuring, to name just a few—suggests our discomfort with the topic. Of course, vocabulary matters, and these positive alternatives to "retrenchment" communicate important aspects of the motivation behind budget reduction; nuanced communication is never more critical than when faced with such challenges. Still, Jon McGee, author of *Breakpoint* and former vice president for planning and strategy at the College of Saint Benedict and Saint John's University (MN), captures well the typical attitude toward institutional pruning as a set of choices ordered from most to least preferred. The most preferred option is to "raise your price—try to capture more," he says. "The second choice, or maybe 1A, is 'We'll raise more money.'" If that isn't feasible, then "the third is 'We'll develop new programs and new markets that allow us to capture more students and more money.'" Examples from previous chapters suggest McGee is right so far. Only when the first three options fail do we arrive at actions involving cuts, "but we're going to do it incrementally in the smallest amount possible in a way that preserves as much of what we are and have been as possible." The last option, says McGee, is major budget and programmatic revision. However, he observes, most institutions only come to this point "kicking and screaming." Kicking and screaming or otherwise, we now arrive at this last option.

Instinctive resistance to size reduction is understandable: for many, perceptions of institutional health and growth are inherently intertwined. Schools struggling with declining enrollments must lack clarity of mission or otherwise fail to support student success, or so the argument goes. The tendency to equate enrollment reduction with institutional effectiveness is undoubtedly shaped and amplified by higher education's history since World War II. From 1954 through 2013, each year brought more enrollments to postsecondary education than had been seen five years prior (NCES 2018, table 303.10).[1] Not only was growth consistent; it was usually robust. For example, from 2001 through 2012, in each year the five-year growth rate never fell shy of 10%. During this 50-year growth episode, perhaps declining institutional enrollments did suggest something meaningful about institutional weakness.

Beginning in 2014, however, we entered a new era of declining aggregate enrollment. In 2017, the latest year for which we have final enrollment data, enrollments were almost 5% lower than in 2012. In fact, year-over-year enrollments have fallen in each year since 2010. To be sure, this decline in part reflects recovery from the Great Recession, which drove many to college classrooms. However, recoveries from recessions earlier in the twentieth century didn't produce five-year declines in enrollment. Surely, declines are more likely now that the number of high school graduates has reached a plateau. In the context of falling national enrollment, we might expect enrollment declines to be more common even at reasonably healthy institutions. An analysis by Zemsky et al. (2020) of data from the Integrated Postsecondary Education Data System (known as IPEDS) indeed suggests just that: many institutions have recently had to navigate contraction. Zemsky et al.'s study examines the years 2008 through 2016, a period of increasing and then decreasing aggregate enrollments. Overall, these years saw modestly higher enrollments at public two-year institutions (up 1%), public four-year institutions (up 9%), and private nonprofit (hereafter "private") four-year institutions (up 8%). Despite aggregate growth, decline was quite common at individual institutions; around two-thirds of public two-year schools, over 33% of public four-year schools, and almost half of private four-year schools had fewer students in 2016 than nine years prior.

Given demographic trends described in earlier chapters, it is unsurprising that losses were geographically concentrated in the Great Lakes, Middle Atlantic, and New England. In the former region, over 30% of four-year public schools saw an enrollment decline of at least 10%. In New England, the Southeast, the Plains, and the Middle Atlantic, more than 20% of such institutions posted similarly deep enrollment reductions. An even greater share of four-year private schools lost more than 10% of their students. In fact, in no region did fewer than 17% of four-year private institutions experience such a decline. With so many campuses experiencing meaningful enrollment contraction in the past decade, surely more than a few such schools do not fit the stereotype of a weak institution suffering justly deserved decline. Changing times call for revised thinking about what we might conclude about a college that chooses to become smaller or even to merge. The examples in this chapter provide alternative pictures of this process, ranging from reorganization to rightsizing to merger. While the method of tightening varies, in most instances institutional leaders came to the process believing it offers them an opportunity to fulfill their missions more completely.

Reprioritization (Program Cuts)

While those who adopt program cuts don't always come to that point "kicking and screaming," as in McGee's description, most do recognize that serious challenges lie ahead. After all, in periods of growing enrollment it is relatively easy to implement a thoughtless expansion that doesn't hobble the institution. Perhaps newly added resources are not in the best position to support the mission, but nothing productive has been cut in the process. By contrast, in periods of scarcity, poorly placed reductions can leave critical departments understaffed at a time when strong performance is at a premium. As a result, plans to cut—even when accompanied by strategic investments in new areas—are best proceeded by comprehensive program review, at least if the decision to cut was made deliberately rather than in a moment of immediate financial pressure.

Careful planning certainly undergirded systematic reprioritization at Simpson College (IA), as described by former president Jay Simmons. From the mid-2000s through fall 2016, Simpson's full-time enrollment declined almost 10%, echoing a similar decline in Iowa's high school graduates as reported by WICHE (2016). In May 2017, the board of trustees approved a comprehensive program review to look at every academic and nonacademic program on campus. To create buy-in, Simmons organized a committee with elected representatives of faculty, staff, and students. The committee, he explains, was charged with examining a wide range of information including "enrollments, long-term trends, economic data about particular majors, [etc.,] as well as our own internal data about numbers of majors in every academic program." Each department also generated a program report to inform the committee's understanding of needs and opportunities for efficiencies.

The process, which spanned most of the 2017–18 academic year, was not without cost. "It was a long, laborious and, I will admit, painful process," Simmons acknowledges. But in return, the study produced "some fairly obvious conclusions for anyone willing to look at the data." At the end of the process, the college eliminated majors in French and German and closed the art department.

Cuts in foreign languages are hardly unique to Simpson. In work with the Modern Language Association, Looney and Lusin (2019) report that the number of language programs at US institutions fell by 651 (or more than 5%) between fall 2013 and fall 2016. In total, foreign-language enrollments were off by more than 9% over the same period. These declines were widespread, with the Modern Language Association documenting enrollment declines in all of the 15 most commonly taught languages with the exception of Japanese and Korean.

Not all institution types experienced the same enrollment pressure. In particular, foreign-language enrollments at two-year colleges declined more (16%) than at four-year schools (7%). Of course, the general trend obscures variation across individual programs. In fact, Looney and Lusin (2019) find that during this three-year period of national decline, one-third of foreign-language programs gained enrollments and another 13% were stable.

With departmental enrollments more or less tracking national trends, Simpson viewed the decision to eliminate majors as a question of responsible resource allocation. Simmons explains, "In those three areas, we had five fully tenured faculty members at roughly $80,000 per year in total compensation. The math becomes fairly simple," he continues, "$400,000 a year in salary and compensation for about two majors graduating per year. It's just not good stewardship." Savings from these decisions have allowed expansions elsewhere in other departments, including human services and sports management, and funded a new full-time disability services coordinator.

Reprioritization initiatives like this one inevitably raise questions about institutional mission and philosophical commitment to college divisions absorbing reductions. Simmons is well aware of the tension, noting that "we're trying to be responsible stewards of our resources while maintaining the integrity of our Arts & Sciences foundation." Still, some faculty are sure to see things differently, and Simmons welcomes that engagement. "Not surprisingly, faculty are advocating for their departments and programs, as you would anticipate—and as they should." Despite varieties of opinions, the reprioritization initiative, founded on the yearlong fact-finding effort, moves forward. "[M]ost faculty appreciate that long-term trends suggest that we will be a smaller institution than we were a decade or 15 years ago, but that doesn't mean we don't have great opportunities . . . and can't be quite healthy."

Champlain College (VT) has essentially institutionalized reprioritization through an annual zero-based budget process. Lisa Bunders, vice president of enrollment management, explains how awareness of demographic challenges in Vermont and New England paved the way for the new budget process. "We really did think about how we fund our overall budget around our students—what they're going to look like, what they're going to need, where they're going to come from," she explains. While the transition to zero-based budgeting took just one year, Bunders argues it followed a much longer process, creating a culture of stewardship and awareness of financial pressures— pressures faced by both the institution and by students and their families. Toward that end, administrators practice consistent communication. For just one example, Bunders cites the nearly annual reminder from high-level administrators to staff at the start of the year that "every dollar you spend at work is some family's hard-earned dollar." Certainly, moves to aggressive processes such as zero-based budgeting require more than periodic emotional rhetoric. But, Bunders argues that consistent communication has been important, as Champlain has developed a "DNA of budget consciousness" that connects a frank assessment of enrollment and budgetary environments with mission-driven goals that compel frugality.

Rightsizing (Decreasing Institution Size)

Given its location in Vermont, it is perhaps fitting that St. Michael's College would be a leader among institutions intentionally targeting lower enrollment. WICHE (2016) figures suggest that the state will have produced just 6,700 high school graduates in 2019, more than 25% off a peak reached in 2008. Looking ahead, WICHE anticipates a brief respite in high school graduate declines through 2025 before continued contraction. Because St. Michaels is ranked near the top of the regional colleges category, HEDI projections suggest that it was not likely to significantly buck these broader population trends. In this demographic context and on the heels of the financial crisis, then president John Neuhauser convened a strategic assessment task force in 2012 to identify and evaluate the various forces, demographic and otherwise, that proved threatening to the institution's middle- and long-range health.

The resulting report emphasized questions relating to the financial model of higher education, demographic change, and competition from eLearning, and led to the decision in 2014 to decrease St. Michael's targeted enrollment from around 1,900 to approximately 1,600 over three or four years (Rivard 2014). Reflecting on the decision process five years later, Neuhauser thinks the analysis in the strategic assessment holds up well. Certainly, concerns about the rate of tuition increase, ballooning student loan debt, and declining prospective student pools in the northeast seem as credible today as when the report was written. (Neuhauser concedes that "the concern about eLearning—particularly the MOOCs [massive open online courses]—was at least premature, not that it hasn't had an effect.") In St. Michael's context, he viewed the enrollment reduction as one of "survival." "I think you can withstand, pretty easily, a 10% to 15% drop in net tuition revenue, maybe even a little more. When it gets to be 25% or 30%, you're in for a major restructuring."

Judging by figures in the Common Data Set, St. Michael's has effectively followed through on its enrollment-reduction plan. In each year since 2014, the number of undergraduates has declined by around 5%, resulting in a reduction from 2,039 in fall 2014 to 1,655 in fall 2018. Of course, getting smaller was only part of the plan. The purpose was to use the change in enrollment to maintain quality despite a contracting pool. Neuhauser argues that it was "very important to maintain the quality of the incoming class because if the perception in the market was that you were moving toward open enrollment and away from a classical liberal arts model, that was going to be very hard to restore." Targeting a smaller class size can permit greater selectivity. Here again, evidence in the Common Data Set suggests that the downsizing plan has played out as designed. For example, as the number of St. Michael's students fell, fewer came with very low board scores. Specifically, the shares of first-time, first-year students with SAT reading, math, and writing scores lower than 500 and ACT scores lower than 18 have steadily declined. At the same time, the twenty-fifth and seventy-fifth percentile scores on these examinations have risen. We cannot know how these measures would have evolved had enrollment targets remained unchanged, but Neuhauser believes that "given the [population] decline, it was unlikely we could do this without getting smaller." (Not surprisingly, not all evidence points toward improving quality. While standardized test scores have risen, the first-year retention rate is off a bit.)

The plan, which included budget cuts accomplished largely through staff and faculty attrition, naturally involved risk and engendered some resistance. (As it played out, Neuhauser says, "We had a good deal of success reducing the staff on a voluntary basis; much less success on the faculty side.") For instance, as late as 2017 one faculty member accused Neuhauser of "not telling the truth about the decline in the number of high school graduates." Given widespread reports of institutional closings and declining enrollment in the Northeast, this perspective might seem difficult to understand. However, Neuhauser thinks that we can appreciate such responses by remembering the historical context. "In retrospect, American higher education from probably 1960 to 2005 was really a golden era. To see that potentially decline was hard for a lot of people to swallow. It's hard for me to swallow."

Resistance also came from some in the alumni community who wanted the college to be more aggressive in marketing, particularly in the large Boston market, making the case for the value of a St. Michael's degree. "There are people who honestly believe you can create new curriculum programs, market more heavily, and you'll be just fine," observes Neuhauser. "I think you should do that. I just don't think you can count on that" to maintain prior enrollment levels.

If it is easy to imagine why some would oppose a smaller campus, what was persuasive in getting to the downsizing outcome? Neuhauser thinks the strategic assessment, and the demographic arguments in particular, actually carried significant weight. More importantly, the composition of the assessment team (which included faculty, staff, and alumni) lent credibility. "This wasn't a randomly selected group," explains Neuhauser. Specifically, he sought out high-status, midcareer faculty. "I thought we should put this in the hands of the people whose institution this would be in 10 years."

The content of the report was then persistently and consistently communicated, particularly at faculty meetings, which are heavily attended. As at many colleges, Neuhauser says that at St. Michael's "the key is really faculty—trying to get faculty to understand that there are things that we can do, but it's much better if we do this together." That messaging was not focused solely on cuts but also articulated the vision for a strong and healthy future. "You had to bet on certain areas and let people know that there was hope," Neuhauser maintains. Even as the college became smaller, St. Michael's could not ignore strategic investment questions faced by all colleges. In particular, like many peers, St. Michaels perceived the need to respond to "growing [student] interest in STEM subjects" and the need to better "prepar[e] students, however you did it, for initial jobs," Neuhauser recalls.

The combination of downsizing with new investments raised important questions of mission for the traditional liberal arts college. Neuhauser contends, "You don't want to turn yourself into something that you're not or you shouldn't be," even as you implement changes to grapple with new demographic and recruiting realities. Despite a healthy appreciation for the challenge of leading the campus through downsizing, Neuhauser still concludes: "I underestimated how hard it was going to be politically."

Were he to do it over again, Neuhauser would take a slightly different approach to hiring. "We absolutely should have held the line on hiring, at least at the beginning, because I think symbolically that was important." Doing so would have helped to communicate the idea "that this was an imminent crisis." Instead, in early years of implementation the college agreed to new hires in several departments with growing course enrollments. Having been a faculty member, Neuhauser says he would have advanced—and as president respected—the arguments that departments made for these new faculty lines. And he recognizes the likely political cost of saying no despite such strong arguments. "You put the provost or dean in a tough position. To some extent you're cutting off your nose to spite your face when you don't hire that chemist because that's where the student interest is." Still, Neuhauser thinks a hiring moratorium would have served the college more effectively. While it would have disrupted campus relations a bit, he sees that outcomes as "a price that was worth paying" to communicate the urgency and necessity of a fundamental change like the one St. Michael's had embarked on.

Taking stock of his entire experience, Neuhauser believes other schools would benefit from St. Michael's example. "I still think it's a good way to go," he says. In fact, based on the evidence since the strategic assessment report, he thinks some important risks were underappreciated in the original analysis. "Because of the decline in the availability of students, we were likely to enter into a price war using financial aid. I think we underestimated what that would do to net tuition." This observation is echoed by a Moody's Investors Service analysis that cites "hypercompetition" for limited students as a cause for stagnant revenue growth in higher education (Seltzer 2019). Ultimately, Neuhauser's advice to other institutions facing similar challenges is direct: "You should be aware that the demographics are real. You should begin as early as you can—set budgets based on what are reasonable demographics." And while institutions should work to "improve marketing and all kinds of competitive programing," Neuhauser cautions, "I think to bank on [those recruitment-oriented efforts] is foolish."

Although Zemsky et al. (2020) find that many institutions have already experienced significant enrollment declines, relatively few have followed St. Michael's example by actively targeting cohort size reductions. The George Washington University (DC) represents a notable and recent counterexample. In July 2019, its board of trustees adopted a five-year plan that anticipates a 20% reduction in undergraduate enrollment. In an open letter to the campus, President Thomas LeBlanc presents a theme: "Better, not bigger."[2] According to Common Data Set reports, between fall 2013 and fall 2018, George Washington's full-time undergraduate enrollment increased by 18%. LeBlanc's message notes how this growth "has stretched our facilities, our services, our staff and our faculty," and argues that the new plan can be seen as "rightsizing." The university's recent recruitment success suggests the strategic plan originates from a position of significant strength; the data certainly don't present a campus with no option other than putting an optimistic frame around inevitable decline. Continued growth into the future might not be sustainable in light of softening demographic trends (not to mention limited real estate), but the university clearly faces a wide range of choices. And in their estimation (as explained in LeBlanc's letter), planning for smaller size will best position the institution for strategic investments in STEM and policy-related fields to "help us offer the high-quality undergraduate experience our students expect and deserve." While the specific investments speak to George Washington's established identity, the broader lines of the argument clearly echo those made at St. Michael's.

Mergers

College and university mergers have become regular items in higher education media coverage as their frequency increases. While the decades of the 1980s, 1990s, and 2000s each saw between 10 and 12 mergers, merger activity has tripled in the 2010s (Azziz et al. 2017; Education Dive 2019; Sapiro 2019). Already 11 mergers have been announced to be completed in the first part of the 2020s, not including the administrative consolidation of a dozen community colleges in Connecticut (Education Dive 2019). Moreover, looking forward, S&P Global (2019) analysts believe the pace of merger activity will increase, particularly in regions most affected by declining student numbers. The resulting interest in mergers has motivated reports analyzing the role of mergers in higher education's future (Azziz et al. 2017; Seltzer 2018).

The term "merger" is used to describe a wide range of activities (Azziz et al. 2017; Boggs 2018; Seltzer 2018). At one end of the spectrum, a merger might be the combination of two equally robust institutions who perceive strategic complementarities—of scope, scale, or both—in their union. At the other extreme, a weak institution might be acquired by a stronger neighbor that sees some advantage in parts of the "target" institution. While these latter mergers are lexically distinguished from a closure, for many staff and faculty this is a distinction with little meaning. For example, when Wheelock College and Boston University merged, more than half of the former's employees were laid off (*BU Today* 2018). (All tenured faculty were counted among the lucky job-keepers.) Azziz et al. (2017) argue that when financial duress motivates merger activity, "available resource are few" and the resulting transition is more likely to be experienced as an acquisition in which the target institution has little control (25). The authors contend that, to realize the most positive results for both parties, merging should be considered more proactively as one of many tactics rather than as a last resort when remaining merger opportunities offer alternatives little better than closure.

This advice, while sensible, may be impossible for most institutional leaders to follow. W. Joseph King, president of Lyon College (AR) and scholar of higher education governance, notes that if a president were to suggest that the board of trustees might profit from a discussion of possible mergers, "the board will be thinking about a new president." This is unfortunate, says King, because new realities in higher education mean that "we have to put some of these things on the table." Particularly in regions more densely populated by small colleges than by prospective students, it seems unlikely that all will thrive independently. Merger may indeed be the best means of fulfilling the institutional mission, but often the topic cannot even be discussed.

Moreover, King worries that too many boards suffer from governance structures ill-suited to contemplating mergers. Board members are too part-time and too disconnected, he says, and governance committees are more often designed for protracted discussion than timely action. Even if a board were willing to take up the question of a merger, King wonders whether these structures preclude a healthy outcome. "[Merger discussion] can't take two years. [If it does,] everyone will just work to kill it."

Perhaps merger discussions would be politically feasible and potentially healthy if the perceived connection between a merger and institutional failure could be broken. As Randall Deike, senior vice president for enrollment management and student success at Cleveland State University, notes (in a broader context), "Crisis is often what drives change." While this observation is true, if crisis is the only context in which fundamental change is debated, then broaching such challenging topics will almost surely elicit counterproductive fears of an imminent crisis—even if no crisis exists. The conversation is over before it begins. King imagines an alternative world in which boards and campuses agree to discuss "verboten" questions on a regular basis as a matter of course. For instance, if taboo topics were preassigned to the agenda every 10 or 20 years, then presidents would not risk losing their jobs just by leading the conversation.

While merger is one such taboo topic, King sees broad applicability of this principle. In the end, "all we need are the faculty and the students," he says. "That is the college. If the campus disappeared, we could still have class tomorrow." With such a perspective, everything else is up for consideration. King sees the willingness to radically reenvision the institution as a necessary antidote to the human problem of myopic hindsight. "Memory is so short," he explains. For example, "for the vast majority of liberal arts colleges, there was a time just before the 1980s or 1990s where campuses were much starker, they had classes on Saturdays, the cost structure was radically smaller." But after just 30 or 40 years, many can't imagine their institutions operating by those standards. "They can't imagine ever being that institution," says King. While there are good arguments behind these and other evolutions in campus life, King argues institutions run risks if they are unable to talk through possible futures that relax some of these assumptions. Ultimately, he worries, "all the things you think that the college is are making the college financially unstable."

The relative infrequency of mergers combined with the typical perception that mergers only follow severe financial duress leave us with relatively few healthy examples of mergers that institutions might want to emulate. Notable exceptions are found in the University System of Georgia, where merger and consolidation have been made more or less routine over the past decade. At the outset, it should be noted that the university system has a single governing body. As such, Georgia is better organized to accomplish mergers than others who approach a union with multiple governing bodies.

John Fuchko III, University System of Georgia vice chancellor for organizational effectiveness, stresses that merger activity within the system has not been dictated by demographic or financial forces.

Rather, the "primary focus was how we can take advantage of where we have two institutions to rationalize what we have [and] increase the scale of what we can provide." This objective is captured by six principles adopted by the system board of regents in 2011: (1) increase educational attainment, (2) improve accessibility and connection to each region, (3) avoid programmatic duplication, (4) create economies of scale and scope, (5) support economic development, and (6) streamline administration. Fuchko and the board believe these broad goals of enhanced effectiveness are facilitated by the all-encompassing nature of the merger process. "The nature of a consolidation is an opportunity to really put everything on the table," explains Fuchko. "You're going to bring two faculties together, two sets of traditions. By nature, there has to be a give and a take, a willingness to reexamine." As a result, institutions can identify and address ongoing (and sometimes unseen) weaknesses.

With so few examples of healthy merger to draw from, it is hardly surprising that the Georgia system would experience a steep learning curve. Mergers involve many moving parts—Fuchko says that the system office now tracks more than 600 distinct tasks as they move through the process—and best practices are not always obvious without experience. For example, while communication and feedback are critical for success, more is not always better. In a widely reported instance from the system's first merger between Augusta State University and Georgia Health Sciences University, the public conversation was overtaken by the question of the new institution's name, crowding out space for other issues more directly connected to education (Gardner 2017). In subsequent mergers, by announcing the board's determined name for the new institution at the outset of a proposed merger, Fuchko says feedback and communication were better focused on strategic questions such as "What are some things we ought to be doing differently? How can we better serve the region?"

Another important lesson: mergers suffer from what Azziz et al. (2017) call a "discordance in timing between gains and costs" (3). In other words, merging institutions face up-front costs related to facilities, marketing, administration, employee training, and more; the potential economies of scale that generate savings are only realized later. Georgia's success in past mergers supports their request for patience from policymakers and stakeholders. While one might hope that schools in other states could point to Georgia's example to ask for the same, the critique of Connecticut's ongoing merger by Adair, Aime, et al. (2019) reminds us that when contexts differ, such arguments may fail to persuade all listeners (particularly when delays add to the up-front costs).

While financial savings were not the primary objective of Georgia consolidations, Fuchko estimates savings of $30 million per year from nine consolidations. "Those are hard numbers that don't include avoidance costs" such as sidestepping a new hire, according to Fuchko. The savings were largely from administration and management in particular. For example, "obviously, if you put two institutions together you don't need two presidents. That by itself is a little over $2 million." In the context of the 18 involved institutions, $30 million is a modest sum—only 0.8% of their aggregate budgets (University System of Georgia 2019).[3] (Even as a share of state appropriations to the combined institutions, the savings is less than 3%.) However, following the principles underlying the initiative, those savings have been reinvested in the affected campuses. As part of consolidation planning, institutions "had to bring a plan forward about how they would use [the savings]." As a result, campuses have seen a net increase in staff, new faculty lines, new academic programs, financial aid office and enrollment management investments, and expansions in advising.

The theory behind the Georgia consolidation program is that these strategic reinvestments along with rationalization and reconfiguration of programs across campuses will lead to better educational outcomes. Russell (2019) formally evaluates this hypothesis in an examination of persistence rates. Using nonmerging campuses as a control group and controlling for observable characteristics such as SAT scores, Russell examines the first five mergers to see how retention and graduation rates changed over time at the merging institutions relative to nonmerging peers. Russell reports that consolidation led to a 10% reduction in first-year dropout rates, an effect size that is "similar in magnitude to effects of increasing financial aid by $1000" (126). Moreover, Russell finds that students were more likely to graduate with a bachelor's degree. Students who were initially enrolled in two-year programs were more likely to switch to four-year programs (perhaps because consolidation facilitated ease in switching). In addition, the four-year graduation rate among students who were initially enrolled in a four-year program rose by four percentage points. To put this effect in appropriate context, Russell (2019) notes that "given that only 14% of students who enroll in a Bachelor's program pre-consolidation end up graduating with their degree within four years, this is a meaningful increase of about 29%" (128).

Given the sheer magnitude of merger work, not to mention the inherent political hurdles, it is perhaps not surprising that full consolidations have been rare. However, some have found it possible to reap many of the rewards (particularly those associated with scale) with partial consolidations. For example, Ross Gittell, chancellor of the Community College System of New Hampshire, has realized gains in his system through collaboration particularly among rural schools facing the greatest demographic pressures. While the schools remain independent, "our colleges work together," Gittell explains. "For instance, each of our rural colleges don't need a full-time institutional researcher. We have a single Banner student record system. We have a single learning management system so students can go from one college to another easily."

These examples represent a common approach to partial consolidation: the combination of back-of-house support functions (Boggs 2018). Gittell's schools have attempted to move their collaboration further into front-facing functions to achieve even greater advantages. "If a rural college can't offer a broad set of humanities course offerings," he explains, "students at rural colleges can take courses at our larger colleges online or by traveling to the other college's location." In addition, cross-institution colleagues have worked together to advance programming initiatives such as guided pathways (see chapter 8), apprenticeship programs, and workforce development. In such curriculum revision work, Gittell argues that the system has been able to accomplish important work that would have been impossible if attempted by an individual campus due to limitations of scale and expertise. "A rural college could not have taken on the guided pathways initiative on its own," he argues, "but working with other faculty from other colleges they can do it."

While some might see such interinstitutional coordination as an incomplete step toward a more desirable goal of merger and consolidation, Gittell takes a different view. Colleges and universities have many objectives. Their mission is not simply to educate the largest number of people at the lowest cost. This is particularly true of public institutions whose locations clearly speak to the additional aims of access and economic development (to mention but two components of the public college and university mission). Based on data from the 2002 Educational Longitudinal Survey, Grawe (2018) finds that the median distance between a two-year college student's high school and community college of attendance is less than 15 miles. Consolidation resulting in campus closures hampers student matriculation and completion. Even when campuses remain open, Gittell argues, complete consolidation generates critical costs beyond the higher education system. For instance, he notes that "presidential leadership at rural colleges is really important because those are leaders of their communities, and they are leaders in education including the K–12 system." As a consequence, systems may find it preferable to pursue partial interinstitutional collaborations that realize significant cost savings and yet stop short of complete merger.

The Opposite of Rightsizing

Undoubtedly, we use euphemisms to describe institutional contraction because they allow us to avoid contemplating some of the more difficult, related realities. But euphemisms also serve to control the narrative. Despite leading the rightsizing at St. Michael's (or perhaps because of it), Neuhauser quickly ticks off the risks inherent to the strategy. "It's a very conservative strategy. You could read this as a sign of weakness. 'We're not going to fight back. We're not going to market our way out of this. Instead we're going to retrench and be-come smaller.'" These perspectives were particularly common in the alumni community. "It's a hard thing to sell, that we're going to get smaller to stay strong," he concludes. Perceptions of weakness are al-ways concerning, but how much more is that concern in the context of enrollment and financial trends that demand top-level recruitment success. If ability to control the narrative of downsizing seems ques-tionable at best, some may instead conclude the path forward lies in the opposite direction: plans for growth that communicate strength and confidence, various forms of which are considered in the next chapter.

TEN

Growth Plans

ONE OF THE more counterintuitive strategies for navigating demographic change may be enrollment growth. This idea may sound like a twist on the joke about the inept businessperson who explains that "we lose money on every sale, but make it up in volume." If institutions are struggling to find students in a demographically depressed era, how can growth be a pathway to success for some? Obviously, this strategy can't possibly work for everyone. However, even as it increases competition, some thoughtful leaders see growth as a means to achieve institutional goals for net tuition revenue in the midst of demographic challenge.

Elites Are Different

Clearly, elite schools face challenges like the current demographic upheaval with a good degree of privilege. As chapters 2 through 4 make clear, rising educational attainment among parents coupled with increasing numbers of Asian American students portend relatively stable demand for this subsector of higher education. Even as other portions of the industry anticipate dwindling prospective student pools, students with the demographic markers of elite attendance are expected to hold steady or increase.

But even this analysis misses two bigger points. First, elite schools are obviously highly selective. They often accept less than one in three applicants. At the extreme, in 2018 Princeton University (NJ) pressed its industry-leading acceptance rate to a new low of 5.5%. If these schools want to grow their undergraduate enrollments, they could easily do so even if the number of applicants fell. Of course, growth in class sizes by definition requires compromise elsewhere. In the context of population decline, it likely requires higher acceptance rates, and average student quality—however conceived by the school—may arguably be sacrificed to a degree. But given the HEDI projections of a rising trend in the elite market, for these schools the trade-offs may exist only relative to a counterfactual in which enrollments were left unchanged: modest growth in enrollments may be accomplished at the same time that rising application numbers permit each admitted class to outshine the last. In this sense, among elites, the institution-level interaction between larger admitted classes and coincident demographic change is less interesting.

Indeed, growth by elites is much more likely to be driven by other mission-related aims. For instance, in 2016 Princeton announced its intention to expand by 125 students per class year as they added a seventh college (Knapp 2016). As explained in Princeton's strategic planning framework, "the expansion . . . will provide opportunities to enhance the diversity of Princeton's undergraduate student body" (Princeton 2016, 11). Similarly, a larger cohort size may allow an institution to achieve critical mass for an otherwise unsustainable program.

Lafayette College (PA) provides a similar example from a top liberal arts college. Former provost Abu Rizvi explains, "We have been embarked on a new strategic direction [since 2015] to increase access and affordability," supported by an enrollment increase of 15% through 2025. If successful, the campus would grow from 2,500 to 2,900 students. Demographic trends provided significant motivation for change, but not the demographics of a declining market. Influenced by national economic forces, Lafayette has experienced a rightward shift in the income distribution of students. Rizvi says that a "desire for greater diversity on campus" necessitated enrollment growth. In addition, larger class sizes will better support Division I athletics and several targeted expansions in the curriculum. Resulting new revenue along with targeted donor support through a capital campaign will allow Lafayette to rededicate merit aid to need-based grants and otherwise deepen resources to support socioeconomically diverse recruitment.

The second point to remember about elite institutions and their potential growth is that they educate a small minority of college-going students. Just over 700,000 students attend top-50 universities and about 100,000 more study at top-50 liberal arts colleges. In total, these institutions account for less than 8% of the more than 10.5 million full-time undergraduates in the United States—to say nothing of the 6.5 million part-time undergraduates (NCES 2018, table 303.70). Yale University's (CT) recently implemented plan to add two new colleges and grow its undergraduate class by 15%—or 200 per cohort—simply can't reshape the higher education market. Of course, institutions with heavy admissions overlap with a modest-sized growing elite school might feel the pressure.

But while the total size of the top tier is small and many constituent institutions draw relatively few students per cohort, some institutions in this category are among the largest schools in the country. And in their markets, growth can have outsize impacts. For example, the University of Michigan at Ann Arbor is home to almost 29,000 full-time undergraduates. While previous classes had numbered around 6,000, with occasional unexpected surges of almost 10%, beginning in the fall of 2015 the university raised its intentional admissions goal to nearly 6,700. Such an increase has greater potential to have an effect on other institutions—directly or indirectly.

According to Kedra Ishop, vice provost for enrollment management, the motivation to grow is completely mission-driven. Consistent with HEDI forecasts that show growth in the market for highly selective education, the Ann Arbor campus has seen "tremendous quality demand for admission." Charged with providing an exceptional education to Michiganders and preparing a trained workforce for the state's industry, Ishop contends, the university would arguably be squandering a vital state resource if it needlessly restricted admission. And so, in approaching the enrollment target, Ishop and her colleagues asked, "What is our true capacity to serve as many students in the state of Michigan as we can [in addition to serving national and international populations]?"

Consistent with its public mission, the implementation of growth balances the needs of prospective students and workforce needs in the state. With a world-recognized reputation, the school could easily fill the additional seats with students from other states or even other countries. (About 7% of Michigan's undergraduates are international students.) Ishop explains that the admissions team continues to make sure they enroll roughly the same percentage of high school graduates from the state of Michigan "even as it has become more competitive to get into the institution because applications have gone from 20,000 to 70,000." As a result, while growth is fueled by an increase in demand that would surely permit the school to hit enrollment targets without increasing aid, Michigan is simultaneously expanding grants to low-income students from within the state. Under the Go Blue Guarantee, Michiganders with family income below $65,000, the median state income, are offered full tuition grants, what Ishop describes as one of many "deliberate actions to reflect our place as a state institution." Even as demand from outside the state has surged, a boon to the state's workforce, "we work really hard to serve our home base," Ishop explains.

So, while admissions growth at elite institutions is likely neither to be driven by demographic change nor to substantially alter the larger picture for most of higher education, growth at a handful of larger elite institutions will create meaningful ripples in local markets. Growth in the modestly sized elite sector is unlikely to represent an existential threat to other institutions. However, what growth does take place is layered atop serious demographic challenges. For example, WICHE (2016) suggests that the number of high school graduates in Michigan has already fallen by more than 15% from highs in 2008, and in the next 15 years the state might expect further reduction of an approximately equal proportion. Even if growth among top-50 colleges and top-50 universities is unlikely to direct the course of higher education, in states like Michigan it may be an important thread in the story with meaningful impacts realized by moderately selective private peers who have significant admissions overlaps with these schools.

Growth beyond the Top

Outside the most selective colleges and universities, HEDI forecasts suggest a decline in potential student numbers in the mid-to-late 2020s that, after a brief rebound in the early 2030s, persists for the foreseeable future. Work in chapters 2 and 3 suggests declines on the order of 10% nationally and deeper in the Middle Atlantic and East North Central, where declines appear closer to 20%. Pursuing a strategy of growth in this context entails greater risk—and, if successful, potentially greater reward.

To understand the logic of this strategy—and to see its potential risks and benefits—consider a very stylized hypothetical school at which, through need or merit aid, only a small minority of the class pays the full fee. Suppose the school's discount rate stands at 47.5%. In an increasingly competitive context, the discount rate might need to rise to 50% to maintain enrollments. With net fee income down about 5%, if our hypothetical school is even modestly selective, it may set out to increase size by an equal degree to offset the loss—more students at a lower net fee supporting the same total budget. For several reasons, our school will likely need to grow more aggressively to avoid declining net revenue in the wake of heightened competition. Most obviously, additional students impose additional costs on the institution. More importantly, the added students are likely to bring in lower net fee incomes than the average. To the degree that the admissions process is sensitive to financial aid costs, marginal students are likely to have relatively less capacity to pay. Moreover, these additional students may be less ardently committed to our hypothetical school. This fact may mean they require slightly greater financial aid to motivate attendance, and they may also be more prone to transfer, both of which reduce their contributions to net revenue. Still, for schools with deep enough application pools or nearby markets that have not been fully tapped, these caveats don't change the nature of the required growth, only the degree.

Obviously, this approach is not without risk. After all, many institutions feel stress today precisely because they adopted budget models founded on unrealized growth. For example, Jon McGee, author of *Breakpoint* and former vice president for planning and strategy at the College of Saint Benedict and Saint John's University (MN), points to the rapid expansion of graduate programs and offerings to nontraditional undergraduates in the 1990s. "There never were any real barriers to entry," he notes. "So, now you have a market stuffed with providers, and any margins you may have had have just gone away for most of those programs." Institutions adopting growth as a response to tightening demographics must believe their program possesses characteristics that somehow set themselves apart.

Wheaton College (MA) has recently adopted growth as one of several approaches to grappling with the declining number of New England students. President Dennis Hanno immediately notes, though, that demographic change is only part of the picture. Developed as part of the college's 2016 strategic plan, the goal to increase student numbers from around 1,600 to 1,800 also reflects the desire to create "more buzz and energy" on the campus, says Hanno. Given Wheaton's location in the small, quiet town of Norton, he notes that the college's larger size will "create the critical mass [required to create the feel of] a college town." The school is even contemplating retail partnerships at the edge of the campus to create parts of the college town that are currently missing—partnerships that are not viable without a large number of undergraduate customers. So, as will surely be true of most institutions looking at growth, Wheaton is not pursuing this strategy solely as a means to offset demographic softness in their New England market.

But this is not to say that the financial benefits were not explicitly considered. Hanno explains that the college has experienced slow growth in net fee income, at a rate of about 1% per year, as a rising discount rate has consumed much of each year's increase in fees. From

2010 to 2016, the years leading up to the recent growth spurt, the discount rate steadily increased from 30% to 40%. Wheaton's growth in enrollment is intended to counterbalance the rising discount rate with increasing numbers of students.

But as noted previously, when a school digs deeper into its application pool to grow the admitted class, further increases to the discount rate may be unavoidable. When I asked Hanno whether Wheaton experienced this effect to some degree, he said: "Absolutely. It skyrocketed." Indeed in 2017, after previously rising by about 1.6 points per year, the discount rate rose almost three points to 42.7%. Hanno is quick to note that close analysis of their data suggests the discount rate would have increased even in the absence of growth, but some of the increase seems due to expanded admissions. In addition, direct costs of growth are evident in the form of a new residence hall, begun in the spring of 2018, which adds almost 180 beds. Hanno's team views these costs as "short-term cost for a long-term payoff," which comes with larger cohort sizes. Certainly, given its comprehensive fee of more than $66,000, collecting even a modest portion of the fee on an additional 200 students may support the college's financial strength if other costs can be held in line.

Regional institutions pursuing growth in a time of contracting pools are unlikely to grow through geographic expansion. At such institutions, the vast majority of applications and matriculations originate in at most a handful of states. Indeed, it is not uncommon for an institution to draw 95% or more of its students from a narrow "core" market. Given the incredible importance of word-of-mouth advertising, breaking into entirely new geographic markets may be all but infeasible. Even if it were possible, overcoming the lack of name recognition would likely require significant aid expenditures that markedly drive up discount rates and mitigate the potential benefit of added numbers. If new geographies are not available, growth may instead come through gaining market share in existing markets. Many institutions can identify high schools within their core recruiting region that produce large numbers of applications—and an additional set of demographically similar schools that produce few if any applications.

A growth strategy based on depth rather than breadth might seek to leverage existing name recognition in the region to extend success from the former to the latter.

Of course, any institution adopting this strategy must answer an obvious question: Why do we expect to succeed while others fail? After all, if the total pool is shrinking, growth at one institution requires even deeper cuts at others. While it is not impossible to imagine some success stories, surely this outcome should not be expected by many.

Cascading Consequences

Insofar as some institutions attempt to grow their way through the challenges of demographic change, the cascading problems of a shrinking market will only be made more difficult for others. As made clear in chapters 2 through 4, the HEDI forecasts are not to be understood as predictions of the number of students who are likely to attend colleges and universities of a given type. Rather, the projections represent the number of students with demographic markers associated with attending schools of various types. Clearly, admissions departments can (and surely will!) revise their practices in response to the changing environment.

While it isn't possible to anticipate all of the changes ahead, we can make some reasonable assumptions that guide our thinking. Schools with any degree of selectivity are unlikely to take on "their share" of enrollment contraction. Rather than dealing with the budget shortfalls associated with shrinking cohort sizes, most of these institutions are likely to admit larger shares of their applicant pool to make their class size (or come as close to this as possible). This decision may lead to decreased selectivity, increased tuition discount rates, or other on-campus adjustments to accommodate a somewhat different student body, but many will view these adjustments to be modest compared with the alternative. Still other schools are likely to find a path that supports growth despite already high acceptance rates.

Of course, to the degree that some colleges and universities respond to softening demographics by increasing enrollment or mitigating losses through higher acceptance rates, other institutions are almost surely left with a larger challenge. While students and institutions can't be ranked perfectly along a single dimension, it seems likely that elite recruiting in declining markets will protect those institutions at the expense of national schools, who will in turn offset losses at the expense of somewhat selective regional schools, and so on down the line. That is, the pressures of demographic change are likely to cascade. This is the unpleasant arithmetic of competition. Of course, not all of our work is competitive. Collaboration, the focus of the next chapter, is also a potential response to demographic challenges.

[ELEVEN]
Collaborative Action

A NUMBER OF years ago, I spoke at a faculty chair's meeting as the chair of a strategic planning subcommittee charged with thinking about what the actions of our competition meant for Carleton College's future. My task was to get feedback on the committee's work. One of my colleagues offered an interesting observation: "I prefer to think of our peers as collaborators rather than competitors." My initial thought was that while I, too, preferred to think of them this way, when we are looking to hire faculty and staff or recruit students, my preference has routinely been disappointed. Though colleges and universities can't avoid the reality that, in some spaces, peers are zero-sum competitors, my colleague made an important point. We overlook collaborative opportunities to address challenges at our collective and individual peril.

To be sure, higher education is exceptional at sharing best practices. Other industries are far more concerned with establishing intellectual property rights to new processes. While that ethic of sharing runs deeply through the academy, other forms of collaboration often remain elusive. Alexander (2019) argues that even the financial pressures of the Great Recession were rarely sufficient to motivate widespread collaboration either in terms of resources or strategy, and he doesn't see that trend likely to change in coming years. "In reality, colleges and universities have a hard time collaborating. They tend to see each other as competitors rather than allies, a perception likely to strengthen as demographic and economic pressures mount" (58). While Alexander enumerates a host of impediments to cooperative initiatives, the potential benefits continue to beckon.

In public higher education, many cite decentralized governance as a hurdle. With that in mind, some states have created centralized bodies that coordinate public institutions within the state. Zakiya Smith Ellis, secretary of higher education in New Jersey, describes how her recently formed Office of Higher Education is "responsible for . . . coordination and planning for what the direction of higher education should be in the state."[1] In her vision, this coordination includes collaborative recruitment activity. "If every college in your state is trying to chase after [students with strong backgrounds for college]," she observes, "that means that we don't have people . . . reaching out to other populations . . . that are really important to reaching our attainment goals." For the system to achieve its potential, McGuinness (2016a) argues that it must move toward "a coordinated, differentiated network of institutions in which the impact of the system is far greater than the sum of its parts" (40).

While some states have pursued centralized governance that facilitates collaboration, "the majority of states lack a venue where key state leaders come together to develop . . . long-term strategic goals" (McGuiness 2016a, 30). Moreover, there is no clear trend toward that model (Sponsler and Fulton 2018). One reason for this is that effective collaboration is difficult to do well—even with centralized governance. State Higher Education Executive Officers Association (SHEEO) president Robert Anderson argues that "if you're developing a state master plan, an attainment strategy that actually has some breadth and depth to it, you have to have [an extensive, wide-reaching] listening tour and you have to have buy-in from your campuses."[2] Defining and communicating shared vision is hardly trivial, and unsuccessful attempts at coordination can easily lead to worse outcomes than the status quo.

Of course, collaborations between independent colleges and universities introduce another level of difficulty because such associations cannot be nudged toward cooperation by a shared authority (which, for public institutions, exists in the ultimate sense of the legislature and governor even if not in a governing body). Arguably, joint efforts between public and private institutions generate even greater complications due to the disparate missions across the public-private divide. Despite these challenges and hurdles, as the examples in this chapter illustrate, a number of institutions are pressing ahead in pursuit of greater student success and institutional viability through shared action.

Advocacy for Higher Education Finance Reform

Attitudes toward education's contribution to society have eroded such that SHEEO's Anderson contends we must now work to "rekindle [a belief in] the public good of higher education." The trend toward viewing higher education as a private good emerges clearly from an examination of public finance data. Duderstadt (2009) captures the progression experienced at the University of Michigan: "We . . . evolved from a state-supported to a state-assisted to a state-related to a state-located university. In fact, with Michigan campuses [outside the United States], we remain only a state-molested institution" (4). While the University of Michigan has been exceptionally successful in attracting alternative revenue streams (less than 4% of their expenditures are supported through state appropriations[3]), SHEEO (2018) documents the national trend. In the 1990s and early 2000s, families paid for only 30% of a public higher education. Then, in the wake of recession, public support pulled back and the family share rose to 36%. After economic recovery, equilibrium at this higher level was established until the Great Recession, when state appropriations fell again and the family share rose to 47% in 2012. Since that time, the families' share has once again been stable, but the pattern is established: in times of financial hardship, higher education is treated less and less like a public good.

The erosion of public support for higher education is felt by private institutions as well. Relative to their share of full-time equivalent students, private four-year institutions receive a proportionate share of Pell Grant dollars and a disproportionate share of funds from the Federal Supplemental Educational Opportunity Grant (FSEOG), Federal Work Study, and Perkins Loans (Baum et al. 2018). Public institutions are more dependent on state coffers, but private schools share in risks associated with declining public support.

Despite broadly shared common interests, collective advocacy is difficult to maintain as the conversation moves from abstract principles to detailed policies. Inevitably, public policies create incentives that run in favor of some institutions at the expense of others. Lapovsky (2019) provides a useful overview of this tension in the context of free-college initiatives. For example, the requirement that recipients of the New York Excelsior Scholarship enroll in 30 credits favors full-time attendance over part-time. The Tennessee Promise encourages attendance in two-year programs but may draw enrollment away from four-year institutions. And free-college proposals generally subsidize public options over independent colleges, who predictably prefer expansions of institution-neutral programs like the Pell grant.

As a consequence, higher education might find it easier to coalesce around student loan reform. According to the Federal Reserve Bank of New York's (2019) *Quarterly Report on Household Debt and Credit*, US households owe more than $1.5 trillion in student loans—up more than 500% since 2003. What is more, Brown et al. (2015) find that about 25% of borrowers default at some point in the first nine years of repayment. The media and presidential aspirants have used this data to advance the narrative of a student loan system in general crisis and in need of massive overhaul.

However, many scholars argue that the dominant narrative misconstrues the problem and so suggests needlessly expensive solutions at the expense of better alternatives. Media stories of six-figure debts distort the picture by focusing on extreme cases. According to Baum et al. (2018), of those with loans, the average debt held by graduates from a public four-year institution was under $27,000; graduates from private, nonprofit schools owed more but still less than $33,000. The former figure rose by 20% over a decade, while the latter rose less than 10%, so growth has been modest. Even when including graduate school debts, only 6% of borrowers owe $100,000 or more, and another 8% owe between $60,000 and $100,000 (Baum et al. 2018).

Not surprisingly, large debts are disproportionately owed by people with advanced degrees. According to Cilluffo (2017), the median student loan among those with only a bachelor's degree totals $25,000—approximately half the median among those with a postgraduate degree. Given the role of professional degrees in generating debt, it is hardly surprising that debt burdens are strongly correlated with income. Baum (2016) finds that families in the top income quartile owe 47% of outstanding student loan debts, and Looney and Yannelis (2015) report that those with debts between $90,000 and $100,000 earn more than three times as much as those who owe less than $10,000. (Gervais and Ziebarth [2019] and Minicozzi [2005] provide further evidence of the positive relationship between income and student loan debts.) Given these facts, Baum (2016) argues that typical undergraduate loan balances are easily repaid with the roughly $1,500 monthly wage premium earned by those with a bachelor's degree. Akers and Chingos (2014) concur, noting that the median share of income devoted to student loan repayment has been stable at about 3% to 4% since the early 1990s.

Still, while the current student loan system works well for many students, Baum (2016) cautions that "everyone doesn't have the same great outcome" (58). She observes that about one in five graduates from four-year institutions earn less than the median income for high school graduates. Despite degree completion, these borrowers earn too little to reliably repay modest loans without significant difficulty. In fact, defaults are about twice as common among those who graduate owing less than $5,000 than among those who graduate owing more than $100,000 (Brown et al. 2015). While high loan balances come with large payments, they also typically signal high educational attainment and high income; we might be better served by worrying about those with lower balances and lower incomes. Moreover, as highlighted in chapter 7, many students fail to earn a degree—they enroll long enough to acquire debt but not long enough to gain the earning power to pay it off. Despite low balances owed by noncompleters, Baum (2016) reports that this group has a default rate that is two to four times higher than that among diploma-holders.

Research suggests that mismatches between loan balances and income affect a range of important life decisions. For example, some suggest that the correlation between debt and income reflects a preference among high-debt students for high-paying careers over "public interest" alternatives such as government and education (Rothstein and Rouse 2011). Additionally, those with loans are more likely to experience health and financial hardships (Despard et al. 2016; Walsemann et al. 2015). While these impacts are not directly related to the work of colleges and universities, their significance calls for attention from the higher education sector that generated the loans. Still other side effects of indebtedness have a direct effect on higher education's future. Researchers report that those burdened with large student loan obligations put off marriage (Gicheva 2016) and delay childbearing (Baum and O'Malley 2003), producing additional downward pressure on the fertility that creates the next generation of college students.

While colleges and universities aren't currently liable for their students' debts, John Neuhauser, former president of St. Michael's College (VT), thinks that could easily change. He worries that if present problems are not addressed, the federal government could reform the student loan system to the detriment of higher education, either requiring institutions to cover a portion of loan defaults or restricting loan balances. Either way, "that could take away a considerable percentage of revenue in a hurry." Before that happens, higher education may prefer to unite behind an alternative policy revision.

Loan forgiveness proposals are currently in vogue, but they seem to miss the mark in several important ways. First, they are expensive. Lane (2019) estimates that one popular loan forgiveness proposal would cost $640 billion. Moreover, because income and loans are positively correlated, the proposal is highly regressive. Pointing to these drawbacks, a number of economists and policy analysts have proposed an alternative reform that is more narrowly tailored to the problems in the current system. As Looney (2019) points out, "Most borrowers use the loan program responsibly." Moreover, because debt levels are modest relative to the college wage premium, Dynarski (2014) argues, "there is no debt crisis. . . . Rather, there is a repayment crisis" (2). Dynarski and Kreisman (2013) explain: "The current system turns reasonable levels of *debt* into crippling *payment* burdens" through misalignment between required repayments and income (2; emphasis in original).

These authors advocate for broadly applied income-based repayment (IBR). (See chapter 3 for examples of institutions that are experimenting on an individual basis with income-sharing agreements that operate much like IBR.) While IBR is presently available to some borrowers, complicated application processes and eligibility rules discourage participation. In fact, Dynarski and Kreisman (2013) find that less than one in seven borrowers choose any payment option other than the ten-year constant payment currently offered by default. Under their plan, borrowers would automatically enroll in an IBR program requiring repayment of 3% to 10% of the borrower's income (with the rate increasing with income) for 25 years. By collecting payment using the same tools utilized to gather income taxes, the plan assures that payments automatically adjust with income. After the 25-year repayment period, remaining loan balances are forgiven.

Looney (2019) analyzes the effect of a similar IBR proposal. He finds that there would be almost no impact on the average level of loan payments. Rather, the program would shift payment burdens from low- to high-income individuals. For example, those in the top quintile of the income distribution would pay almost $2,000 more per year, while those in the first and second quintiles would pay about $650 and $850 less, respectively. Because aggregate payments would be unchanged, the scheme is viable for lenders. And because repayments would be radically realigned to match incomes, default risk and repayment-induced hardships would be mitigated.

Of course, those who have persistently lower incomes over the 25-year repayment period would not fully repay their loans. This may add a new cost to the system when outstanding debts are forgiven. While

Looney doesn't formally estimate this cost of forgiveness, it will be modest. Most households experience income growth over the life cycle, which means few remain in the lowest quintile for 25 years. And those who do experience persistently low incomes are already prone to default, so the "cost" of forgiveness may not be an additional burden at all. Finally, those with low incomes typically have low balances, and so the size of defaulted loans will be relatively small.

While repayment reform is likely part of the solution, higher education might also reexamine loan practices. While those with extreme loan balances remain the minority, their share has increased following regulatory reform that lifted and then eliminated limits on PLUS and graduate student loans (Looney and Yannelis 2018). Looney (2019) cautions that too often large loans are packaged even when the intended degree has no reasonable prospect of repayment. If higher education does not formulate standards of practice that reduce the incidence of these disproportionate loans—or work with the government to craft regulations that accomplish the same end—consumer backlash reminiscent of that directed at mortgage lenders following the Great Recession may impose significant costs.

Advocacy for International Student Regulatory Reform

Faced with declining numbers of domestic prospective students, institutions may look to maintain enrollments by expanding international student programs. Indeed, international students have been a tremendous growth market for higher education since World War II, increasing steadily over seven decades from around 25,000 students to more than 1 million (Institute of International Education [IIE] 2019). The 5.6% average annual growth in international students is nearly twice the 3% average growth rate among domestic students over the same period (NCES 2018; table 303.10). As a result, the share of students at US institutions who come to us from abroad has steadily increased from just over 1% in the late 1940s to 5.5% today (IIE 2019).

Not all institutions have tapped equally into the international market, of course. Disaggregating the data by Carnegie classification, doctoral universities lead the way; almost 11% of their enrollments come from abroad.[4] Master's colleges and universities and baccalaureate colleges draw less than half that share (just over 4%). Similarly, some regions of the country have attracted more international students than others. Not surprisingly, California, Massachusetts, and New York top the list (NAFSA, n.d.). But while these three coastal states account for one-third of all international students, six interior states—Texas, Illinois, Pennsylvania, Ohio, Michigan, and Indiana—fall among the top ten international student destinations and account for almost 30% of the international market.

Unfortunately, recent developments suggest that significant collective work is necessary if higher education is to deepen international markets. Over the last three years of available data covering academic years 2016–17 through 2018–19, the number of new international undergraduate student enrollments has declined each year for a total loss of more than 10% (IIE 2019). (Doctoral universities with very high research activity are an outlier to this trend, though even in this group the growth in total international students fell to 2.7% in 2018–19, down from 7.2% growth in 2015–16.)

At least two factors help to explain the recent contraction. First, the world is increasingly competing with us. For example, in 2018 Canada welcomed almost 600,000 international students, a 16% increase over the previous year (Canadian Bureau for International Education, n.d.). What's more, China and India, which account for 80% of all US international students (NCES 2018, table 310.20), have built new institutions designed on the US liberal arts model to retain students at home (Dattagupta 2018; Pickus and Godwin 2017). So, US institutions must increasingly beat out foreign competition. While external competition is undoubtedly important, recent regulatory proposals and changes have also made the United States a less interesting educational destination (Redden 2018).

The potential risks of declining international student numbers were recently made very tangible by the University of Illinois's purchase of insurance to mitigate the threat of declining tuition revenue should enrollments decline. The university paid over $420,000 for up to $60 million in coverage that would begin to pay out should international enrollments fall by more than 20% (Bothwell 2018). For an institution that enrolls more than 10,000 students from abroad, the potential fallout from a major realignment in international student interest is clear. Of course, even institutions with smaller numbers of international students have a significant interest in maintaining the country's identity as a top destination for higher education students from other countries.

The potential for lobbying in this area seems high. While economists stress that gains from trade are *not* measured by net exports, policymakers on both ends of the political spectrum seem fixated on boosting this figure. Because only one in six international students receives institutional financial aid (NAFSA, n.d.), they contribute disproportionately to net tuition revenue. Public universities alone take in an estimated $9 billion, or one-quarter of all tuition revenue, from international students (Loudenback 2016). In total, international student expenditures on tuition, fees, housing, food, and other retail purchases exceed $40 billion (NAFSA, n.d.), an export market similar in size to those for telecommunications capital equipment or pharmaceutical preparations (Bureau of Economic Analysis 2019).[5] While policy serves many goals and must consider the interests of American workers, NAFSA points out that international students become job creators as well as employees: among US start-up companies valued in excess of $1 billion, one in four was founded or cofounded by someone who came to the United States as an international student (NAFSA, n.d.). As we move steadily toward the mid-2020s, when domestic students will become increasingly scarce, it would benefit higher education greatly to speak consistently to the value of international students to our economy.

Data Collaboration

In advocating for energetic and effective reforms to address student retention, Kirp (2019) persuasively argues that "decisions should be based on data rather than a hunch" (135). The stakes are too high and the costs too great for misdirected action. However, for small institutions, the limitations of modest sample sizes can make it difficult to gather compelling statistical evidence that supports decision-making. Through data-sharing collaborations, smaller institutions might overcome this barrier by leveraging networks of similar schools. This goal will be of increasing importance as institutions seek to promote student success and retention to offset declines in new enrollments.

Achieving the Dream (ATD) has partnered with a network of tribal colleges and universities (TCUs) in one such effort to advance student success goals through data sharing and collaborative discussion. Participating schools collected data in 2017 using the Survey of Entering Student Engagement (SENSE) and in 2018 using the Community College Survey of Student Engagement (CCSSE). Data was then shared and discussed at annual meetings organized by ATD. Because TCUs have long recognized elements of shared mission, discussions of common points of success and opportunities for growth are not new to these institutions. However, Ace Charette, director of research, assessment, and accreditation at Turtle Mountain Community College (ND), argues that the recent partnership is distinct in that it is the "first time we really saw a collective data approach where not only were the vast majority of the TCUs participating in the exact same national assessment, [but] they were doing so at the exact same moment in time."

Peering into the statistical mirror brought much to light. First, the network was able to celebrate distinctive success that ran across colleges and universities. "The amount of student satisfaction we're seeing within the tribal colleges is out of this world," says Charette. As previously noted in chapter 7, almost 90% of students reported feeling a sense of belonging (Adair, Azure, et al. 2019). Comparison with CCSSE responses of Native American students at nontribal colleges further showed that TCU students were more likely to feel close relationships with faculty, staff, and peers (CCSSE 2019).

Second, the group was able to identify common challenges around which they might share best practices. For example, Charette points to the pressing issues of food insecurity. "It was something that we kind of anecdotally knew," he says, but seeing the data "hit people really hard." Among tribal college students, 34% report that in the previous year they have worried about being left without food when money runs out, and one-quarter have actually experienced this crisis (CCSSE 2019). Charette saw some professors, spurred on by the daunting statistics, take immediate, personal action. For example, he shares the story of a professor who even before the CCSSE study responded to concerns around food security by bringing healthy snacks to class on exam days to make sure all students "have some fuel in the tank prior to taking a heavy exam." Of course, comprehensive solutions to student hunger will likely require a systemic approach, but systemic approaches are often born out of individual action.

Institutions also learned by comparing their data with that of peers. Scott Friskics, director of sponsored programs, shares the power of data sharing from the perspective of Aaniiih Nakoda College (MT), a community with fewer than 200 students. Like peer TCUs, Aaniiih Nakoda students report a very strong sense of connection to the school; in the spring CCSSE administration, 91% of all students indicated that they had a sense of belonging (Adair, Azure, et al. 2019). However, Friskics and his colleagues noted that only 77% of fall-term, first-year students said the same, notably lower than the 88% recorded at peer TCUs. They realized that despite the intimate campus size and overall success, sense of belonging "was something that had to be cultivated and nurtured" right from the start of fall term. As part of a broader strategic initiative, one concrete action the school has taken is to institute a new "Fall Fling"—a community-wide party with food and activities modeled after a popular, existing Spring Fling that concludes the academic year (Adair, Azure, et al. 2019). Friskics explains that the hope is that creating a connection point with the community early in the year will "speed up the process by which students feel like they belong and are part of the campus."

Ultimately, the goal of the ATD collaboration is transformational change, says Cindy Lopez, ATD's director of tribal college and university programs. "Building data capacity is just a part of that," she observes. At many institutions, data structures have been built for compliance; ATD wants to support efforts that instead put data to use informing effective action, particularly around student success initiatives. Lopez cautions that "it's a long game and you have to stay the course; you don't build data capacity and transformational change attitudes and practices overnight." Charette, for one, certainly shares this big-picture perspective on the potential power of shared and democratized data. He points to the Ojibwe colleges, which, despite shared linguistic and cultural heritage, have had little opportunity to work with and learn from one another: "There really is no mechanism for us to cross-pollinate our ideas and ways of achieving some of the most core aspects of our mission statements." He argues that these structural issues follow as a consequence of federal jurisdiction that has "painted tribes within lines of reservation systems," effectively turning schools inward toward the local reservation. While service to the local community is an important part of the TCU mission, this focus has diminished Ojibwe schools' opportunities to work and learn with one another to achieve some larger, commonly held aims. Charette contends that "data is what can crack open that system of non-collaboration" and promote broader goals of the Ojibwe people.

Enrollment Connections between Two- and Four-Year Institutions

Much has already been done to facilitate transitions between two- and four-year institutions, particularly in the public system. System-wide course numbering and articulation agreements have made it easier for students to move from public two-year schools into institutions offering four-year degrees, and vice versa. Reverse transfer agreements allow students who make the transition to four-year schools prior to two-year degree attainment to earn that degree through courses at the new institution.

And still, students who begin at two-year institutions complete degrees at alarmingly low rates. According to the Community College Research Center at Columbia University, of the approximately one million students who begin at two-year institutions each year (NCES 2018, table 305.10), about 80% do so hoping to complete a bachelor's degree. But despite these aspirations, in the six years following enrollment less than one-third transfer to a four-year institution, and only 13% earn a bachelor's degree (National Student Clearinghouse Research Center 2019b). While these statistics are sobering, they also represent opportunity, as chapter 7 notes. If higher education can address the barriers that limit student success, enrollments can increase despite shrinking cohorts. This offers hope for two- and four-year campuses alike, as students beginning studies at a two-year institution ultimately go on to earn both two- and four-year degrees.

Recent efforts have moved from articulation agreements to integrated admissions. Rather than merely offering a list of courses that will be accepted for transfer credit, four- and two-year schools collaborate to educate students who seamlessly move from one institution to the other. Kirp (2019) provides a detailed description of the University of Central Florida's (UCF) partnership with Valencia College. Overwhelmed by rapid growth, UCF needed to find new strategies to make it accessible to a growing market. In addition to an online initiative that relieved pressure to build facilities, they found a solution in collaboration. By committing to admitting nearby Valencia College graduates, UCF was able to extend its reach by having many students complete the first two years of college through a two-year partner. UCF advisors embedded on the Valencia campus further prepare students for the transition to the four-year campus.

While the UCF-Valencia story was born out of an overabundance in interested students, many institutions are finding the lessons of collaboration useful when wrestling with declining enrollments. Collaborations between two- and four-year institutions are developing new responses to admissions applications. In addition to the well-established answers of "yes" and "no," Nancy Griffin, vice president for enrollment management at the University of Southern Maine, describes a novel third response: "You'll get here, but not today." Of course, the challenge is how to keep students in the pipeline to that successful outcome.

That is where intimate partnerships between two- and four-year institutions are creating new paths. For example, the University of Massachusetts–Lowell has developed a "reserved placement program" in conjunction with five community colleges. One of these partners is

Middlesex Community College, just a mile away. Through the program, students who are not admitted directly to Lowell are instead offered deferred admission—a guarantee of a place at Lowell so long as the student successfully completes a semester of community college. As in the UCF-Valencia partnership, advising is important. Lowell advisors work with students in the program to ensure they are taking community college courses that prepare them for success after transfer. As discussed in chapter 7, however, academic preparation is only one part of the student success equation. To create a sense of belonging, students in the reserved placement program are welcomed into the Lowell community right from the start. They are issued student IDs and are encouraged to participate in Lowell campus programs even as they take community college classes.

St. Cloud State University (MN) and neighboring partner St. Cloud Technical and Community College (SCTCC) have developed a similar relationship in their Community College Connection (CCC) program. In addition to engaging students in the university's campus programming while studying at SCTCC, the collaborative venture moves the students physically onto the university campus. SCTCC staff offer courses on the university campus, and CCC students are actively encouraged to consider living in St. Cloud State University campus housing. This holistic integration of CCC students allows them to be placed in the educational environment best suited for their success—whether that is immediate admission to the university or deferred admission while preparatory work is completed. And yet, from the student perspective, the ultimate goal of connection to a four-year degree program is achieved right from the start. Collaborations such as these have the potential for a win-win-win as they attract new enrollments to both the two- and four-year partners while supporting student success.

Though the majority of work to facilitate two- and four-year partnership has been undertaken by public institutions, independent colleges are increasingly getting involved through articulation agreements with neighboring two-year institutions. As valuable as bilateral agreements might be, they are obviously limited in scale and scope. For example,

Dickinson College (PA) has established relationships with five nearby community colleges and has achieved a 100% graduation rate among about a dozen transfer students.[6] This work clearly demonstrates the potential for selective, independent colleges to benefit from partnerships with two-year institutions if such programs can be scaled.

North Carolina Independent Colleges and Universities (NCICU) have worked since 1996 on an alternative, collaborative approach. Under their Independent Comprehensive Articulation Agreement (ICAA), students who complete an associate's degree at any of North Carolina's two-year colleges enter the four-year institution of their choice as juniors having completed all general education requirements. In the most recent revision of the ICAA, completed in 2015, 30 of NCICU's 35 independent colleges and universities signed on to the agreement. Hope Williams, president of NCICU, says the result has been "a much more streamlined process" for students and for institutions, some of which transfer in as many as 300 students per year. "We're finding this is especially important for traditional students," explains Williams, because "they are not place-bound—they can transfer all over the state—and so it is important that they know that what they are taking [during their first two years at a two-year college] will transfer wherever they go."

Understandably, articulation agreements that cover general education requirements pose challenging questions regarding the curriculum at independent colleges. Often, these requirements speak to institutional identity such that it is difficult or impossible to outsource them to other institutions. For example, Williams points to requirements for religion courses that are not replicable at some two-year colleges. Working with registrars and chief academic officers, she explains that these requirements were reconceived as graduation requirements as opposed to general education requirements so that students completed them in their final two years enrolled at the independent institution. "It was a major step forward to see how quickly that dissolved some of the concern about adopting a comprehensive agreement," Williams shares.

As important as it is to complete general education requirements, progress toward a major is also a critical goal in the first years of college. Without clear connection to a major, too often students end up taking elective credits that don't move a student toward a diploma, Williams notes. The additional coursework weighs heavily on financial and time constraints that we know hamper student persistence. To address this problem, NCICU has recently developed discipline-specific agreements within the broader ICAA. The first such programs developed were RN to BSN, music, theater, and fine arts with an agreement for teacher education under development. Beginning in fall 2019, with support from the Council of Independent Colleges and the Teagle Foundation, agreements are being crafted for psychology and sociology. As major tracks proliferate, advising becomes more critical. And so, just as in the partnerships between public institutions, additional resources are being devoted to advising students prior to the transfer decision to ensure that they make the best use of their time at the two-year college prior to the transition.

The Teagle Foundation's involvement flows from its recognition of the two-year transfer pathway as critical both for achieving access and for financial sustainability of independent colleges. Loni Bordoloi Pazich, program director for institutional initiatives at the foundation, argues that higher education has done a good job promoting access in the broadest sense. "If you want to go to college," she says, "there's a place for you." But, as noted in chapters 1 and 2, a disproportionate share of access success has been achieved through enrollment at community colleges. While that success story must be told, Pazich points to the data on student aspirations: most students beginning at a two-year college hope to earn a four-year degree. "There are systemic issues at play," she contends, that have meant that most of these students don't reach their ultimate goal. Given the systemic nature of the problem, Teagle is looking to support consortial approaches rather than "boutique," bilateral agreements. When successful, the foundation hopes to nurture one part of the systemic solution to achieving broader equity in educational attainment with two-year students achieving their four-year education goals. And at the same time, independent colleges and universities that participate in this work will develop new or deeper connections to a large submarket that may become increasingly important in a period of demographic contraction.

Mutual Insurance

Chapter 9 describes how some institutions are engaging in reprioritization, reorganization, merger, or downsizing as they grapple with market adjustments. While the ultimate goal of this work is realized financial savings, the transition process often involves up-front costs. When engaged in a proactive fashion while the institution is healthy, these costs often can be self-financed. Unfortunately, sometimes the realization that fundamental change is required comes too late for that. Campuses then find themselves in a difficult position. Evidence that the status quo is unsustainable abounds, and yet transition to a new, viable future might be prevented for lack of the resources to effect necessary change. As a consequence, the only remaining viable options involve one-sided mergers and closure.

James Galbally Jr., former associate dean at the University of Pennsylvania's School of Dental Medicine and current president of the Galbally Group, likens higher education's situation to a broken healthcare system that overutilizes the emergency room. In higher education's emergency room, lopsided mergers and closure usually lead to a diminished future. Resulting costs are immense to individual institutions and our system as a whole, which loses what might otherwise have been a thriving contributor to a diverse higher education network. Galbally argues that "more and more colleges are in need of urgent care," which can set them aright while healthy recovery remains a realistic probability—"a quick and dirty assessment of finances, enrollments, and assets" that undergird a midterm reform plan, setting the institution on a path to renewed sustainability. With timely intervention, he believes many institutions can be revived at modest cost (at least as measured against the alternatives of one-sided merger and closure).

Of course, a turnaround plan is not worth much if it isn't paired with the investments necessary to move the troubled institution onto firmer footing. To overcome this hurdle, Galbally proposes to create something akin to an International Monetary Fund (IMF) for higher education. Just as the IMF provides resources to sustain troubled economies through periods of reform and transition, the new organization would "bail out" institutions on the brink. Of course, there would be little point pledging resources toward a continuation of failed strategies. Just as in the example of the IMF, Galbally's imagined higher education lender of last resort would require institutional commitment to meaningful reforms in exchange for funding that would serve as a bridge to a new, credible, sustainable path. (Based on the IMF's experience, one might expect the new organization to have mixed reviews from recipients who are pushed to make fundamental changes to their business and educational practices.)

Galbally sees precedent for this model in public higher education. For example, in response to challenges caused by declining numbers of high school graduates in the Northeast and Midwest, the board of governors of Pennsylvania's State System of Higher Education has developed a plan to expand infrastructure for online offerings and deepen collaborations around data and other campus services (Schackner 2019). The ultimate goal is to regain enrollments and reduce costs. Even supposing the proposed pivot would place the system on a sustainable path, they can't get from their present position to the new future without overcoming steep transition costs. The board has requested from the state a one-time investment of $100 million (on top of an annual operating allocation of almost $500 million)—a request paired down from alternative proposals that reached as high as $300 million (Schackner 2019). While such restructuring costs are significant, averaged over the 14 institutions overseen by the system, the sums are plausible—just about $7 million per institution. While nontrivial, a sum of that magnitude seems eminently affordable if the alternative is system-wide decline. (Of course, this conclusion presumes the proposed reforms are sufficient to the challenge, something the state will no doubt examine in depth.)

To create an IMF-like organization for higher education, Galbally imagines creating an endowment to sustain the work. Sources of funding could include foundations that support higher education, legislators that recognize independent colleges' importance to local economies, and healthy institutions that pay premiums in good times in the event that they may find themselves in need of bridge funding at some point in the future. Insofar as the first two of these sources presumably involve diverting resources that might otherwise support higher education, each revenue source represents a form of mutual insurance. As with any insurance project, the challenge will be to convince a large and disparate group of institutions that each is better off participating rather than attempting to self-insure. Clearly, this is a nontrivial hurdle that may be hard to overcome. Feasible or not, this outside-of-the-box idea points to a missing market in higher education that cannot be addressed by institutions acting individually.

When You Want It Done Right and You Can't Do It Yourself

While much work in higher education necessarily takes place in the context of an individual campus, the activity described in this chapter underscores that some forms of critical transformation are only possible in collaboration with peers. Turtle Mountain Community College's Charette well captures the potential for even greater change flowing from the intersection of ideas described previously. Reflecting on the missions of TCU institutions, he notes that the dominant model is to serve and support a local community. While this is one important goal, Charette worries that it can have an unintended consequence as each institution more or less replicates all others in program offerings despite "having some programs that are really strong and others anemic." He wonders whether that individualistic approach means TCUs are missing out on the opportunity to better serve their collective community. Informed by data on student success, might it be possible to develop sophisticated articulation agreements that allow students to move more freely between TCU campuses to tap into the best the system has to offer? For example, he considers the case where one tribal college develops a highly effective business program. "Should all of the other tribal colleges in that region try to create another business program as well?" Given different communities and campus assets, Charette thinks this outcome is not the best use of collective resources. And yet, most current incentive structures nudge higher education toward replication. Perhaps the shift from ever-increasing new enrollments to an era of flat or declining student numbers invites a different, more cooperative response.

[TWELVE]

Something between Chicken Little and Pollyanna

To say that HEDI projections have elicited a wide range of responses would be an understatement. Two exchanges that took place in the same month illustrate the point. At a conference, I was pulled aside by a president's cabinet-level administrator from a national four-year institution located in the Midwest. With his background, he was well-informed about demographic trends long before any contribution from me. His concern was that while my work clearly illustrated the challenges that higher education faces, the overview of potential responses could be read optimistically. Readers might come away thinking that there was some hope for navigating demographic change without fundamental disruption. The second interaction came by email from an alum of a regional four-year school in the East. She informed me that "your work is being bandied about as a reason" to close her alma mater. So, a wide range of responses to be sure.

Previous chapters invite similarly disparate readings. Updated HEDI projections show the same general patterns and extend the period of low student numbers into the mid-2030s. So, the early chapters of the book could be read as a version of Chicken Little's warning. But the second half of the book is filled with examples of ways that institutions are proactively attempting to work their way through the problems of demographic upheaval. Even the chapter on retrenchment includes positive approaches to budgetary cutbacks and planned enrollment contraction. One could read these chapters and see a touch of Pollyanna.

In the regions most affected by declining birth rates, is it simply necessary that the market correct for decades of expansion in institution numbers and seat counts through closures and consolidation? Is it possible to hold simultaneously to both parts of the story—demographic decline and responsive institutional adaptation—or is this tantamount to wishful thinking in the face of existential peril, a combination that only heightens the threat to institutional sustainability? Any credible answer to these questions must begin by confronting uncomfortable facts.

Unavoidable Facts

The low fertility rates of the past ten years all but ensure at least a decade of lower prospective student numbers beginning in the middle of the 2020s. Demographer Kenneth Johnson (2019) asks an interesting hypothetical question: What if fertility rates had not declined, instead holding steady at 2007 levels? Because the number of women in their 20s and 30s rose by 8% in the subsequent years, we would have expected a steady increase in births. Instead, of course, we've seen persistent decline. Johnson estimates that the country saw 800,000 fewer births in 2018 than we would have had fertility rates held constant. In total, during the decade following the Great Recession, lower fertility rates account for 5.7 million "foregone births." Whatever may be possible to mitigate the consequences of declining fertility going forward, one option we don't have is to add to the birth cohort of, say, 2010.

Additional immigration could cushion that decline. However, given the current size of the nonnative population ages 15 to 19, we would need to triple the number of such young people to make up for lost domestic births. In parts of the country with disproportionately steep declines in fertility, the increase in immigration would, of course, need to be larger. Even if this immigration influx were realized, it would not suffice because natives and the foreign-born have different college attendance patterns. In other words, the size of the fertility decline is realistically too large to be overcome through this channel, even if the country were broadly supportive of a sizeable increase to immigration. Similarly, additions of international students could lessen the consequences of low fertility. But even were it possible to quadruple international student numbers (which is approximately what would be required), as with increased demand via additional immigration, it's clear that their distribution across institutions would not match the decline in domestic prospective students.

Expanded access is also unlikely to offset lower birth rates. The elimination of the college attendance gap previously experienced by Hispanics should certainly be celebrated. And success in overcoming this inequality should spur us on to tackle the problem of falling attendance rates among African Americans. But even a 10-point gain in rates of college-going among non-Hispanic blacks (achieving parity in attendance rates with non-Hispanic whites) would have a modest effect on overall enrollments. In addition, the correlation between income and demographic markers of nonattendance means we would need to grow total enrollments to maintain net tuition revenue. Without a doubt, higher education should seek to expand access because it is right, and some may seek to expand access because it helps address demographic pressure on their institution, but as a whole we cannot expect access initiatives alone to overcome fertility decline.

In short, Johnson's (2019) missing 5.7 million young people (and counting) are very difficult to replace.

The Possiblist View

Bowen and Staley (2019) point to Rosling (2018) for a constructive way to view challenges we face. Rosling explains, "I'm not an optimist. That makes me sound naïve. I'm a very serious 'possiblist.' . . . It means someone who neither hopes without reason, nor fears without reason, someone who constantly resists the overdramatic worldview. [Visible progress] fills me with conviction and hope that further progress is possible. This is not optimistic. . . . It is having a worldview that is constructive and useful" (69). The possiblist response to Johnson's forgone children rejects silver bullet thinking but still sees paths toward a healthy future in higher education through concerted work on multiple fronts.

For example, for institutions with a student audience that extends (or might newly extend) beyond the traditional age, it is certainly possible to imagine offsetting the effects of declining fertility with engagement of the market for adult learners. A little arithmetic makes the case. Of the almost 20 million students enrolled in postsecondary education, about 12 million are of traditional age and 8 million are over the age of 25 (NCES 2018, table 303.40). To offset a 10% reduction in the former group, enrollments of adult students would need to increase by around 15%. Placed in the wider perspective of employment figures, this task seems plausible. According to the US Bureau of Labor Statistics, there are more than 100 million workers in the country between the ages of 25 and 54. If a bit more than 1% of these workers newly return to postsecondary education for retraining, it would balance the decline in enrollments in the traditional market. Of course, students of nontraditional age are more likely to attend part time, so outreach to adult learners would need to be several times this large to maintain the same number of credits. Still, the sheer size of the adult market offers opportunities to make up a portion of the lost ground.

Improvements to retention and attrition similarly provide opportunities from the possiblist perspective. Judging by the average first-year retention rates and six-year graduation rates at four-year schools (NCES 2018, tables 326.30 and 326.40), reducing attrition rates by one-quarter would increase enrollment levels enough to offset a 5% decline in the prospective student pool. While it will clearly take work to accomplish, that degree of improvement seems achievable in light of a similar increase in first-year retention achieved over the past decade (NCES 2018, table 326.30). Admittedly, insofar as student success is advanced through more efficient courses of academic study, higher retention will coincide with fewer excess credits, reducing the net increase in enrollment. But the point remains that a meaningful portion of higher education's demographic stress might be relieved through continued focus on retention.

More than a belief that any one tactic will constitute a silver bullet, the possiblist argument rests on the philosophy embodied by the successful slogan of English supermarket Tesco: "Every little helps." In the face of substantial challenge, rarely is any one action "the" solution. While it is tempting to discard one solution after another in search of the single "thing to be done," resolutions of large problems often involve the combination of many partial solutions. Institutional commitments to carbon neutrality, for example, never identify a single action that accomplishes the whole. So, too, might successful paths through demographic change be comprised of a range of incomplete parts that add up to a larger whole.

One of these partial measures may be a manageable reduction in size, perhaps facilitated by recent aging of faculty and staff. Given the national rise in prospective students we've experienced in the recent past and the expected increase in young people leading up to the mid-2020s (reflective of the increase in births leading up to 2007), some reduction in the next decade might be understood as right-sizing. Implemented by deliberate attrition as baby boomers near retirement, some colleges and universities might be well-situated for this approach. In addition, recent higher education practices, whether intentional or not, seem designed to make such adjustment easier. In particular, the share of professors covered by tenure is on a decades-long slide. While the share of institutions offering tenure has recently rebounded to around 55% from a low of 45% in 2011, the share of full-time faculty at those schools with tenure has steadily declined—from 56% in 1993 to 46% in 2016 (NCES 2018, table 316.80). Institutions public and private, four-year and two-year have participated in the trend away from tenure. It would be a welcome silver lining if a modest reduction in institutional size coincided with a return to traditional models of tenure that support faculty governance and academic freedom. (Retirement of physical capital is somewhat more complicated because buildings don't typically leave campus without expenditure.)

Moreover, if a range of adaptations mitigate (though not eliminate) the need for contraction, experience suggests that many institutions can continue to fulfill their missions despite the need for change. Recall the findings by Zemsky et al. (2020) summarized in chapter 9. In the nine years leading up to 2016, around one-third of public four-year schools, one-half of private nonprofit four-year colleges, and two-thirds of public two-year institutions experienced enrollment declines, and many of these saw declines of 10% or more. However challenging it has been to grapple with lower enrollments, most of these institutions have innovated and adapted using a variety of tactics such as those described in preceding chapters. Though many of these stories remain incomplete, institutions of higher education appear more innovative and capable of navigating periods of rapid change than credited by popular perception.

The fact that adaptation is possible hardly makes it easy, but this realization is not news to those who lead. Zakiya Smith Ellis, secretary of higher education in New Jersey, recently reflected on her time serving as senior advisor for education on the White House domestic policy council.[1] "President Obama used to remind us that all of the decisions at an executive level involve some kind of trade-off," she says. "If there is ever something that is just rainbows and bunnies and unicorns and it's wonderful, it's not usually a decision. Somebody already did it; it's taken. The only thing you are dealing with at [the executive level] are trade-offs—and difficult trade-offs. You're trying to figure out 'Is what we are going to do and the potential negative things that may happen better than the negative of the status quo?'" The choices discussed in previous chapters involve changes to institutional practices, union contracts, institutional mission, and even the sacred academic calendar. Each option involves risks as all leadership decisions do.

The constructive work of so many institutions and the undeniable need for and power of higher education lead me to a possiblist point of view—not a blind faith that ignores the demographic facts but an informed trust based on the collective experiences across higher education. As previous chapters make clear, innovation is prevalent. From admissions, to the budget office, to enrollment management, to student financial services, to the faculty, numerous creative and proactive responses are progressing at campuses of all types and sizes. Given the importance of higher education to the future of the country, we will continue to need a network of diverse and innovative institutions through the twenty-first century and beyond, whatever challenges lie ahead. With student-centered, mission-focused reform, institutions may emerge, not untouched by demographic change but reshaped into better, if sometimes leaner, versions of themselves, prepared to serve students for generations to come.

The methodological appendix in Grawe (2018) provides a complete description of the methodology underlying the Higher Education Demand Index (HEDI). The forecasts in this book were constructed in the same manner with modest revisions, and so that content will not be repeated in its entirety here. Instead, the first section of this appendix provides an overview of the HEDI model. Following the overview, the second section explains revisions to variable definitions and modeling choices that followed from differences between the 2002 Education Longitudinal Study (ELS) and 2011 American Community Survey (ACS), which were used in Grawe (2018), and the 2009 High School Longitudinal Study (HSLS) and 2017 ACS, used here.

Overview of the HEDI Model

HEDI projections combine head counts of children, which are taken from the 2017 ACS, with probabilities of college-going, which are estimated using data in the 2009 HSLS. To illustrate, table A.1 provides a hypothetical, simplified example in which there are just two demographic groups. While both groups are more or less equally represented among the 17-year-olds observed in 2017, an examination of the number of children in each group by age shows that Group 1 is declining in number while Group 2 is growing. Because Group 1's decline is faster than the growth of Group 2, the total number of 18-year-olds looks likely to decline between the years 2018 and 2034.

While the total, hypothetical population in table A.1 is generally declining across birth cohorts, this doesn't mean that the number of prospective college students should be expected to shrink. In the example, members of Group 2 are more than three times as likely as Group 1 members to attend college. As a result, the potential demand for college depends more on movements in the expanding Group 2. Because of this, the expected number of college-going students, which is shown in the rightmost column, increases despite a falling population. The change in the composition of the population overcomes the decline in its size.

Table A.1. Hypothetical, Simplified Example of the Higher Education Demand Index for Illustrative Purposes

Age in 2017	Birth Year	Year of HS Graduation	Number of Children (1000s)			Probability of College-Going		College-Going (1000s)		
			Group 1	Group 2	Total	Group 1 (%)	Group 2 (%)	Group 1	Group 2	Total
17	2000	2018	500	501	1001	20	75	100	376	476
16	2001	2019	496	504	1000	20	75	99	378	477
15	2002	2020	491	506	997	20	75	98	380	478
14	2003	2021	485	509	994	20	75	97	382	479
13	2004	2022	480	512	992	20	75	96	384	480
12	2005	2023	475	515	990	20	75	95	386	481
11	2006	2024	470	518	988	20	75	94	389	483
10	2007	2025	465	522	987	20	75	93	392	485
9	2008	2026	460	524	984	20	75	92	393	485
8	2009	2027	455	527	982	20	75	91	395	486
7	2010	2028	450	530	980	20	75	90	398	488
6	2011	2029	445	534	979	20	75	89	401	490
5	2012	2030	440	536	976	20	75	88	402	490
4	2013	2031	436	540	976	20	75	87	405	492
3	2014	2032	431	542	973	20	75	86	407	493
2	2015	2033	425	545	970	20	75	85	409	494
1	2016	2034	420	548	968	20	75	84	411	495

HEDI projections rest on observations of children ages 1 to 17 in the 2017 ACS. Collected by the Census Bureau, the ACS surveys more than 3.5 million households over the course of a year. Using ACS data provided through the Integrated Public Use Microdata Series (Ruggles et al. 2019), counts of children by birth cohort are broken down by geography—the 28 largest metropolitan statistical areas (MSAs) and the residual, nonmetropolitan portions of states.* The MSAs used in the study are Atlanta, Boston, Charlotte, Chicago, Cincinnati, Cleveland, Dallas, Denver, Detroit, the District of Columbia, Houston, Kansas City, Los Angeles, Miami, Minneapolis–St. Paul, New York City, Orlando, Philadelphia, Phoenix, Pittsburgh, Portland, Sacramento, San Antonio, San Francisco, Seattle, St. Louis, and Tampa. After separating out populations living in these cities, some nonmetropolitan portions of states have very small populations. (This is also true of entire states such as Wyoming, even though no metropolitan area is separated from the rest of the state.) To reduce projection errors resulting from small sample sizes, contiguous areas of nonmetropolitan portions of states are combined to form larger regions with populations of at least two million. These combined nonmetropolitan areas are: Alaska and Hawaii; Colorado and Wyoming; Connecticut, Massachusetts, and Rhode Island; Delaware, Maryland, Virginia, and West Virginia; Idaho and Montana; Kansas, Nebraska, North Dakota, and South Dakota; Maine, New Hampshire, and Vermont; New Jersey and Pennsylvania; and Oregon and Washington. In total, the country is divided into 64 cities and nonmetropolitan portions of states.

Note that the geographic variable captures the location of the student, not the location of the postsecondary institution(s) attended. The model projects the number of students with demographic markers associated with college attendance who grew up in each of the 64 locations.

While the hypothetical example in table A.1 includes only two groups, the HEDI allows for the probability of college attendance to vary by a set of demographic markers: sex, race/ethnicity, family income, parent education, geographic location, family composition (whether living with mother, father, both, or neither), and nativity (whether born in the country). For each child included in the ACS, each of these markers is noted.

---

*For confidentiality reasons, the Census Bureau reports residents' location by public use microdata areas (PUMAs) or, when migration is a consideration as is the case here, larger amalgams of PUMAs called migration PUMAs. As explained in Grawe (2018), I perform a crosswalk between migration PUMAs and MSAs. As a result, the geographic area associated with an MSA differs slightly from the actual boundary of the metropolitan area in question.

Head counts from the ACS are combined with estimates of the probability of college attendance derived from the 2009 HSLS. A Department of Education longitudinal survey, the HSLS studies choices of more than 23,000 students who attended the ninth grade in 2009 at almost 950 schools. The latest wave of data available includes information through February 2016. Assuming on-time graduation and immediate postsecondary matriculation, the survey covers outcomes through as much as the third year of college. The restricted portion of the dataset includes detailed information on college attendance including IPEDS codes of institutions attended. This makes it possible to estimate probabilities for a range of college-going outcomes, distinguishing between attendance at various institution types (not only two- versus four-year institutions but also subsets of the latter group based on rankings by *US News & World Report*) as well as whether an institution is the first attended by the student, whether the student has been retained at the institution of first attendance and/or persists toward a degree at some school in February 2016.

For each college-going outcome, a logit model predicts the probability of that outcome conditional on sex, race/ethnicity, parent education (of parents living with the child), family income, and geographic location—both region and whether in an urban or nonurban setting. Three separate models were fit, one for each of the following three subsets: children living with both parents, children living with either mother or father (for whom only one parent's education is observed and so included in the model), and children who are either living with neither mother nor father or who are not native-born. (See the next section for even greater detail on these logit models.) Given the rich data available in the HSLS (including high school transcripts and standardized test scores), it is certainly possible to find better predictors of college-going outcomes than these broad demographic measures. However, because the estimated probabilities are intended to be matched with individuals in the ACS, the models are restricted to variables observed in that Census source.

Having estimated probabilities for each college outcome conditional on observed demographic characteristics, these values are then applied to ACS observations to find the expected number of young people achieving each college outcome in each MSA or nonmetropolitan portion of a state. These expected values form the core of HEDI forecasts. Because a three-year-old observed in Kansas in 2017 is likely to grow into an 18-year-old in the year 2032, the expected number of Kansans achieving a given college-going outcome among the three-year-old birth cohort in 2017 is a reasonable projection for that outcome in 2032. Of course, reality is more complicated than that. As described in detail in Grawe (2018), adjustments are made to account for:

- mortality between the age of observation and age 18,
- retention to the first year of high school (because the HSLS is representative of this group),
- migration between geographic areas,
- immigration into the country, and
- changes in family composition.

Updates and Adjustments to Modeling

For several reasons, the present work incorporates modest revisions to the model presented in Grawe (2018). First, variable definitions in the more recent 2009 HSLS and 2017 ACS sources sometimes vary slightly from those in the sources used in the prior work. Second, the updated work considers several college-going outcomes not studied in the original. Third, readers of the prior work have suggested refinements. Finally, in a few instances data suggested modest improvements to model specification. These modifications are described here.

College-Going Outcomes

Chapters 2 and 3 look at a range of postsecondary enrollment outcomes. Chapter 2 updates projections of measures explored in Grawe (2018): attending any postsecondary institution, attending a two-year institution, and attending a four-year institution. Four-year schools are disaggregated into three subgroups: those ranked between 1 and 50 on *US News & World Report*'s top national colleges and universities (this collection of 50 colleges and 50 universities—100 in total—is termed "elite" schools), those ranked between 51 and 100 on the same two lists ("national" schools), and all other four-year institutions ("regional" schools). HSLS respondents are counted as attending a postsecondary institution if they enrolled in any institution after completing high school. This is a modest change from Grawe (2018), which counted students who ever attended an institution, including dual enrollees who did not later attend an institution of the same type. Note that many students transfer between two- and four-year schools or between one category of four-year institution to another. As a result, it is quite possible for a single respondent to be coded in several of these subcategories. And so, for example, projections of the number of college-going students is not equal to the sum of those attending two- and four-year schools.

Chapter 3 considers several additional categories of college-going outcomes. The market for four-year colleges is divided between public, private non-profit, and for-profit sectors. (The two-year sector was not similarly divided because it is so heavily dominated by the public sector that few respondents reported attendance at private institutions.) Those who attended some postsecondary institution after high school were coded as attending a public institution if any postsecondary institution of attendance was under public control. Private nonprofit and for-profit attenders are identified in analogous fashions.

Chapter 3 also distinguishes attendance patterns of first schools of attendance versus attendance involving a transfer. An HSLS respondent who attended a postsecondary institution following high school is noted as first attending a two-year institution if the first postsecondary institution they attended is categorized as a two-year institution. First-attenders at four-year schools are identified in an analogous fashion. By contrast, an HSLS respondent is counted as a transfer into a two- or four-year school if they ever attended a two- or four-year school that was not the first postsecondary institution of attendance.

Next, chapter 3 considers persistence and retention. This analysis focuses on first postsecondary enrollments beginning between June and November of 2013 (i.e., the summer and fall following on-time high school graduation). An HSLS respondent is counted as "retained" if in the February 2016 wave of the survey they report either (1) having earned a degree from that institution or (2) ongoing enrollment there. Respondents are coded as "persistent" if, in that same wave of the survey, they report either (1) having earned a degree from any institution or (2) ongoing postsecondary enrollment anywhere.

Finally, chapter 3 reports projections of dual enrollment attendance. HSLS respondents are counted as dual enrollees if they enrolled in any postsecondary institution while still in high school.

Probability Models

The probability of each college-going outcome is estimated from HSLS data using logit regressions with the panel weight variable W4W1W2W3STU. Separate logit regressions are estimated for (1) students living with both parents, (2) students living with only one parent, and (3) students living with no parent and nonnative students. (The combinations in regressions 2 and 3 mitigate problems associated with small numbers of HSLS students living with father alone or with no parent.) The predictors in each regression analysis are essentially the same: sex, race/ethnicity, the interaction between sex and race/ethnicity, parent education (of parents living with the child), family income, and geographic location—both Census division and whether living in an urban or nonurban setting. Due to the fact that parent education is reported in the ACS only for parents in the household and due to small sample sizes in some subsets of the data, several modest modifications to this general model were made. The following provides details:

- children living with both mother and father: the full set of predictors listed earlier without amendment
- children living with only one parent (either mother or father): In a few of the regressions (specifically those with lower probabilities such as attending a national or elite four-year institution), living in the East South Central perfectly predicted the outcome, and so all persons in that division would have been excluded from the estimation procedure. To avoid this loss of data, the East and West South Central divisions were combined into a single geographic region in all models for children living with only one parent. Similarly, small sample sizes and regression coefficients motivated a simplification of parent education into two categories: associate's degree or less and bachelor's degree or more.
- Children living with neither parent and nonnative children: Small sample sizes and regression coefficients motivated a simplification of location to Census region (as opposed to division), a parsimonious, four-category version of family income ($\leq$ \$55,000, \$55,001–\$75,000, \$75,001–\$115,000, > \$115,000), and the exclusion of race/ethnicity. Parent education is excluded because parent education is not observed for children living with neither father nor mother and the meaning of parent education data is unclear for nonnatives.

Mortality
Mortality rates have been updated to reflect more recent data reported by the Centers for Disease Control and Prevention (2018a).

Changes in Family Structure
The analysis of changes in family composition using data from the Panel Study of Income Dynamics (PSID) was updated using the 2015 Parent Identification File and observations gathered in 2011 and 2015.

Among those with mothers holding a college degree or more, the sample size is relatively modest. In particular, there is only one individual in this PSID subsample who was living with father alone in 2011. As it happens, that child was living with mother alone in 2015. Based on this experience, the model described in Grawe (2018) would assume all children of college-educated mothers living with father alone will transition to living with mother alone. Given the sample size of one, imposing that assumption seems unwise. Instead, the model assumes that all such children continue to live with father alone.

Migration

In Grawe (2018), mother's education was found to be the strongest predictor of migration between states or cities in the study. However, in the 2017 ACS, father's education is a stronger predictor. (Note, however, that the parent education measures are highly collinear.) As a result, in the present study father's education is used to predict migration probabilities.

In addition, an examination of migration patterns in the most recent ACS samples (2016 and 2017) shows some variation across the two years. For example, at the Census division level, while 2016 saw modest (−0.1%) net outflows from the East South Central, 2017 saw modest (0.2%) inflows. More importantly, while 2016 saw substantial net outflows (−0.5%) from New England, 2017 recorded modest inflow (0.2%). While chapter 3 shows that HEDI projections are robust to alternative assumptions about migration such that these differences have limited impacts, to mitigate the potential influence of migration patterns from a single year, migration probabilities were estimated as described in Grawe (2018) for both the 2016 and 2017 ACS, and then averaged.

High School Persistence

The HSLS tracks outcomes of ninth graders where the ELS used in Grawe (2018) studies a sample of high school sophomores. As a result, early departure from high school creates fewer issues of nonrepresentative samples in the HSLS than in the ELS. Among respondents to the 2017 ACS, 97.9% of 15-year-olds were in school as compared with 95.4% of 16-year-olds. Nevertheless, just as in Grawe (2018), adjustments are made to account for school-leaving prior to the ninth grade. However, the school-leaving (logit) probability models have been adjusted slightly based on patterns observed in the data. Among natives, the probability of school-leaving is modeled as a function of sex, race/ethnicity (simplified into two groups: non-Hispanic blacks and all others), the interaction between sex and race/ethnicity, the educational attainment of parents living with the child (simplified by combining those with a bachelor's and those with greater than a bachelor's), and urban location status. Separate regressions are estimated for children in the four different family composition types.* Guided by the data, the model for persistence among nonnatives is estimated as a function of parents' education (with the missing parents' education estimated as described in Grawe [2018]) and family income.

Race/Ethnicity
In response to reader feedback, in the present study those who indicate race as Hawaiian or Pacific Islander are categorized as "Other" rather than "Asian."

Parent Education
While the ELS reports years of parent education, which allows some parents to be categorized as "some college but no degree," the HSLS records degrees attained. In the present study, parent education in both the HSLS and the ACS is grouped into five categories: less than high school, high school (or equivalent), associate's degree, bachelor's degree, and degree beyond a bachelor's.

Family Income
As in the ELS, the HSLS only reports income by bracket. Here as in Grawe (2018), the brackets are reduced to 8 categories (population share given in parentheses): <=$15,000 (12%), $15,001–$35,000 (21%), $35,001–$55,000 (18%), $55,001–$75,000 (15%), $75,001–$95,000 (10%), $95,001–$115,000 (13%), $115,001–$235,000 (9%), and >$235,000 (3%).

---

*In the analysis of those living with father alone, a group accounting for less than 5% of the population of children, the regression chi-square value is not statistically significant, indicating that these predictors do not well-predict the rare event of school-leaving prior to ninth grade for this very small subpopulation. Because the regression chi-square was significant among the three other family composition subgroups, and to maintain consistency of the model across groups, I nevertheless used the logit model to estimate the (small) probability of school-leaving in this subgroup.

APPENDIX 2: *Comparison to WICHE Forecasts*

The Western Interstate Commission for Higher Education (WICHE) is the clear leader in forecasting the future of education. Through its *Knocking at the College Door* project, WICHE has produced and regularly updated projections of high school graduates. While it is useful to differentiate higher education demand by institution type, separating, for example, the markets of two-year schools from those of highly selective four-year institutions, WICHE's high school graduation data is of great value and widely used. For that reason, it is useful to consider how HEDI projections align with and deviate from those of WICHE.

WICHE's (2016) forecast of high school graduates is compared, in figure A2.1, with HEDI's projection of postsecondary enrollers for the years 2018 through 2032 (with HEDI forecasts through 2034 for context), the years of overlap between the two sources. The same is done in figure A2.2, broken down by Census region. Because one model looks at high school graduates while the other measures college matriculants, to aid comparison the figures plot the percentage changes from 2018 rather than levels. Clearly, HEDI and WICHE tell very similar stories. Between now and the mid-2020s, we might expect modest growth nationally, led by advances in the South and West offsetting losses elsewhere. Between 2018–19 and 2024–25, the expected growth rates foreseen under the two models are within one or two percentage points of each other in all four census regions. After that point, all regions face declines driven by falling population through 2029–30. With the exception of the Northeast, where WICHE anticipates a 7% decline and the HEDI projects a loss of 10%, again the two models are within a point or two of each other in every region. Within this general agreement, the HEDI projects a larger bump in the early 2030s, a reflection of the much larger number of 4-year-olds than 5-year-olds in the 2017 ACS. Given the potential importance of the early 2030s rebound (brief as it is), I replicated the HEDI forecasts replacing 2017 ACS data with the equivalent observations from 2016. The resulting 2030 forecasts were little changed. The rebound in WICHE forecasts is closer in magnitude to that in births reported by the CDC, which might argue in favor of WICHE's more modest rebound.

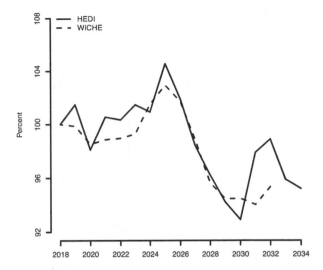

Figure A2.1. Comparison of Percent Change in WICHE Forecasts of High School Graduates and HEDI Projections of Postsecondary Enrollers, 2018 to 2032. *Source:* WICHE (2016) and author's calculations based on data from the American Community Survey (2017), Centers for Disease Control and Prevention (2018a), 2009 High School Longitudinal Study (restricted and unrestricted), and the Panel Study of Income Dynamics (2011, 2015)

The forecasts are least congruent in the West. A very similar divergence is found when comparing WICHE forecasts with HEDI projections of population, so the modest disagreement is apparently driven by the two models' assumptions for immigration and migration in the West rather than by HEDI adjustments for the probability of college-going. Of course, both models include errors, and so it is possible the difference is simply noise. While the differences between the WICHE and the HEDI data in the West in the early 2030s are meaningful, the broader picture is still clearly one of agreement.

Forecasts at the state level are compared in figure A2.3.* Naturally, as projections are pushed to a more granular level, divergence increases because

---

*Because the HEDI forecasts are divided by metropolitan area and sometimes-combined nonmetropolitan portions of states, the figure presents data on the least common denominator, sometimes merging contiguous states to achieve a common point of comparison. Those cases are Alaska and Hawaii; Connecticut, Massachusetts, and Rhode Island; Delaware, Maryland, Virginia, and West Virginia; Kansas, Nebraska, South Dakota, and North Dakota; New Jersey and Pennsylvania; and Oregon and Washington. In addition, some metropolitan areas straddle state boundaries and must be assigned to states: Boston (Massachusetts), Chicago (Illinois), Cincinnati (Ohio), Kansas City (Kansas), Minneapolis–St. Paul (Minnesota), New York City (New York), Philadelphia (Pennsylvania), and St. Louis (Missouri).

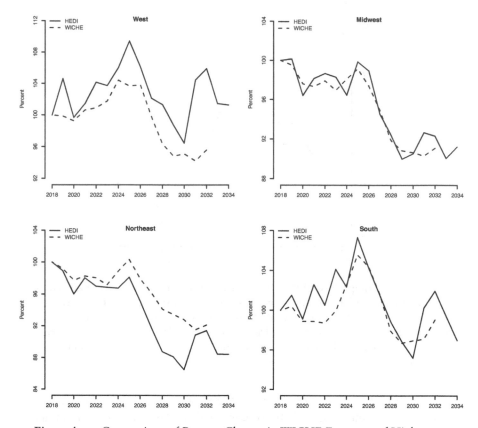

Figure A2.2. Comparison of Percent Change in WICHE Forecasts of High School Graduates and HEDI Projections of Postsecondary Enrollers by Census Region, 2018 to 2032. *Source:* WICHE (2016) and author's calculations based on data from the American Community Survey (2017), Centers for Disease Control and Prevention (2018a), 2009 High School Longitudinal Study (restricted and unrestricted), and the Panel Study of Income Dynamics (2011, 2015)

both forecast error and differing assumptions about migration and immigration become relatively more pronounced. The fact that HEDI projections are created for metropolitan areas that are then attributed to single states even when they cross state lines adds an additional source of disagreement between the two studies. The greatest differences occur in the West, where migration and immigration play a disproportionate role in the context of many sparsely populated areas. Notably, the two locations of greatest forecast divergence, Arizona and Nevada, have been disproportionately shaped by immigration and cross-state migration. When western locations (squares

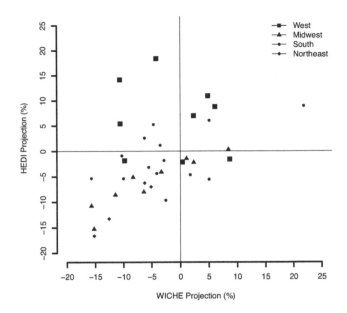

Figure A2.3. Comparison of Percent Change in WICHE Forecasts of High
School Graduates and HEDI Projections of Postsecondary Enrollers by State,
2018–19 to 2031–32. *Source:* WICHE (2016) and author's calculations based on data
from the American Community Survey (2017), Centers for Disease Control and Prevention (2018a), 2009 High School Longitudinal Study (restricted and unrestricted), and the
Panel Study of Income Dynamics (2011, 2015)

in figure A2.3) are excluded, the correlation between the respective studies'
state forecasts increases from 0.48 to 0.70.

In conclusion, both models speak clearly to the same domestic market
for higher education. Not surprisingly, projections of high school graduates
and postsecondary enrollees follow similar tracks: because broad college-
going rates are generally high across all demographic groups, there is little
space between conversations about the population of high school graduates
and the population of college attendees. And so, for access-oriented institutions that attract more or less representative subsets of the population, the
WICHE forecasts undoubtedly serve very well. Most of the variation between the two forecasts follows from differences in expectations of population growth due to migration and immigration rather than accounting for
college-going probabilities. While the HEDI's disaggregation of higher education provides nuance in considering differences between submarkets, for
two-year and regional four-year schools it is not clear that one set of forecasts, particularly at the local level, are preferable to the other.

Chapter 1. Evolving Demographic Trends

1. At the time of the 2016 WICHE report, official tallies of high school graduates by state were only available through 2010–11. WICHE's forecasts anticipate much greater decline than those published by the Department of Education in the *Digest of Education Statistics*. The WICHE forecasts, like my own, track much more closely with the numbers of young people in each respective birth cohort.

2. The US Census Bureau asks more than 3.5 million households to complete the ACS each year. For the purposes of this work, we are especially interested in questions about basic demographic characteristics—data that can be matched to items included in the Department of Education's longitudinal studies of college-going.

3. Readers interested in a detailed description of the HEDI's construction including detailed variable definitions and model specifications should see chapter 3 and the methodological appendix in Grawe (2018). Appendix 1 of this work provides an abbreviated description of the methods along with an explanation of how the model in Grawe (2018) was modestly revised to accommodate differences between the datasets used there and in the present work.

4. After separating out the metropolitan areas, some nonmetropolitan portions of states held very small populations. As described in Grawe (2018), I combined contiguous nonmetropolitan portions of states within Census divisions until I reached a geographic area that included a population of at least two million people. The combined nonmetropolitan areas are: Alaska-Hawaii, Colorado-Wyoming, Delaware-Maryland-Virginia–West Virginia, Idaho-Montana, Kansas-Nebraska–North Dakota–South Dakota, Maine–New Hampshire–Vermont, Massachusetts–Rhode Island–Connecticut, New Jersey–New York, and Oregon-Washington.

5. Because the HEDI projects college-going in the years immediately following high school graduation, it is an analysis of traditional-aged college students. Of course, 18-year-olds become 30-year-olds at some point, but the limitations of the data used here don't permit study of the college-going behaviors of nontraditional students.

6. These comments were made at the 2018 Liberal Arts Illuminated conference held at the College of St. Benedict and St. John's University. McGee currently serves as head of school at St. John's Preparatory School (MN).

7. The official count of international students, however, continues to rise because that tally includes those in optional practical training.

8. The total fertility rate is a common summary of fertility. It measures the number of children a woman would have if at each age of her life she had the average number of births among women of that age in the year of measurement.

9. All of the college attendance rates cited here from the NCES pertain to attendance in the fall following high school graduation. Unless noted otherwise, the HEDI considers a slightly broader measure of college-going—whether the student ever attended college between high school graduation and the 2016 HSLS follow-up survey.

Chapter 2. Updated Projections of Higher Education Demand

1. While the ACS covers millions of people every year, only about 650,000 of these are children. And each birth cohort includes around 36,000. While this is hardly a small sample size, to reduce potential variability caused by randomness in sampling, here and in the chapters that follow I combine cohorts in the first and last two years of the projections.

2. Given the nature of sampling error, projections exhibit greater error variance the finer the data are parsed. In these figures, for instance, data are divided by geography and then by institution type. The number of people from low-population geographies with markers of attending a given type of institution (particularly elite institutions) can be quite small. As a consequence, projection error is inherently larger in local than national projections. Aggregating up from the state or city to the Census division reduces these concerns by averaging projection errors across several locations, but this choice comes at a cost to accuracy when locations within a Census division are heterogeneous. Moreover, the geographic area of interest for some institutions may draw from parts of multiple divisions. The maps in figure 2.3 are shared so that readers can make their own trade-offs between precision and accuracy and define regional boundaries in ways that serve their needs.

3. The forecasts differ from one another in level due to attendance differences between the time periods studied and methodological differences between the studies. The former is likely driven by different economic circumstances. Still in the shadow of the Great Recession, the summer of 2013 saw unemployment rates for 20-to-24-year-old high school graduates above 16%—up 60% from the same season of 2004. This weak labor market likely explains a slight increase in college-going observed in the HSLS relative to the ELS.

Methodological difference represents a larger source of deviation in enrollment levels between the two studies. As described in detail in appendix 1, differences in how variables were coded in the ELS and HSLS require somewhat different categorizations. For example, the former records parents' years of education, allowing for identification of those who had some college but less than a bachelor's degree, while the latter reports degrees completed. These differences lead to different crosswalks with data reported in the ACS, which, in turn, lead to stronger or weaker concordance in the distributions of variables between the longitudinal sources of college-going probability models and the Census head count data. Moreover, in response to feedback to Grawe (2018), the present study distinguishes dual enrollments from postsecondary attendance. While the original study measured whether a student ever attended an institution of a given type, the present work only counts enrollments following high school completion. (Dual enrollment is separately examined in chapter 3.) These methodological differences affect comparisons of the forecasts' levels. For this reason, comparison here focuses instead on the models' projections for percentage change in prospective student numbers relative to 2018.

Chapter 3. New Lenses for Higher Education Demand

1. This conception of "transfer student" differs from formal definitions. A student might attend institution A but earn no credits. When entering institution B, the work in this section considers the student a transfer. Formal definitions of transfer require completion of prior credit hours.

2. This definition misses retained or persistent students who arrive to a campus after the fall following high school graduation. While this selection is regrettable, an alternative definition that allowed for later arrivals would introduce an offsetting problem: late-arriving students might be said to persist even if they only stayed in higher education for a short time. For example, consider the student who first enrolls for fall term in 2015. By persisting for a single term, they report continued enrollment in February 2016. This short duration of enrollment doesn't seem to capture the intent of what is meant by "persistence." By contrast, the proposed measure requires either degree completion or enrollment spanning more than two years for a student to be defined as persistent.

3. https://www.census.gov/data/tables/2016/demo/foreign-born/cps-2016.html.

4. See the methodological appendix in Grawe (2018) for a complete explanation.

5. Slightly more—2.3%—moved across boundaries defined by the 64 cities and nonmetropolitan portions of states used in the HEDI.

Chapter 4. A Detailed Examination by Race

1. https://www.census.gov/data/tables/2016/demo/foreign-born/cps-2016.html.

Chapter 5. Strategies and Tactics for Tackling Disruptive Change

1. I thank Mike Hemesath, former president of Saint John's University (MN), for this observation.

Chapter 6. Recruitment and Financial Aid Policies

1. These comments were made at Inside Higher Ed's 2018 Leadership Series titled "The Admissions Challenges Facing Private Colleges."

2. These comments were made at Inside Higher Ed's 2018 Leadership Series titled "The Admissions Challenges Facing Private Colleges."

3. These comments were made at Inside Higher Ed's 2018 Leadership Series titled "The Admissions Challenges Facing Private Colleges."

4. In the pilot study, these measures of adversity were summarized in a single index score. Some critics objected to the idea of simplifying a complex range of experiences into a single measure, and so the College Board eliminated this summary statistic in 2019. All of the experiences described here preceded this change. It is not clear whether similar effects will follow from the use of the tool without this simplification.

Chapter 7. Retention Initiatives

1. https://studentsuccess.uiowa.edu/what-we-do/past-committees-and-initiatives /pick-one/.

2. https://www.depauw.edu/commitment/.

3. https://www.morningside.edu/admissions/why-morningside/.

4. These comments were made at Inside Higher Ed's 2018 Leadership Series titled "The Admissions Challenges Facing Private Colleges."

5. In addition to providing financial aid, the program gathers students in a cohort and provides additional emotional and academic counseling. These program elements contribute to a deeper sense of belonging as discussed in this chapter.

Chapter 8. Program Reforms

1. These comments were made at the 2018 Liberal Arts Illuminated conference held at the College of St. Benedict/St. John's University.

2. These comments were made at Inside Higher Ed's 2018 Leadership Series titled "The Admissions Challenges Facing Private Colleges."

Chapter 9. Reorganization, Rightsizing, and Other Names for Retrenchment

1. This description must be modestly revised if for-profit enrollments are excluded. With this exclusion, 1996 and 1997 also posted contractions, though these declines were of less than 1%.

2. https://gwtoday.gwu.edu/message-president-leblanc-strategic-planning -process.

3. Because the goal of consolidation was not budget savings, the $30 million figure should be viewed as a lower bound. It may well be that consolidation made possible other savings that would have had little impact on quality. Had savings been a primary objective, perhaps the system would have exercised the newly available option. As it was, with educational quality as a primary aim, the savings realized by Georgia may not be representative.

Chapter 11. Collaborative Action

1. These comments were made at Inside Higher Ed's 2019 Leadership Series titled "The Future of Public Higher Ed."

2. These comments were made at Inside Higher Ed's 2019 Leadership Series titled "The Future of Public Higher Ed."

3. https://obp.umich.edu/wp-content/uploads/pubdata/factsfigures/finance _umaa_18-19.pdf.

4. These figures are based on a comparison of international and total enrollments by Carnegie classification presented in IIE (2019) and the Center for Postsecondary Research (2019), respectively.

5. NAFSA's calculations conservatively measure only direct expenditures; they exclude indirect "multiplier" effects in which economic activity might further expand as those who receive revenue from international students use that added income to augment their own consumption.

6. This collaboration was described at Inside Higher Ed's 2018 Leadership Series titled "The Admissions Challenges Facing Private Colleges" by Dickinson's Tara Fischer, associate dean of academic advising and college dean and coordinator of the community college partnership initiative, and Catherine McDonald Davenport, interim vice president for enrollment management and dean of admissions.

Chapter 12. Something between Chicken Little and Pollyanna

1. These comments were made at Inside Higher Ed's 2019 Leadership Series titled "The Future of Public Higher Ed."

Adair, Kathy, Liza Azure, Scott Friskics, Charles Roessel, and Leah Woodke, with Cindy Lopez. 2019. "Survey Data from Students Spurs Tribal Colleges and Universities to Action." Achieving the Dream. https://www.achievingthedream .org/news/17659/survey-data-from-students-spurs-tribal-colleges-and-universities -to-action.

Adair, Stephen, Lois Aime, Charlene LaVoie, Colena Sesanker, Patrick Sullivan, and Matt Warshauer. 2019. "Troubling Numbers: The Cost of 'Saving.'" CT Mirror, April 2.

Akers, Beth, and Matthew M. Chingos. 2014. "Is a Student Loan Crisis on the Horizon?" Brookings Institution, Washington, DC: Brown Center on Education Policy.

Alexander, Bryan. 2019. Academia Next: The Futures of Higher Education. Baltimore: Johns Hopkins University Press.

American Academy of the Arts and Sciences. n.d. "Humanities Indicators." Accessed March 1, 2020. https://www.humanitiesindicators.org/content /indicatorDoc.aspx?i=10.

———. 2018. The State of the Humanities 2018: Graduates in the Workforce and Beyond. Cambridge, MA: American Academy of the Arts and Sciences.

American Community Survey. 2011. Washington, DC: United States Census Bureau.

———. 2017. Washington, DC: United States Census Bureau.

American Iron and Steel Institute. 2015. Profile 2015. Washington, DC: American Iron and Steel Institute.

Avery, Christopher, and Sarah Turner. 2012. "Student Loans: Do College Students Borrow Too Much—or Not Enough?" Journal of Economic Perspectives 12, no. 1: 165–192.

Azziz, Ricardo, Guilbert C. Hentschke, Bonita C. Jacobs, Lloyd A. Jacobs, and Haven Ladd. 2017. "Mergers in Higher Education: A Proactive Strategy to a Better Future?" New York: TIAA Institute.

Bailey, Thomas, Shanna Smith Jaggars, and Davis Jenkins. 2015. "What We Know about Guided Pathways." New York: Community College Research Center.

Baker, Peter. 2017. "Trump Supports Plan to Cut Legal Immigration by Half." New York Times, August 2. https://www.nytimes.com/2017/08/02/us/politics /trump-immigration.html.

Barrow, Lisa, and Cecilia Elena Rouse. 2018. "Financial Incentives and Education Investment: The Impact of Performance-Based Scholarships on Student Time Use." *Education Finance and Policy* 13, no. 4: 419–448.

Baum, Sandy. 2016. *Student Debt: Rhetoric and Realities of Higher Education Pricing*. New York: Palgrave Pivot.

Baum, Sandy, Jennifer Ma, Matea Pender, and C. J. Libassi. 2018. *Trends in Student Aid 2018*. New York: The College Board.

Baum, Sandy, and Marie O'Malley. 2003. "College on Credit: How Borrowers Perceive Their Education Debt." *Journal of Student Financial Aid* 33, no. 3: Article 1.

Baumol, William, and William Bowen. 1966. *Performing Arts—The Economic Dilemma: A Study of Problems Common to Theater, Opera, Music and Dance*. New York: Twentieth Century Fund.

Berwick, Donald M., David R. Calkins, C. Joseph McCannon, and Andrew D. Hackbarth. 2006. "The 100,000 Lives Campaign: Setting a Goal and a Deadline for Improving Health Care Quality." *Journal of the American Medical Association* 295, no. 3: 324–327.

Bird, Kelli A., Benjamin L. Castleman, Jeffery T. Denning, Joshua Goodman, Cait Lamberton, and Kelly Ochs Rosinger. 2019. "Nudging at Scale: Experimental Evidence from FAFSA Completion Campaigns." Working Paper No. 26158, NBER Working Paper Series.

Boatman, Angela, and Bridget Terry Long. 2016. "Does Financial Aid Impact College Student Engagement?" *Research in Higher Education* 57, no. 6: 653–681.

Boggs, Bennett G. 2018. "A Legislator's Toolkit for the New World of Higher Education." Paper No. 3, National Council of State Legislatures.

Bothwell, Ellie. 2018. "Insuring against Drop in Chinese Students." *Inside Higher Ed*, November 29.

Bowen, Melanie, and Rich Staley. 2019. "Transforming for the Next Generation of Students." CONNECTED19: Student Success Collaborative Summit from EAB, Washington, DC, November 5.

Brown, Meta, Andrew Haughwout, Donghoon Lee, Joelle Scally, and Wilbert van der Klaauw. 2015. "Looking at Students Loan Defaults through a Larger Window." *Liberty Street Economics* (blog), Federal Reserve Bank of New York, February 19.

Bureau of Economic Analysis. 2019. "US International Trade in Goods and Services, December 2018." News release. March 6. https://www.bea.gov/news /2019/us-international-trade-goods-and-services-december-2018.

BU Today. 2018. "Wheelock Merger Results in Layoffs." March 15.

Canadian Bureau for International Education. n.d. "International Students in Canada." Accessed April 28, 2020. https://cbie.ca/infographic.

Center for Community College Student Engagement. 2019. *Preserving Culture and Planning for the Future: An Exploration of Student Experiences at*

Tribal Colleges. Austin: University of Texas at Austin, College of Education, Department of Educational Leadership and Policy, Program in Higher Education Leadership.

Center for Postsecondary Research. 2019. "The Carnegie Classification of Institutions of Higher Education: 2018 Update Facts and Figures." Center for Postsecondary Research, Bloomington: Indiana University School of Education.

Centers for Disease Control and Prevention. 2010. *National Vital Statistics Reports* 58, no. 24.

———. 2012. *National Vital Statistics Reports* 61, no. 3.

———. 2013. *National Vital Statistics Reports* 62, no. 1.

———. 2018a. *National Vital Statistics Reports* 67, no. 7.

———. 2019. *National Vital Statistics Reports* 68, no. 13.

Christensen, Clayton M., and Henry J. Eyrling. 2011. *The Innovative University: Changing the DNA of Higher Education from the Inside Out.* San Francisco: Jossey-Bass.

Chronicle of Higher Education. 2017. *The Tuition Pricing Crisis: How College Leaders Are Responding and Preparing for the Future.* Washington, DC: Chronicle of Higher Education.

Cilluffo, Anthony. 2017. "5 Facts about Student Loans." *Factank: News in the Numbers* (blog), Pew Research Center, August 24.

Clotfelter, Charles T., Steven W. Helmet, and Helen F. Ladd. 2017. "Multifaceted Aid for Low-Income Students and College Outcomes: Evidence from North Carolina." *Economic Inquiry* 56, no. 1: 278–303.

Cohn, D'Vera, and Andrea Caumont. 2016. "10 Demographic Trends That Are Shaping the U.S. and the World." *Factank: News in the Numbers* (blog), Pew Research Center, March 31.

Cohodes, Sarah R., and Joshua S. Goodman. 2014. "Merit Aid, College Quality, and College Completion: Massachusetts' Adams Scholarship as an In-Kind Subsidy." *American Economic Journal: Applied Economics* 6, no. 4: 251–285.

Cooperrider, David L. 1986. "Appreciative Inquiry: Toward a Methodology for Understanding and Enhancing Organizational Innovation." PhD diss., Case Western Reserve, Cleveland, OH.

Dattagupta, Ishani. 2018. "How Private Universities Are Reviving Liberal Arts Education in India." *Economic Times*, January 25.

Davis, Glenn M., Melissa B. Hanzsek-Brill, Mark Carl Petzold, and David H. Robinson. 2019. "Students' Sense of Belonging: The Development of a Predictive Retention Model." *Journal of the Scholarship of Teaching and Learning* 19, no. 1: 117–127.

Deming, David, and Susan Dynarski. 2010. "College Aid." In *Targeting Investments in Children: Fighting Poverty When Resources are Limited*, edited by Phillip B. Levine and David J. Zimmerman, 283–302. Chicago: University of Chicago Press.

Department of Homeland Security. 2018a. "Legal Immigration and Adjustment of Status Report Fiscal Year 2018, Quarter 1." Accessed November 1, 2019, https://www.dhs.gov/immigration-statistics/special-reports/legal-immigration#File_end.

———. 2018b. "Legal Immigration and Status Report Quarterly Data." Accessed November 1, 2019. https://www.dhs.gov/immigration-statistics/readingroom/special/LIASR.

———. 2018c. *Yearbook of Immigration Statistics 2017*. Washington, DC: Department of Homeland Security.

Despard, Mathieu R., Dana Perantie, Samuel Taylor, Michal Grinstein-Weiss, Terri Friedline, and Ramesh Raghavan. 2016. "Student Debt and Hardship: Evidence from a Large Sample of Low- and Moderate-Income Households." *Children and Youth Services Review* 70, November: 8–18.

Drew University. 2017. *Drew University Fact Book 2017–18*. Madison, NJ: Drew University.

Driscoll, Anne K., Michelle J. K. Osterman, Brady E. Hamilton, Joyce A. Martin. 2020. "Quarterly Provisional Estimates for Selected Birth Indicators, Quarter 1, 2017–Quarter 3, 2019." National Center for Health Statistics. National Vital Statistics System, Vital Statistics Rapid Release Program.

Duderstadt, James. J. 2009. "Current Global Trends in Higher Education and Research: Their Impact on Europe." Dies Academicus 2009 Address, Universität Wien, Vienna, Austria. https://deepblue.lib.umich.edu/bitstream/handle/2027.42/88580/2009_U_Vienna_Dies_Academicus.pdf?sequence=1.

Dynarski, Susan M. 2014. "An Economist's Perspective on Student Loans in the United States." ES Working Paper Series, September 2014, Brookings.

Dynarski, Susan M., and Daniel Kreisman. 2013. "Loans for Educational Opportunity: Making Borrowing Work for Today's Students." Hamilton Project Discussion Paper 2013–15, Brookings.

Dynarski, Susan M., and Judith Scott-Clayton. 2013. "Financial Aid Policy: Lessons from Research." *Future of Children* 23, no. 1: 67–92.

EAB. 2016. "Incentivizing Behavioral Change with Aid Dollars: Targeted Interventions to Promote Persistence." Enrollment Management Forum. https://eab.com/research/enrollment/study/incentivizing-behavioral-change-with-aid-dollars/.

Eddinger, Pam. 2019. "Don't Call Our Students Kids!" *Perspectives*, Ferris State University Alliance for Community College Excellence in Practice, October.

Edelman. 2019. "2019 Edelman Trust Barometer: Special Report: California." https://www.edelman.com/sites/g/files/aatuss191/files/2019-02/2019_Edelman_Trust_Barometer_Special_Report_California_0.pdf.

Education Dive. 2019. "How Many Nonprofit Colleges and Universities Have Closed Since 2016?" Updated August 2, 2019. https://www.educationdive.com/news/tracker-college-and-university-closings-and-consolidation/539961/.

Education Longitudinal Study. 2004. Washington, DC: United States Department of Education.

Fain, Paul. 2019. "Employers as Educators." *Inside Higher Ed*, July 17.

Federal Reserve Bank of New York. 2019. *Quarterly Report on Household Debt and Credit*. Federal Reserve Bank of New York Research and Statistics Group, May.

Frey, William H. 2018. "US White Population Declines and Generation 'Z-Plus' is Minority White, Census Shows." *The Avenue* (blog), Brookings Institution, June 22.

———. 2019a. "US Foreign-Born Gains Are Smallest in a Decade, Except in Trump States." *The Avenue* (blog), Brookings Institution, October 2.

———. 2019b. "US Migration Still at Historically Low Levels, Census Shows." *The Avenue* (blog), Brookings Institution, November 20.

Gardner, Lee. 2017. "Georgia's Mergers Offer Lessons, and Cautions, to Other States." *Chronicle of Higher Education*, June 19.

———. 2018. "How Maine Became a Laboratory for the Future of Higher Ed." *Chronicle of Higher Education*, February 25.

Gervais, Martin, and Nicolas L. Ziebarth. 2019. "Life after Debt: Postgraduate Consequences of Federal Student Loans." *Economic Inquiry* 57, no. 30: 1342–1366.

Gicheva, Dora. 2016, August. "Student Loans or Marriage? A Look at the Highly Educated." *Economics of Education Review* 53: 207–216.

Grawe, Nathan D. 2018. *Demographics and the Demand for Higher Education*. Baltimore: Johns Hopkins University Press.

Gurantz, Oded, Jessica Howell, Michael Hurwitz, Cassandra Larson, Matea Pender, and Brooke White. 2019. "Realizing Your College Potential? Impacts of College Board's RYCP Campaign on Postsecondary Enrollment." Working Paper No. 29-40, EdWorkingPaper Series.

Guthrie, Kevin M. 2019. "Challenges to Higher Education's Most Essential Purposes." Issue Brief, Ithaka S+R April 9.

Hacker, Andrew. 2012. "Is Algebra Necessary?" *New York Times*, July 28. https://www.nytimes.com/2012/07/29/opinion/sunday/is-algebra-necessary.html.

High School Longitudinal Study. 2009. Washington, DC: United States Department of Education.

Institute for Healthcare Improvement. 2006. "5 Million Lives Campaign: An Initiative of the Institute for Healthcare Improvement." Accessed March 1, 2020. http://www.ihi.org/about/documents/5millionlivescampaigncasestatement.pdf.

Institute of International Education. 2019. *Open Doors 2019: Report on International Education Exchange*. Accessed March 1, 2020. https://www.iie.org/en/Research-and-Insights/Open-Doors/Open-Doors-2019-Media-Information.

Johnson, Kenneth. 2019. "U.S. Fertility Rate Hits Record Low and Births Continue to Diminish." Data Snapshot, University of New Hampshire, Carsey School of Public Policy Data Snapshot, May 16.

Kirp, David. 2019. *The College Dropout Scandal*. New York: Oxford University Press.

Knapp, Crystal. 2016. "Princeton University Will Add One More Residential College, Expand Undergraduate and Graduate Student Body." *Planet Princeton*, February 2.

Krogstad, Jens Manuel, Jeffrey S. Passel, and D'Vera Cohn. 2019. "5 Facts about Illegal Immigration in the U.S." *Factank: News in the Numbers* (blog), Pew Research Center, June 12.

Lane, Sylvan. 2019. "Warren Bill Would Wipe Out Nearly All Student Debt in US." *The Hill*, June 13.

Lapovsky, Lucie. 2015. "Tuition Reset: An Analysis of Eight Colleges That Addressed the Escalating Price of Higher Education." Accessed March 1, 2020. http://lapovsky.com/wp-content/uploads/2015/11/TuitionReset.pdf.

———. 2019. "Free College Programs Are Not the Best Way to Provide College Access." *Forbes*, August 28.

Lederman, Doug. 2018. "A Quarter of Private Colleges Ran Deficits in 2017." *Inside Higher Ed*, June 27.

Leighton, Joy. 2019. "CS+X Pilot to be Discontinued End of Spring Quarter." *Stanford News*, January 24.

Lipka, Sara. 2014. "Colleges, Here Is Your Future." *Chronicle of Higher Education*, January 24.

Looney, Adam. 2019. "A Better Way to Provide Relief to Student Loan Borrowers." Brookings Institution Up Front. April 30. https://www.brookings.edu/blog/up-front/2019/04/30/a-better-way-to-provide-relief-to-student-loan-borrowers/.

Looney, Adam, and Constantine Yannelis. 2015. "A Crisis in Student Loans? How Changes in the Characteristics of Borrowers and in the Institutions They Attended Contributed to Rising Loan Defaults." *Brookings Papers on Economic Activity*, Fall: 1–68.

———. 2018. "Borrowers with Large Balances: Rising Student Debt and Falling Repayment Rates." Brookings Institution Economic Studies, February.

Looney, Dennis, and Natalia Lusin. 2019. "Enrollments in Languages Other Than English in United States Institutions of Higher Education, Summer 2016 and Fall 2016: Final Report." Modern Language Association Web Publication, June.

Loudenback, Tanza. 2016. "International Students Are Now 'Subsidizing' Public American Universities to the Tune of $9 Billion a Year." *Business Insider*, September 16.

Ma, Jennifer, Sandy Baum, Matea Pender, and C. J. Libassi. 2018. *Trends in College Pricing 2018*. New York: The College Board.

Marcus, Jon. 2018. "Panicked Universities in Search of Students Are Adding Thousands of New Majors." *Washington Post*, August 9. https://www .washingtonpost.com/news/grade-point/wp/2018/08/09/lots-of-new-college -majors/.

McGuinness, Aims. 2016a. *State Policy Leadership for the Future: History of State Coordination and Governance and Alternatives for the Future.* Denver, CO: Education Commission of the States.

———. 2016b. "The States and Higher Education." In *American Higher Education in the Twenty-First Century*, edited by Michael N. Bastedo, Philip G. Altbach, and Patricia Gumport, 238–280. Baltimore: Johns Hopkins University Press.

Minicozzi, Alexandra. 2005. "The Short Term Effect of Educational Debt on Job Decisions." *Economics of Education Review* 24, no. 4: 417–430.

Monaghan, David, Tammy Kolbe, and Sara Goldrick-Rab. 2018. "Experimental Evidence on Interventions to Improve Educational Attainment at Community Colleges." In *Handbook of the Sociology of Education in the 21st Century*, edited by Barbara Schneider, 535–559. Cham, Switzerland: Springer.

Moody's Investors Service. 2015. "Moody's: Small but Notable Rise Expected in Closures, Mergers for Smaller US Colleges." Announcement, September 25.

NAFSA: Association of International Educators. n.d. "NAFSA International Student Economic Value Tool." Accessed March 1, 2020. http://www.nafsa .org/Policy_and_Advocacy/Policy_Resources/Policy_Trends_and_Data /NAFSA_International_Student_Economic_Value_Tool/.

National Association of College and University Business Officers. 2018. *The 2018 NACUBO Tuition Discounting Study*. Washington, DC: National Association of College and University Business Officers.

National Center for Education Statistics. 2000. *Digest of Education Statistics*. Washington, DC: US Department of Education.

———. 2004. *The Condition of Education 2004*. Washington, DC: US Department of Education.

———. 2016. *Remedial Coursetaking at U.S. Public 2- and 4-Year Institutions: Scope, Experience, and Outcomes*. Washington, DC: US Department of Education.

———. 2017. *Digest of Education Statistics*. Washington, DC: US Department of Education.

———. 2018. *Digest of Education Statistics*. Washington, DC: US Department of Education.

———. 2019a. *Dual Enrollment: Participation and Characteristics*. Washington, DC: US Department of Education.

———. 2019b. *Status and Trends in the Education of Racial and Ethnic Groups*. Washington, DC: US Department of Education.

National Student Clearinghouse Research Center. 2019a. "Snapshot Report: First-Year Persistence and Retention." Snapshot Report, Summer.

———. 2019b. "Tracking Transfer." Signature Report, September 26.

Nienhusser, H. Kenny, and Toko Oshio. 2017. "High School Students' Accuracy in Estimating the Cost of College: A Proposed Methodological Approach and Differences Among Racial/Ethnic Groups and College Financial-Related Efforts." *Research in Higher Education* 58, no. 7: 723–745.

Oreopoulos, Philip, and Uros Petronijevic. 2019. "The Remarkable Unresponsiveness of College Students to Nudging and What We Can Learn from It." Working Paper No. 26059, NBER Working Paper Series.

Page, Lindsay, Bruce Sacerdote, Sara Goldrick-Rab, and Ben Castleman. 2019. "Financial Aid Nudges: A National Experiment with Information Interventions." Working Paper No. 3, The Hope Center Working Paper Series.

Page, Lindsay C., and Judith Scott-Clayton. 2016. "Improving College Access in the United States: Barriers and Policy Responses." *Economics of Education Review* 51, no. 2016: 4–22.

Panel Study of Income Dynamics. 2005. Ann Arbor: University of Michigan.

———. 2009. Ann Arbor: University of Michigan.

———. 2011. Ann Arbor: University of Michigan.

———. 2015. Ann Arbor: University of Michigan.

Parthenon-EY. 2016. "Strength in Numbers: Strategies for Collaborating in a New Era for Higher Education." Parthenon-EY Education Practice. https://cdn.ey.com/parthenon/pdf/perspectives/P-EY_Strength-in-Numbers -Collaboration-Strategies_Paper_Final_082016.pdf.

Patel, Reshma, Lashawn Richburg-Hayes, Elijah de la Campa, and Timothy Rudd. 2013. "Performance-Based Scholarships: What Have We Learned? Interim Findings from the PBS Demonstration Project." Manpower Demonstration Research Corporation Policy Brief, August.

Pickus, Noah, and Kara A. Godwin. 2017. "Liberal Arts Innovations in Chinese Education." *Inside Higher Ed*, November 20.

Pope, Loren. 2000. *Colleges That Change Lives: 40 Schools You Should Know about Even If You're Not a Straight-A Student*. New York: Penguin Books.

Potter, Halley. 2014. "What Can We Learn from States That Ban Affirmative Action?" The Century Foundation, June 26.

Powell, Farran. 2018. "See Which Private Colleges Have Lowered Tuition Prices." *US News & World Report*, November 1.

Princeton University. 2016. "Princeton University Strategic Framework." January 30.

Purdue University. 2019. "Purdue Back a Boiler." Accessed January 2, 2019. https://www.purdue.edu/backaboiler.

Radford, Alexandra Walton, Laura Burns Fritch, Katherine Leu, Michael Duprey, and Elise M. Christopher. 2018. "High School Longitudinal Study of 2009 (HSLS:09) Second Follow-Up: A First Look at Fall 2009 Ninth-Graders in 2016." Report No. 2018-139, US Department of Education, National Center for Education Statistics.

Redden, Elizabeth. 2018. "New International Enrollments Decline Again." *Inside Higher Ed*, November 13.

Reed, Matt. 2015. "Is Indentured Servitude Really a New Idea?" *Confessions of a Community College Dean* (blog), *Inside Higher Ed*. August 30.

Rivard, Ry. 2014. "Shrinking as a Strategy." *Inside Higher Ed*, April 9.

Rosling, Hans. 2018. *Factfulness: Ten Reasons We're Wrong about the World—and Why Things Are Better Than You Think*. New York: Flatiron Books.

Rothstein, Jesse, and Cecilia Elena Rouse. 2011. "Constrained after College: Student Loans and Early-Career Occupational Choices." *Journal of Public Economics* 95, no. 1-2: 149–163.

Ruff, Corinne. 2016. "Computer Science, Meet Humanities: In New Majors, Opposites Attract." *Chronicle of Higher Education*, January 28.

Ruggles, Steven J., Sarah Floor, Ronald Goeken, Josiah Grover, Erin Meyer, Jose Pacas, and Matthew Sobek. 2019. *IPUMS USA: Version 9.0 American Community Survey*. Minneapolis: IPUMS.

Russell, Lauren. 2019. "Better Outcomes without Increased Costs? Effects of Georgia's University System Consolidations." *Economics of Education Review* 68, no. 2019: 122–135.

Rutschow, Elizabeth Zachry. 2018. "Making It Through: Interim Findings on Developmental Students' Progress to College Math with the Dana Center Mathematics Pathways." New York: Center for the Analysis of Postsecondary Readiness.

S&P Global. 2019. "Consolidation or Closure: The Future of U.S. Higher Education?" S&P Global Ratings Direct, March 14.

Sáenz, Rogello. 2015. "A Transformation in Mexican Migration to the United States." National Issue Brief No. 86, University of New Hampshire, Carsey School of Public Policy.

Sapiro, Virginia. 2019. "When the End Comes to Higher Education Institutions, 1890–2019: A Data Source." http://blogs.bu.edu/vsapiro/files/2019/02/Sapiro WhentheEndComesDataSource-3.pdf.

Schackner, Bill. 2019. "PA's 14 State Universities Requesting $100 Million to Overhaul System." *Pittsburgh Post-Gazette*, October 17.

Seemiller, Corey, and Meghan Grace. 2016. *Generation Z Goes to College*. San Francisco: Jossey-Bass.

Seltzer, Rick. 2018. "The Growing Role of Mergers in Higher Ed." Inside Higher Education Special Report. https://www.insidehighered.com/content/growing -role-mergers-higher-ed.

———. 2019. "Moody's Maintains Negative Outlook for Higher Ed." *Inside Higher Ed*, August 14.

Shear, Michael D. 2019. "Trump Immigration Proposal Emphasizes Immigrants' Skills over Family Ties." *New York Times*, May 15.

Sponsler, Brian A., and May Fulton. 2018. "Modern Era Trends in State Higher Education Coordination, Governance, and Alternatives for the Future." In

The State Higher Education Executive Officer and the Public Good:
Developing New Leadership for Improved Policy, Practice, and Research,
edited by David A. Tandberg, Brian A. Sponsler, Randall W. Hanna, and
Jason P. Guilbeau, 219–254. New York: Teachers College Press.

St. Olaf College. n.d. "Enrollment Demographics, Entering Cohorts 2002–
2019." Accessed March 1, 2020. https://wp.stolaf.edu/ir-e/institutional-data
-and-information/students/.

State Higher Education Executive Officers Association. 2018. *State Higher*
Education Finance: FY 2017. Boulder, CO: State Higher Education Executive
Officers Association.

Strada and Gallup. 2018a. *From College to Life: Relevance and the Value of*
Higher Education. Washington, DC: Strada Network and Gallup.

———. 2018b. *Why Higher Ed? Top Reasons US Consumers Choose Their*
Education Pathways. Washington, DC: Strada Network and Gallup.

Strayhorn, Terrell L. 2018. *College Students' Sense of Belonging*, 2nd ed. New
York: Routledge.

Strumbos, Diana, Donna Linderman, and Carson C. Hicks. 2018. "Postsecondary Pathways out of Poverty: City University of New York Accelerated Study
in Associate Programs and the Case for National Policy." *Russell Sage*
Foundation Journal of the Social Sciences 4, no. 3: 100–117.

Taleb, Nassimo Nicholas. 2012. *Antifragile: Things That Gain from Disorder.*
New York: Random House.

Tavernise, Sabrina. 2019. "Immigrant Population Growth in the US Slows to a
Trickle." *New York Times*, September 26. https://www.nytimes.com/2019/09
/26/us/census-immigration.html.

Tinto, Vincent. 1987. *Leaving College: Rethinking the Causes and Cures of*
Student Attrition. Chicago: University of Chicago Press.

Turner, Lesley J. 2014. "The Road to Pell is Paved with Good Intentions: The
Economic Incidence of Federal Student Grant Aid." University of Maryland
working paper. http://econweb.umd.edu/~turner/Turner_FedAidIncidence
.pdf.

University of South Carolina. 2018. "Gamecock Guarantee Program: Facts and
Figures at a Glance." Accessed March 1, 2020. https://www.sc.edu/about
/offices_and_divisions/financial_aid/grants/gamecock_guarantee/facts_and
_figures_ggg.pdf.

University System of Georgia. 2019. "Fiscal Year 2020 Operating Budget."
Accessed March 1, 2020. https://www.usg.edu/fiscal_affairs/functions
/budgeting.

Venit, Ed. 2018. "Is Your Student Success Strategy Ready for the Next Decade?"
Student Success Insights (blog), EAB, November 12. https://eab.com/insights
/blogs/student-success/is-your-student-success-strategy-ready-for-the-next
-decade/.

Vigo, Julian. 2017. "Student Loans, the Indentured Servitude of the 21st Century." *CounterPunch*, December 14. https://www.counterpunch.org/2017/12/14 /student-loans-the-indentured-servitude-of-the-21st-century/.

Walsemann, Katrina, Gilbert C. Gee, and Danielle Gentile. 2015. "Sick of Our Loans: Student Borrowing and the Mental Health of Young Adults in the United States." *Social Science and Medicine* 124, January: 85–93.

Western Interstate Commission for Higher Education. 2012. *Knocking at the College Door: Projections of High School Graduates, December 2012.* https://files.eric.ed.gov/fulltext/ED540129.pdf.

———. 2016. *Knocking at the College Door: Projections of High School Graduates, December 2016.* https://static1.squarespace.com/static/57f269e 19de4bb8a69b470ae/t/5a4bf94f24a694d32cfe41ab/1514928467746 /Knocking2016FINALFORWEB-revised010218.pdf.

Whistle, Wesley, and Tamara Hiler. 2018. "The Pell Divide: How Four-Year Institutions Are Failing to Graduate Low- and Moderate-Income Students." Third Way, May 1.

Zemsky, Robert, Susan Shaman, and Susan Campbell Baldridge. 2020. *The College Stress Test: Tracking Institutional Futures across a Crowded Market.* Baltimore: Johns Hopkins University Press.

Page numbers in *italics* refer to figures and tables.

industry partnerships, 147–48
inmates, programs for, 109–11
Institute for Healthcare Improvement, 100,000 Lives Campaign of, 90–91
Institute of International Education, 18
institutions: diversification by type of, 39; examples from, 89–90; fiscal conditions of, 5; size or scope of, 4–5, 210–11; threats to, 5, 89–90; types of, 28–29, 29. *See also* competition between institutions; elite institutions; national institutions; regional institutions; two-year institutions; *specific institutions*
interdisciplinary programs, 142–43
international students, 1–2, 18, 192–94, 208
internships, 151, 156
Ishop, Kedra, 178–79

Johnson, Kenneth, 207, 208

King, W. Joseph, 100, 108, 169, 170
Kirp, David, 134, 136, 194, 198
Kreisman, Daniel, 191
Kyle, Michael, 102–3, 118

Lafayette College, 143, 177–78
Lane, Sylvan, 190
language programs, 161
Lapovsky, Lucie, 99–100, 188
leadership: change and, 86–88, 156–57, 211; at rural colleges, 174
LeBlanc, Thomas, 167
Leighton, Joy, 143
liberal arts education, 153–55
loan repayment, models of, 100–102
Long, Bridget Terry, 130
Looney, Adam, 189, 191–92
Looney, Dennis, 161–62
Lopez, Cindy, 196–97
Lusin, Natalia, 161–62
Lyon College, 108

major fields, reforms in, 142–43
Marcus, Jon, 139
market for higher education: declines in, 1–2; diversity of, 28; at regional and local levels, 32–36, 33, 34; subsectors

of, 28–30, 29, 49, 50–53, 52, 64–65; transfer market, 53–55
markets, expansion into new, 102–11
Massa, Robert, 97, 99, 100, 130
math courses, required, 139–42, 149
McGee, Jon: on context, 81; on curricular change, 138–39, 181; on diversification of students, 117–18; on models, 16; on regional markets, 104; on responses to change, 83–84, 87, 157, 158–59; on tactics and strategies, 82
McGovern, Amy, 122–23
McGuinness, Aims, 186
mental health services, 129–30
mergers, 168–74
Middlesex Community College, 198–99
migration, interstate, 18–19, 62–64
missions, rethinking, 86–88
Modern Language Association, 161
Monaghan, David, 132–33
Moody's Investors Service, 5, 167
Morgan, Jeff, 144, 146
Morningside College, 124–25, 149–50

NAFSA, 194
National Association of College and University Business Officers, 98
National Center for Education Statistics (NCES), 5, 27, 31, 50
national institutions: definition of, 28–29; projected attendance at, 29, 30, 33, 34, 35–36; race/ethnicity of students of, 68, 69–70, 71–72, 75
national perspective, 27–30, 28, 29
National Student Clearinghouse Research Center, 115
Neuhauser, John, 163–67, 174–75, 190
Nicholas, Jason, 123
Nienhusser, H. Kenny, 96
North Carolina Independent Colleges and Universities (NCICU), 200–201
Northeast: enrollments in, 133, 163; fertility rates in, 12, 13, 14, 20; propensity to attend college in, 16
Northern Michigan University, 123

Obama administration, 16–17
online programs, 109, 144–46